Drowning in Now:

A Search for God and Humanity
at the Top of the World

By Alicia Jean Demetropolis

Drowning in Now: A Search for God and Humanity at the Top of the World

The Global Humanity Initiative
P.O. Box 1484
Sequim, WA 98382
www.GlobalHumanityInitiative.org

Fifteen percent of the proceeds from the sale of this book goes to support homeless and impoverished elders around the world.

Some names and places have been changed for privacy reasons. Some events from different dates have been combined for brevity.

ISBN: 979-8-21-827566-2

Cover photograph © Alicia Jean Demetropolis
Sang Ngag Phurbaling Monastery, Pharping, Kathmandu, Nepal.
Cover designed by Barbara Gottleib, www.GottGraphix.com

For my parents.

Contents

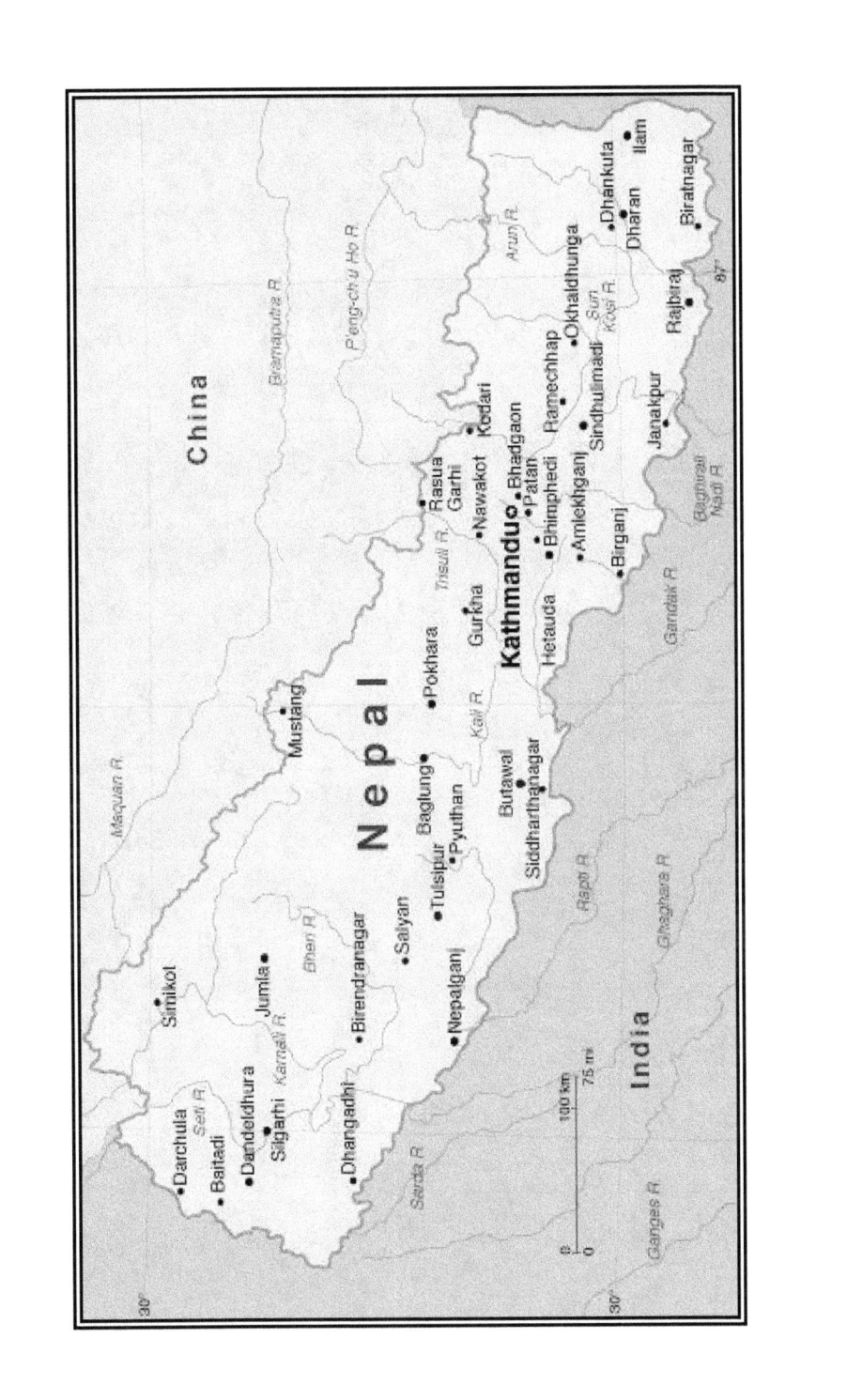

I. Where it Begins

"Humanity is not perfect.
There are imperfections in every human being,
and you will always become unhappy
if you look towards the people themselves.

But if you look towards God,
you will love them and be kind to them,
for the world of God is the world of perfection
and complete mercy."

~ 'Abdu'l-Bahá

The Lie of Shangri-La

ACCORDING TO THE UN Human Development Data report, Nepal is on the long list of Third World countries. To many passing through, it seems as if it's developing; to those who stay longer, it's almost stagnating.

Nestled at the top of the Himalayas, Nepal spreads across a scant 54,363 square miles. In 2020, its estimated population of 29,349,065 people means that approximately 540 people are stuffed into every square mile. Nepal is small, isolated, and landlocked. It has limited natural resources, most of which are untapped, so the Nepali people must rely on imports for many of their basic goods and materials. Their two primary choices for those imports are the much-larger countries of China to the north, and India, which wraps Nepal's eastern, southern, and western borders. China and India have long-simmering tensions with each other, most of which revolve around their shared borders to the northeast and southwest of Nepal, leaving the Nepalis stuck in the middle of the conflicts—as if they don't have enough of their own problems to deal with.

&

I was probably ten years old when I watched a rerun of the 1973 movie-musical version of James Hilton's *Lost Horizon*. Hunkered down in front of the tube television at my aunt and uncle's house during a big family gathering, I was captivated by the legend of Shangri-La, hidden high in the snow-covered peaks of the Far East. There, at the top of the Kunlun Mountains, happy and carefree people lived for hundreds of years in an enchanted land free from worldly strife. At my young age, it was easy to suspend disbelief while watching a movie, even though it was ridiculous that this land in the Far East was somehow populated by white men and women, as the movie portrayed. I wanted to believe that somewhere out in the snows of the most exotic place in the world, was a land free of troubles.

While the movie took place in the Kunlun Mountains (the longest mountain range in China), most people place Shangri-La in the Himalayas, which is home to Mount Everest. These mountain ranges, taken together, are considered part of the "Rooftop of the World," or just the "Top of the World."

Through my formative years, I believed that Nepal was a happy place, populated by generous and kind people, living free of strife. I ignored the reality of the caste system, which Nepal abolished in the 1960s but which still exists if one pays attention, and I disregarded the fact that women were expected (or forced) to burn themselves alive on their husband's funeral pyre in a practice known as *sati.*

I had fallen victim to the myth of a Nepal which the former Nepali monarchy and current government had carefully crafted over the past seventy years, specifically to feed their tourist industry.

It was easy for me to want to believe this myth. A land free of strife meant a life free of bigotry, hatred, and racism. It meant there was a place in this world where I wouldn't experience the ugly side of humanity, which I'd already witnessed in grade school. As I am of Greek descent, my olive skin was darker than the other kids' in school, and my mother's attempts to control my kinky-curly hair usually failed. For most of the fourth grade, many of the other kids in class called me "nigger." This was what they'd learned at home. They did it on the playground, out of earshot of the teachers, and the other kids in my class followed along with the bullying.

During this period, I wasn't allowed to play on certain playground equipment, or to join games with the other kids in my class. Since I didn't know anyone else in the other grades, I played by myself on whatever equipment I could find—until some classmate would chase me down and force me to keep moving.

I recall a very short time when another young boy joined our class. His name was Roger, and he was also darker-skinned than the other kids. One day during recess on the playground, I was called over to a group of children huddled together. Roger was packed in the middle of the group. One of the young boys handed me a bar of soap and asked if I could wash my skin and convince Roger to do the same. He said maybe we'd be white if we washed. The other kids laughed.

Roger and I exchanged sad looks. Looking back on that moment, I wasn't sad for ourselves, but sad for these other kids, and for the whole situation. Even at the age of eight or nine, I couldn't understand what difference it made whether my skin was black or white or purple.

The bullying and name-calling formed me into the person I am today. I refuse to judge someone based on their skin color or ethnic background.

2.

The History that Forms Us

THE PEOPLE OF NEPAL haven't had much of a chance to enjoy any real peace and quiet in their world, especially since the end of the last century.

A small segment of the population decided they no longer liked the constitutional monarchy in power, and so, in the early 1990s, they formed the Communist Party of Nepal. Driven by these self-described Maoists, a bloody civil war—which they referred to as "The People's Movement"—erupted in February, 1996. In September of 2000, the Maoists killed fourteen policemen; just seventeen months later, they killed seventy policemen *in one day*. In 2001, the Crown Prince of Nepal purportedly gunned down nine members of his own family, including his parents, the King and Queen, before turning the gun on himself. In early 2002, Nepal's tourism industry collapsed, with the Peace Corps withdrawing from Nepal two years later.

Finally, in June 2006, Nepal officially abolished its monarchy, and a peace agreement was signed in November 2006, effectively ending the civil war. This peace agreement was carefully crafted with help from India, but the subsequent interim Constitution that was drafted and signed in Nepal made the government of India uneasy.

India felt that the interim Constitution didn't do enough to acknowledge the rights of a tribe of people known as the Madhesis, who had lived along the India-Nepal border since long before modern borders were declared. The Madhesis began to protest, and India supported them. In April 2015, a devastating earthquake struck the country. Half a year later, a five-month-long protest blockade took place along the Madhesis portion of the Nepal-India border. The blockade caused both a humanitarian and economic crisis for the Nepali people, since everything from medicines to fuel were held up at the border. Nepal blamed India for inciting this blockade, while India claimed no involvement.

ॐ

That 2015 earthquake was one of the worst the area ever had seen. Measured at a magnitude of 7.8, it killed eight thousand people and injured twenty thousand more. Less than three weeks later, just when Nepalis thought the aftershocks were over, and as they tried to move back into whatever homes remained standing, a massive aftershock hit, measuring 7.3 on the Richter scale.

Nepali construction consists of either concrete blocks or bricks bound together by loose mortar. This is the way the people have always built, and being fiercely independent, they are resistant to change. The country is in one of the most seismically active regions in the world, yet even after the 2015 earthquake, there has never been a national push for the government to update its building practices and codes.

The quake destroyed more than six hundred thousand landmarks, buildings, and homes, and caused nine billion dollars in damage. In a country where bulldozers are rare, people resorted to digging through the rubble by hand in a desperate search for loved ones trapped alive.

ॐ

Seeing clips of the disaster on the news, I became frantic. I told my husband, Nelson, that I had to go to Nepal. I said that I needed to be there to help. My outburst came as a surprise to both of us. I had never actually told anyone I wanted to go to Nepal. I'd thought about it, sure, and toyed with the idea, but never discussed it with anybody. The panic I felt after the earthquake was something I'd never expected. I became irrational during our conversation, and had trouble thinking straight. It seemed that once

6

I opened my mouth about this need to go to Nepal, I couldn't stop talking about it.

Nelson raised excellent points about my sense of urgency to go help: I didn't know anyone there, wouldn't know where to go or how to get to where I was needed, and would probably just get in the way. He was right, of course. I tried to put the thought out of my mind.

A year later, precisely twelve months after that massive 7.3 aftershock struck Nepal, my mother passed away. As I lay in bed that night, I considered the synchronicity of the date—my mother's death and the one-year anniversary of the quakes. I don't believe in coincidences.

When I thought about the fact that both my parents were gone, I felt a kind of separation. A freedom washed over me—a sense of lightness and ease. I heard a voice in my head say, *"Now."*

It was time to go to Nepal.

ৡ

The internet is full of horror stories about people being stranded in remote areas of foreign countries by shady non-governmental organizations, or NGOs. An NGO is simply a nonprofit that is not influenced by any government or governmental organization, and which is generally formed by civilians with the intention of improving their community.

These organizations collect hefty program fees from their global volunteers, and in exchange promise an immersion experience for the volunteer in the country, including living as the locals do, and working to supposedly improve life for people around them. The NGO's promise is shiny and glossy, but the reality can be a shock. Volunteers arrive in the country, are taken through a quick orientation by the NGO, and then are often dropped in a remote location for a long period of time with no support, no way out, and no recourse. In other instances, volunteers arrive in their chosen country only to discover that the NGO to which they paid their fee doesn't exist. They're stuck in a Third World country and forced to figure things out on their own.

As part of my private fantasy about visiting Nepal, I had started following one Nepali NGO several years before my mother died. I searched for reviews and governmental actions against this specific NGO, called Create Good Nepal (CGN), and they seemed to come out spotless. CGN offered a variety of volunteer programs, including working with children on different projects, teaching English to Buddhist nuns in exchange for meditation practices, and doing elder care in and around Kathmandu, the capital city.

When the time finally comes to take the plunge, I send an email to the address listed at CGN's site, explaining my seven years of experience in elder care, my training in diabetes care (diabetes is rampant in Nepal), and my certification as a Nurse Delegate. Geetu, CGN's volunteer coordinator, responds within a day. She tells me they don't have any certifications such as mine in Nepal, and they don't have people who do in-home elder care, either. Still, she says, my skills could be of value, and she encourages me to fill out an application, which requires paying a nonrefundable application fee.

Geetu adds that CGN's elder care program is their least popular one, a comment which should have caused me to sit up and take notice. I can understand that elder care isn't popular work, either in the West or in a Third World country. If it's their least popular program, though, does that mean it may not be well supported?

CGN arranges for their volunteers to stay in a hotel near their offices in Kathmandu for the first week, during which they hold daily orientation sessions. After that, the volunteers are shipped off to their assignments in various parts of Kathmandu and the valley. Volunteers are housed either at their assignment, or with a family that lives close to their assignment. For example, if I'd chosen to teach English to nuns at a Buddhist monastery, I would stay in the monastery as their guest.

As I will be doing elder care, it is unclear whether I'll be staying at the elder care home or with a host family near to the home and walking back and forth to my assignment. It's unclear because CGN hasn't figured that out yet, even as my departure date approaches.

3.

Making Preparations

THE FIRST FAMILY MEMBER I talk to about my Nepal adventure is my cousin. We are more like sisters and best friends than cousins. Connie squeals on the phone, "This sounds so like *you!*" My two closest girlfriends have a similar reaction, as do my two closest male friends, but without the squealing. There is a consensus: *It sounds like something I'd do.* Maybe my friends know me better than I know myself, because this doesn't sound like me when I think about it. I don't feel as if I'm a particularly exciting and adventurous person. I'm going to Nepal because I have this urge to go. There's no real rational explanation. I just have to go, so I'm going.

People who don't know me well, ask—with a mild sneer—what my husband thinks of this. I reply that I would support him if this were something he felt he needed to do.

My husband has always been my biggest fan. Nelson encourages me and supports any of my plans and ideas, regardless of how harebrained they may seem. Very early in our relationship, we dedicated ourselves to supporting each other, making a vow not to limit the other person or require the other person to live by our own rules. He is excited for me to have this experience and to explore this driving need I feel to be in Nepal, but he is not excited for me to leave him and travel to the other side of the world for three months.

Emotionally flooded and lost in a fog, I begin to focus only on how I'll survive in this great unknown.

~

I start to tell my closest friends that I want to go home, and I become anxious to finally get there. *I'm going home to Kathmandu*, I say. While different places around the US and around the world have felt familiar and comfortable to me, nothing has felt like home. Somehow, I know Kathmandu will.

Maybe I won't recognize myself when I get back from Nepal. I don't know. I can't see past the plane flights, and don't know what to expect once I get there, much less imagine what my life will look like on my return.

What I can't foresee now, is that within two years of my return from Nepal, I will allow several long-term relationships to splinter and collapse. I will simply stop being the glue that binds myself to others. Other people will drift away from our friendship. It will feel as if they no longer know how to relate to me. Now, though, none of this has happened.

A good friend of mine suggests I talk with her astrologer. I'm game. Towards the end of our two-hour conversation, I mention that two people have told me my next spiritual teacher is in Saudi Arabia, but that every time I think of going there, I panic.

The astrologer, Tim, tells me about astrocartography. He tells me that both George H.W. Bush's and George W. Bush's Mars go through Kuwait. Tim says they'll be fighting that battle into eternity unless they deal with the overall spiritual issue. He tells me that my Mars goes through Saudi Arabia. He says I could go, but it might not go very well for me.

Then he tells me my Saturn goes through Kathmandu. He says, "Going to Nepal, arriving in Kathmandu, will feel like going home."

4.

Jumping In

THROUGHOUT ALL THESE PREPARATIONS, no one asks me why I have this driving need to go to Nepal. People either sneer a bit at the idea, or tell me how envious they are about my adventure, or want to give me unsolicited, uneducated advice about my trip. Yet no one stops to ask me *why* I'm going.

If they did, I doubt I'd have the answer. During my head-down, full-speed-ahead preparations, I doubt I'd be able to stop long enough to search my brain for the reason.

It will be more than a month into my trip before someone asks me this question. I will be staying at a hotel, awake late at night, staring out at the neighborhood, feeling out of time and out of place. In the semi-darkness, I will check my email, and my friend Ronni will have sent me a challenge. *It's time to address the reason why you had to take this trip, Alicia,* she'll tell me.

The mental and emotional temper tantrum will start. I will be forced to reckon with this seemingly mad idea which pushed me to leave everything I knew behind. I will be forced into an honest assessment of my behavior and my actions. Like a frustrated, angry, hurt child, I will have to work to find my words.

Because I want to prove something (what, I don't know) to someone (whom, I don't know).

Because I feel called to do this.

Because I need to close out unfinished business from previous lifetimes.

Because I am running from something in the US.

Because I am running to something here.

Because I'm hoping to make someone's life a little better, even if it's only for the short time I'm here.

Because the midlife crisis that started nine years ago has never ended.

Because all the cool kids are doing it.

Because I'm adrift in the world, and this seems like a good shore on which to beach for a while.

Because I want to do something. Something. Anything.

Because I'm seeking something that I hope will find me now that I am here.

Because it is my destiny.

Because I want to start living.

᠀

Life on Washington State's Olympic Peninsula is tranquil. It's filled with the sound of crashing waves as we stroll along the beach, and an awareness of wildlife around us as we hike high into the mountains, up to near-hidden lakes and snow-capped peaks. Folks on the peninsula let other drivers into traffic, hold doors for other customers, and—for the most part—try to be pleasant to one another.

My husband and I have settled into life on the small ranch he manages. We indulge our rescued rat terrier/Chihuahua mix, Daisy, and take her for long walks. We share the acreage with the ranch owners—the elderly architect, Herb, who designed and built the ranch, and his wife, June. Daisy considers Herb and June's home her own, marching through their always-open front door and jumping up onto the furniture to visit with Herb, who will set down his book and have a chat with her. Every Wednesday at 7:00 p.m., I leave our apartment and head up to their house to play bridge with June and two others.

By contrast, the Federal Democratic Republic of Nepal is a hard country. Drivers don't even slow down for a woman holding her infant as she crosses the street at a marked pedestrian crossing. Nepal is where seniors are put out in the street by their own kids, who claim they can't afford to feed their parents anymore, and where children are being left behind in education. This is a country where the people are so detached from their humanity that homosexuality remains illegal. It is a land where some villages are so remote they can only be accessed via a two-hour flight followed by a days-long trek.

In Nepal, the have's continue to get more and the have-not's are moved out into the garbage dump. Study after study shows the poorest ten percent of Nepal's population growing poorer, while the rich get richer, with the wealthiest ten percent claiming an increasing percentage of the wealth over the past thirty years.

Nepalis who have access to social media complain that government officials are buying expensive helicopters to chauffer themselves around, while the average Nepali drowns under the weight of increasing taxes—the same taxes that pay for the expensive helicopters of the government officials. Social media accounts and online newspapers are overrun with detailed complaints by Nepalis who want to know where their money goes and why their country struggles to survive, while few pay attention to the woman whose husband kicks her out of the house when her pregnancy miscarries.

It's a country that desperately wants to come into the modern age, but fights against itself for who can get there first.

And I'm about to jump into the fray.

II. A Month of Fresh Hell

"Deeds of kindness weigh as much
as all the commandments."

~ Talmud Yerushalmi, Peah 1:1

"Always meet petulance with gentleness
and perverseness with kindness.
A gentle hand can lead even an elephant by a hair.
Reply to thine enemy with gentleness."

~ Zoroaster

5.

Coming Home

HOME IS WHERE YOU find *yourself*. It's where you discover that you've been waiting for *you* to arrive all along.

This feeling isn't something that's easy to describe. It's a sigh of relief. A realization that you are comfortable for the first time in your life, and a sudden recognition that you never noticed you'd been *uncomfortable* to begin with.

A recognition that you've not merely been here before, but that you were meant to come back. My friend Katherine says the moment she set foot on the tarmac in South Africa, she "wanted to lie down and hug the earth." For me, stepping out of the airport terminal in Kathmandu and into the dust and dirt and sun and noise, my urge was to drop to my knees and dig in the hard soil to find the pieces of myself I'd left behind.

Standing in my hotel room that afternoon, during my first hours in the country, this feeling was unlike anything I'd expected.

After CGN's driver dropped me at the hotel, I had all afternoon and evening to myself. I didn't venture out into the streets, look for something to eat, or familiarize myself with the area. I didn't go up to the roof for dinner, where I'd likely meet the other CGN volunteers.

Instead, I stayed in my room, unpacking and snacking. As I basked in that quiet time to myself, the feeling deepened. I was supposed to come back. I was finally back.

I had been waiting for myself.

ॐ

I saw the quintessential Kathmandu yesterday afternoon on the drive from the airport: A mass of traffic, streets jammed car door to bicycle pedals to rickshaws to knees on motorcycles. No lanes. Just try to stay to the left. It seems the rule of the road is: "He who blinks first, loses." It's a game of chicken with no kindness or consideration shown to others—no pause or gesturing to let the other person into the flow of traffic as I'm used to back in the US. It's all about getting to where you're going, and screw the other person.

Akkal, CGN's driver, had picked me up from the airport in a tiny, beat-up rental car. With us was a young Nepali woman who introduced herself as another volunteer. We crept along, inch by inch at times, at other times maybe reaching three miles per hour. The roads finally opened up as we came through the main street, into what I would soon recognize as Tri Devi Marg. We drove on through Thamel, weaving in slow motion through pedestrians, tourists, and rickshaws on the way to the hotel with me in the back seat, smiling. Rude traffic and all, I was overjoyed to be back to a home I'd never visited.

Kathmandu is a mess of old and new. Of plain brown punctuated by bursts of color. Of ancient, hand-carved brown wood on buildings, windows, and doors, and concrete pillars covered in flyers or painted yellow or blue or just left plain. Of decaying brown bricks or shiny, red-painted bricks or mortar-covered concrete blocks. Brightly-colored wares hang next to doorways, marigold strands everywhere. Signs the size of small billboards punctuate the scene, red for a popular American soda, blue for a popular Russian vodka. Single-level shops cluster side-by-side, with blue steel rolling doors, or faded steel doors, some that once held logos. Konica. Castrol. Kodak.

The city is graffiti, both as elaborate artwork, and as confrontational phrases. *"THINK NEPAL,"* and *"Nature is dead."* Rippled aluminum sheets rise on beams, used as makeshift overhead covers in front of shops and on the flat rooftops of homes. As industrious humans, we make living space wherever and however we can.

Black cables run everywhere. Thousands of lifelines looped at poles and sagging from point to point, store to store, home to home. There's not enough room for all the people who've overtaken the once-quiet neighborhoods, turning the ancient land into a dirt version of an asphalt jungle. In some areas, second floors now rise above shops. Intricate, ancient buildings made of wood and brick are torn down in favor of four-story concrete block blobs, uninspired rectangles rising from the dust, some painted green, pink, or yellow, but most left plain. Rubble from construction sites spills into the streets.

Garbage is everywhere in Kathmandu. It's poured out by business owners and residents at designated areas throughout the city. On pickup days, it's shoveled into trucks and hauled away.

If the stench of garbage doesn't overwhelm a first-time visitor's senses, the smell of urine and feces from dogs and bulls just might. Tens of thousands of stray dogs roam the streets, and bulls are considered sacred, but useless since they don't produce milk. They're all put out into the streets to try to survive, feeding on whatever they can find or beg from passers-by.

And it's not just the smell that makes it hard for a visitor to breathe. On the list of cities with the worst air quality in the world, Kathmandu ranks up towards the top. The country sits in a geographical basin, where fresh winds rarely blow through, and Kathmandu sits in a bowl of its own within that basin. This causes the fumes from burning garbage and exhaust from cars and motorcycles to lie heavy on the land.

Then there's the noise. Between the echo of motorcycles in the closed-in spaces of narrow streets, and the nonstop honking of horns, there's no relief from the racket. Drivers are constantly on their horn for one reason or another. It's how they communicate with each other. They honk when they come to a blind turn, or when they pass in traffic, or to acknowledge someone passing them. They even honk to tell a driver who's attempting to pass that he should just back off. It's a constant cacophony.

Taken all together, Kathmandu is overwhelming. A mass of confusion for any first-time visitor, or for any visitor who hasn't seen the space for ten years or thirty years. It is smelly, dusty, dirty, hot, poverty-stricken, and noisy. Yet in an inexplicable way, I feel more at home here, amidst this controlled chaos in a country I've never visited, than I have ever felt anywhere else. For the first time in my life, even though I'm immersed in uncertainty, I feel at peace in my world.

There is no possible way to capture it all in words, or in pictures. As I stand on the corner outside the hotel this morning, on my first full day here, I watch as Kathmandu life passes by. People saunter to work, stopping for tea or a bite to eat along the way. Shop owners and shoppers visit with each other. Parents drive their kids to school, with three or four of them piled on a motorcycle or scooter.

I had been scheduled to arrive days earlier, when a group of six other young volunteers from Lithuania and Spain arrived. My snafu with a transit visa for India resulted in me missing the first four days of orientation. But I'm here now, standing on the corner outside the hotel, watching the world go by.

Traffic works hard to get around the hill of garbage piling up at the corner. Poor men in tattered clothes climb up and pick through the heap. They open plastic bags, drain them, then pack the bags with scavenged treasures to take home. It's rancid in the morning heat, and the day is only going to get hotter. The daytime temperature will hover above 90°F for at least another month, and September isn't nearly the hottest month here.

Although times are changing with the younger adults, most women here continue to dress conservatively. It is rare to see a woman wearing a sleeveless kurta—a long, tunic-styled top—outside of her home. Traditionally, a kurta's sleeves come down past the elbows, and the suruwal—a woman's traditional, billowing, cotton pants gathered at the ankles—modestly covers the legs. Men's attire is equally conservative, with the exception of t-shirts exposing their arms. Only the tourists flash skin by wearing tank tops and shorts.

I have brought very few clothes with me. My plan is to purchase some kurtas and some of the leggings now popular with the young women here. Until I can do that, I'm in my short-sleeved t-shirt and my yoga pants, which are too long, so I must stuff them into my shoes under the heels. There's just no way I'm letting any item of clothing touch the filthy roads here.

When a group of young people drift out of the hotel, I recognize CGN's logo on their t-shirts. These are the volunteers who arrived earlier this week. As I begin to introduce myself, I realize I am an old woman in a young person's game.

We are supposed to start at 10:00 a.m. My phone says it's already past that, as the others begin to wander up and down the street, getting coffee or tea, snacks or water. They socialize, and I stand to the side, in a bubble, observing.

I try to pay attention when we finally head out, leaving the hotel behind us for our daily orientation at CGN. We cross the street, head down to a steep and narrow dirt road, take that down to a busy intersection with the equivalent of four or six lanes of traffic flying past. Here in Kathmandu, however, there are no lanes.

Since pedestrians don't have the right of way here, and since there are no real traffic controls, we step forward together in a scattered mass of our own, into the rush of cars and trucks, motorcycles and scooters. Most of the others move without batting an eye.

Next, into Naya Bazar. A maze of streets, dirt and rubble and garbage, and stray dogs and bulls. Gutters run alongside either edge of the roads. It's a twisting, winding trip from the hotel, and it's familiar and new at the same time.

CGN's offices are still being finished inside, and construction debris is everywhere. The first floor has the kitchen, a small bathroom, and two other rooms—one filled with debris, one somewhat cleaned out. As the kids scatter, some sitting in the stairwell to get on Wi-Fi and chat with family or check social media, I look for CGN's staff. Heading up the stairs, I pass the second floor where the hostel will be, and go up to the offices on the third floor, then track down Geetu, the volunteer coordinator, to introduce myself.

She introduces me to Manesh, the volunteer manager. Next, I meet Sunjiya, the orientation coordinator. Sunjiya is responsible for giving the volunteers Nepali lessons, and for teaching us all a bit about Nepali customs and history. Both Geetu and Sunjiya strike me as kind and warm-hearted. Quick to smile, they tell me that the day's orientation will be held in the classroom downstairs, but they are not ready to get started just yet.

I wander back downstairs and sit on the front stoop with the dog who calls this property his home. Many businesses and people here allow dogs to remain on their property during the day or evening, often feeding them leftovers of rice or vegetables. They'll never feed a dog meat, though, because it's too expensive to waste on a dog. This large, lovable mutt, whom the kids have named "Kathmandu," lounges on the dirt in the shade outside, sleeping off last night's adventures. Much to his dismay, he is not allowed inside.

‍ঽ

A couple of hours of Nepali lessons and my brain is hurting. The kids seem to know so much more than I do about everything. It seems as if they've been studying for weeks, and they know where to change money, where to buy SIM cards for their phones, where specific shops are. I've been here only eighteen hours, though, so I should give myself a break. Plus, I will soon learn they also feel lost and frustrated. They were expecting some kind of coordinated, organized program, but nothing here is organized, it seems. Welcome to Nepal.

My insecurity demons pounce on me after my arrival at CGN's offices. Compared to these kids, I feel as if what I'm doing is nothing big. Yes, I'm here in Kathmandu for three months, but they've chosen to stay in Okhaldhunga for five months on their assignments. Okhaldhunga is a minimum ten-hour drive from Kathmandu on a good day, and they'll be away from potable water the entire five months, while I'll be near shops where I can buy bottled water and other sundries. Still, I am an anomaly here and will learn to be patient with the younger volunteers' fascination with me. I am a married, fifty-two-year-old woman, traveling to Nepal, alone, for three months.

We all lounge together outside, in the sun and in the shade, as we nibble a barely-recognizable lunch. I decide to return to being vegetarian for this trip when I spit out what appear to be chicken's feet.

6.

Glitter and Lies

WHAT I WILL SOON learn is that Nepalis lie to each other as a regular course of business. It's the main reason most Nepali businessmen dislike doing business with other Nepali businessmen, and yet no one seems to know how to stop doing it. Over the course of the next three months, I will never hear about women business owners lying to others this way, and I will never experience it myself.

During the weeks before my arrival, CGN had announced that they were still working on finding a suitable elder care home where I could live and work. Then they announced they were still trying to find a suitable host family where I could stay. Then they said I would stay at their new hostel.

A few days ago I arrived in Nepal to find no elder care home, no host family, and nothing close to a completed hostel. Today, however, Manesh swaggers into the classroom during our Nepali lesson, plops himself down on the couch next to me, leans in, and smiles. He believes he's found an elder care home that could use my help. We will go tonight to see if it will be suitable.

Sometime around 4:00 p.m., the winds shift, the temperature starts to drop, and the clouds move in. I pray for rain, hoping it will cool the temps a bit. Before long, I get my wish with an earth-shattering thunderstorm. It's been a long time since I've heard the crack and peal of thunder, since we don't get big storms where I live on the Olympic Peninsula, and I fight the urge to run outside and dance in the rain. I'm overjoyed.

Then reality hits: Manesh rides a motorcycle. I climb onto the seat behind him, nestle beneath the double raincoat specifically made for motorcyclists, and we head out in the downpour, riding through the narrow streets of

Kathmandu in the dark of rush hour. We weave around pedestrians trying to avoid the rivers forming in the dirt roads, skim past other motorcyclists and cars, many of whom aren't using their headlights, and slow and turn to avoid stray dogs. I am so comfortable with Manesh's driving skills that it's long minutes before I realize I'm not holding onto anything—not the back of the bike, nor Manesh. I am safe, racing through the streets of Kathmandu, with my new brother.

Eventually he turns through wide steel gates and into a courtyard. Two small temples sit to each side, and before us is a multi-story building with an open-air shrine room on the first floor. Manesh eases the bike forward towards the shrine room and parks under a rippled aluminum overhang. We dismount as if we've shared a bike for years. Beneath this overhang, it sounds as if thousands of jackhammers are ebbing and flowing with the downpour. It's deafening.

The shrine room is replete with glittering gold statues, sparkling lights, colored flower strands, and strings of decorative vinyl flags. The building resembles an old motel, with three levels of rooms opening onto long balconies, and an open outdoor stairwell. I'm guessing the elders live in the rooms above this ground level shrine room.

The temples in the courtyard look ancient. One is painted red and white, and the other is yellow and red, with an old fig tree growing up through one wall. It could be a photo straight out of a tourist guidebook. Also in the courtyard is a statue of the Buddha in a glass case, perched on a stand, surrounded by a decorative and spiked steel fence. All this—the elder care home, the two small temples, and the courtyard—are referred to as the temple grounds.

People are sitting around in the courtyard on red plastic, outdoor chairs, waiting for a service to begin. An older man with thinning, dyed-black hair motions us over. This is Pradeep, the man who runs the elder care home.

Pradeep still stands to his full height of about five feet, eight inches tall. He's not stooped from hard work or a hard life. Skinny with broad, bony shoulders, he looks as if he's pushing eighty years old. During my stay this next month, Pradeep will always wear a vest with either a long- or short-sleeved shirt, and he will always be too hot. He walks only the half block from his apartment up the street to the temple grounds, and back again. If he needs to go anywhere else, one of his nieces will drive him.

Manesh and Pradeep shout at each other over the noise of the rain as we sit and talk, and again as we climb the building's outdoor staircase to check things out. We climb up past the second floor, lit by lightbulbs, to the third floor, which has no bulbs in the many outdoor sockets. Manesh uses the flashlight on his smartphone as Pradeep opens a few doors. Each one reveals a grimy room with platform beds stacked against a wall.

My room is nowhere near ready for a resident. It is still a dusty, concrete block room, with a filthy cement floor and an equally-filthy platform bed standing on its end against the wall. The interior wall to the right doesn't go all the way to the ceiling for some reason, and Manesh and I exchange looks as we both observe the two-foot gap between the top of the wall and the ceiling. My toilet is in a closet just a little bigger than the toilet itself. Coming from the wall next to the toilet is a handheld water sprayer, similar to those found on kitchen sinks in the West. This is the Nepali bidet.

In Nepal, there's something about their plumbing that requires the toilets to be raised above the rest of the floor by about ten inches. At hotels, the guest steps *up* into the bathroom. The situation is no different here at the elder care home, and running along the back wall of the room is a cement step about ten inches high and three feet deep, just deep enough to accommodate the toilet closet. There's no hot water here, and no shower or shower wand, but none of these facts have registered with me yet. A thin, aluminum-and-wood-framed door opens out onto the cement step, closing off the toilet closet from the rest of the room. The room itself measures about nine by thirteen feet.

This entire third floor is empty, as is the floor above. Only the second floor, directly above the shrine room, is occupied by elders, and only a few rooms on that floor are occupied.

Even though there are no lightbulbs in the sockets on this floor, or the floor above, there is a working bulb in my room. Pradeep flicks on the one light with pride, and also shows us that the toilet flushes. He tells Manesh that he can have the room ready in two days. Manesh will bring me on his motorcycle that first day, and CGN's driver, Akkal, will deliver my bags for me.

By the time our tour ends and we regroup downstairs in the courtyard, the rain has ended, but the noise continues. Their nightly service is underway in the shrine room. One man plays a harmonium, which is a wood box with a two- or three-octave keyboard on top that is played using one's right hand. The back of the harmonium opens as a bellows, which the person pumps with their free left hand. The pumping action forces air through metal reeds inside the box, creating a unique keyboard sound that is both ancient and haunting. Another man plays two small drums, known as a tabla. The drums are played with the palms, fingers, and heel of the hand.

Each musician sits on cushions on the floor in the shrine room, with microphones in front of their instruments. The harmonium player is singing as though he is half-asleep, leaning into the microphone perched above his hands. Two large speakers inside the tiny room blast our eardrums, along with two speakers hanging outside in the courtyard where we sit along with most of the small crowd that has arrived for the service. The shrine room itself can accommodate only about a dozen people, but because it has open walls, everyone in the courtyard can also be part of the ceremonies. Pradeep's sister, Garima, is in front of the altar, leading the service tonight.

Pradeep and Manesh lean in towards each other to yell over the noise. Although Pradeep hasn't spoken a word of English yet, he has told Manesh I will have daily Nepali lessons, and has promised that I will be fluent in Nepali by the time my stay ends. From what I can tell, though, Manesh hasn't told him how long I'll be staying here. Come to think of it, I don't know, either.

More yelling as they work out the details, and finally Pradeep holds out his right hand, rubs the tips of his fingers together. Manesh takes out his wallet, pulls out a few bills, and hands them to Pradeep. No receipt. It could be my imagination, but Manesh looks a bit annoyed at the request for money. Then Manesh leans into me, yells that we're done, and that he'll take me back to the hotel.

All this noise from the rain and the music masks the truth of the facility.

7.

The Growing Darkness

THE FIRST NIGHT OF my stay in the elder care home, I begin unpacking in the growing darkness as Pradeep's sister, Garima, arrives at my door. She has brought my evening tea, and uses her big lungs to talk to me in near-fluent English over the sound of the music playing downstairs. Garima tells me that my name will be easy for her to remember because her granddaughter's name is Alisa, and I decide not to correct her. She invites me down to the service, and though I say I will be down soon, she tells me more than once to be sure to join them.

The evening tea is a gracious welcome for a guest. Tea is served with light cookies, also known as biscuits. Here in Nepal, tea and biscuits are served at breakfast and in the afternoon. It sounds very British because it is British. It's a holdover from the days of India's colonization, and an imported custom which the Nepalis continue to enjoy.

I am unpacking without the room light because I'm trying to get used to the rolling blackouts that are a part of life here in Kathmandu. Pradeep and Garima have had the room decorated. Covering the floor and the cement step along the back of the room is very thin, royal blue carpeting, the style used in office buildings in the West. On my bed is a flimsy and very small pillow in a colorful floral pillowcase; there is a flat sheet of the same material covering the thin cotton mattress. Beds here are wooden platforms. Nothing fancy. There is also a heavy blanket, decorated with the Chanel logo, folded at the foot of the bed. Hanging from a stretch of twine across the window is a makeshift curtain made from thin fabric.

With the music blasting from the shrine room below, and the knowledge that I'm home at last, I'm full of joy and hope.

Downstairs I am greeted by a small crowd of participants who have come from the neighborhood, many of whom are regulars who gather every evening for the service. Two lanky, elderly men in traditional Nepali attire turn to greet me with bright smiles as I stand on the stoop in the stairwell landing, taking it all in. Men and women alike turn to see me, also pressing their palms together in greeting. Inside the shrine room, others call me in to join them, so I slip off my shoes and bless myself, touching the first two fingers on my right hand first to the floor in the shrine room and then to my forehead, according to the Hindu tradition. After repeating this blessing three times, I look up to see the joy on the congregants' faces as I step into the shining room.

As the music and singing continue, I am transported by the noise, by the sound, the incense, the lights. There is something powerful and familiar in this service. Something light and brilliant, but sinister at the same time.

Garima stands before the altar of golden statues and incense and candles, while the congregants sing and the musicians perform. I stand with others around the altar, all of us in our bare feet.

Hinduism dates back four thousand years. As with any religion, beliefs have splintered through the centuries as humans massaged the core message to fit their needs. Just as in Christianity, Hinduism also acknowledges the Holy Trinity. Brahman is the Unchanging Truth, and an intelligence of sorts that transcends human comprehension, but Brahman is not a god. Brahma (not Brahman) is the Creator and the first god of the Hindu trinity. Vishnu, the second god in the trinity, is considered to be the protector. Shiva, the third trinity deity, is the destroyer. He has the power to destroy all things should the universe be overtaken by evil.

Each of the three forms of God has various incarnations, and here at this temple they worship Krishna. In a few weeks, Pradeep will lecture me about there being one God, and yet Krishna is the eighth incarnation of Vishnu.

At the end of the service, Garima heads outside, still praying and singing, ringing a small bell, and taking the incense holder with her as she walks clockwise around the courtyard. She pauses first in front of the red and yellow temple before moving on to the well-lit statue of Buddha. From there she moves to the red and white temple, followed all the while by two women dispensing incense behind her.

The presence of Buddha fascinates me. Contrary to popular belief, Siddhartha Gautama (the Buddha) was born in Nepal, not India. To be precise, he was born in Lumbini, which was not quite in Nepal at the time of his birth since Nepal wasn't Nepal yet.

Many Christians and Jews use Buddhist teachings to deepen their faith and to bring them closer to God. Hindus consider the Buddha to be a reincarnation of Vishnu, which makes him one of their own. This is why Buddha is represented in statue and image everywhere in Nepal, right alongside the other Hindu gods and goddesses. He is worshipped as any other manifestation of the one God, and their original Hindu practices continue.

The irony is that Buddha's enlightenment and subsequent teachings revolved around leaving the old ways behind and recognizing that *we* cause our own suffering, not outside influences, and that we can't manifest a better life for ourselves by appeasing the gods. In other words, stop sacrificing animals and worshipping multiple manifestations of God in an effort to be freed from your suffering. On top of this, he emphasized that we all are born equal and that the caste system should be abolished.

Lots of folks never got that memo.

After Garima and the two women return to the shrine room, the music shifts. The bell ringing stops. The musicians stop playing. Now everyone is singing a hypnotic melody—a fascinating, mesmerizing melody.

At the end of it all, Garima walks around holding the little incense holder with three small oil lamps in it. One by one, people bless themselves by sweeping the smoke from the oil lamps and incense up to their face. A few people bless Garima first, then themselves. Someone else collects the food offerings from the altar and begins to pass them around. Little fried pieces of dough strips. People accept them, palms open, with their right hand resting on top of their left hand.

As people are preparing to leave, I notice a dirt-poor little girl take her very young brother by the hand and walk out into the dark streets, heading home alone. Pradeep and Garima are arranging the chairs towards the back of the courtyard, though, and are calling me to go sit between them. There isn't time for me to process more than the thought, "Is that safe for those kids?"

Women come to me, bowing to me, greeting me. I try to bow to the oldest of the old, reaching to touch their feet or the bottom of their saris, but they are alarmed and stop me. No, *they* want to bow to *me* for traveling so far, for being here, for being me when I haven't done anything yet to merit this honor.

People greet me as if I'm royalty. I'm aware of being on display. A few women pull up their own chairs and sit with me. Everyone is introducing themselves, clasping my hands. With great pride, Pradeep is telling them about me. I have no clue what version of the truth he's giving them. One woman declares that she will teach me Nepali. She used to teach English, she says, and so she can help me—and her English is quite good. As with the other women who will promise this, though, I will never see her again.

Garima takes my face in her hands and kisses me on each cheek before she leaves. She calls "Radi, radi!" to everyone as she walks towards the outside gate. Pradeep begins to stagger off towards his own home on his creaky knees, calling out, "Radi, radi!" as he goes. It seems to be a phrase that serves as both "hello" and "goodbye," but I'll never find the phrase in any Nepal-English dictionary.

I rush to help the elderly woman, who is bent at the waist, as she creeps her way up the stairs. I am useless, though. This woman, whom I will nickname Hajuraama, a formal term for "grandmother," doesn't need my help, nor does she want it. Soon I am sitting with just the old woman who lives here with her daughter, who is my age.

Downstairs, the folding metal gate is being dragged, screaming and protesting, across the open wall of the shrine room to lock it up. The last plastic outdoor chairs are being stacked on the landing. Traffic noise continues, unabated now, even at 7:00 p.m.

8.

Life in the Cement Mixer

On the two-burner countertop range, a large pressure cooker angrily pops and hisses. Rosa, the young woman who cooks for us, stirs the curried vegetable and potato dish in a huge, wok-style pan on the second burner. Raju, her husband, cleans and does maintenance at the home. Their two teenaged children must be downstairs, in the room where their family lives next to the shrine room.

Dinner is served on a massive round steel plate, similar to a cafeteria-style plate with three sections. The largest section is overloaded with steaming bhat (rice). There is a reasonable pile of tarkari (curried vegetable and potatoes) in one of the two smaller sections, and a little steel bowl of dal (lentil soup) perched in the second small section. Rosa also hands me a cup of hot milk. Raju sits to my right at the end of the table up against the wall beneath massive filthy windows. The old woman I will nickname Mahti sits to my left. They offer me a spoon, for which I'm grateful. They eat with no utensils, using their right hand instead.

The dal doesn't taste quite right, but I finish it anyway, afraid of being ungracious. There is so much food, and the tarkari is spicier than anything I've ever eaten. I tell myself that if I don't get used to the spice, I don't eat.

Raju knows quite a bit of English and explains that he and Rosa are both twenty-eight years old. He says they've been married twenty years. Something is getting lost in translation, or is it? Children are promised in marriage sometimes immediately after birth. Plus, the Gregorian calendar we use in the West is far different from the Samvat calendar here in Nepal, so it's hard to know how long they've been married, or how old they are. Raju and Rosa have a daughter who is fourteen, and a son who is eight but looks like he's twelve.

Smiling, Raju talks about eating with his fingers because he can taste the food better that way. I look at how steaming hot everything is and can't even consider sticking my delicate, pampered fingers into this hot mess. Later on, though, during my three-month stay, I will plunge my right fingers into some recently served food and discover that it actually does taste better when you don't use utensils.

Nepalis eat with their right hand because toilet paper isn't part of their life here. That's what their left hand is for, and that's why it supposedly never touches food during meal preparation or during eating.

I'm stuffed. Rosa offers me more, but I hold up my hands. "Pujyo," I say— "Enough!"—and they laugh with delight at my casual Nepali. I say dinner was "mitho sah"—"very good," and Rosa beams. I add, "Bholi, kuhm bhat dinus," asking for less rice tomorrow, and Rosa nods, unoffended.

I head up to my room to get ready for bed, all the while trying to figure out how many elders live here. There is this woman I have named Mahti and her daughter Daya, who is my age; an ancient couple who live at the far end of the second floor; and a man who lives by himself but goes back and forth to work each day. Technically, four elders live in this so-called elder care home.

Pradeep told Manesh and me that nine elders live here.

౨

I am sick from the dal this first night. All night. It wasn't Rosa's cooking. I'm certain of that. I have a ridiculously sensitive digestive system, and I've been plagued by issues all my life.

Right off, I discover my toilet doesn't flush, in spite of Pradeep's earlier proud demonstration. Anything added to the bowl just pretty much sits at the bottom while the water swirls around. The sewage does drain bit by bit from the base of the unsealed toilet bowl into the floor drain nearby, even though nothing actually flushes. Also, the toilet isn't bolted down, and the seat and lid are hanging on by a thread of plastic, which makes sitting on the toilet a precarious venture.

I'm in for a very long night. Along with clogging my own toilet, and the toilet in another room down the hall, I am startled by two, four-inch-long red and black cockroaches in the other room (technically, we startled each other). Through all this, I discover that the traffic noise here doesn't quiet down at night, in contrast to my experience at the hotel. Instead, it somehow gets louder. Large trucks move through, rattling up and down the bumpy hill; gears are shifted down or up. Brakes screech and metal clatters, and I swear I hear tanks rumble past at one point. The noise ping-pongs between our building and the one across the intersection, slamming into our windows and into my psyche.

Also, the bed isn't actually a bed. It's the usual wooden platform, but topped with simple cotton batting that flattens to nothing when I lie down on it.

And then there are the miniscule Nepali mosquitoes. They seem to have a taste for American blood, since no one else was getting bitten this evening. Now that they have unfettered access to me through the open window with no screen, I'm being eaten alive. When I close the window, the temperature in the room skyrockets to stifling.

I can't do this.

Long after midnight I'm asking myself why I'm here. Why I feel I can't stick it out. This was *my* adventure, no one else signed me up for it, and I need to see it through.

An hour later, I realize I can't do it.

Finally, at about 8:00 a.m., I call Manesh. I tell him about being sick and about the noise. I say I'm heading back to the hotel, at least for the night. I tell Rosa and Raju that I've been sick, that I'll be gone tonight. Rosa's feelings are hurt, but tomorrow I'll have the chance to explain that it is just my sensitive tummy and it wasn't her cooking. I'll buy her chocolate-dipped shortbread cookies to make everything better between us, and she'll declare us Nepali "didis"—Nepali sisters. I'll do this tomorrow. Right now, though, I'm just focused on getting out of here.

Back at the hotel, I spend hours lying on the cold, white tile of the bathroom floor in my new room. It's quiet here. Peaceful. Pigeons coo outside my open window. No screens here, and no mosquitoes, either.

At dinnertime, I use the chrome railing to pull myself up the stairs to the roof, feeling every fiber of my weak muscles. With each step, I am soothed by gentle ukulele strumming. One of the girls from Spain softly sings *Over the Rainbow* in delicate Spanish as she plays.

The young nurse from Lithuania sees me and asks how I'm feeling. She is genuine in her concern. I tell her I will be fine, I am eating, and will get through it. I am stubborn and determined.

≈

Manesh cringes when he visits me the next day at the elder care home.

"It is very noisy," he says. It's something you don't notice until you have to spend time here. He ends up giving me three chances to leave the elder care home. While part of me wants to leave, the rest of me believes we are *where* we're supposed to be, *when* we're supposed to be there. I believe I'm supposed to be here.

We are fast approaching Dashain, the biggest holiday in Nepal. I tell Manesh I'll do my best to stick it out until the end of the fifteen-day holiday, making my stay in this home one month long. It's clear that there's no place else for me to stay anyway. The young Lithuanian nurse gave me earplugs to try, and there's a mosquito net I can use back at CGN's offices. I can do this, I tell myself.

The next morning, however, I am again questioning my decision and my sanity.

I don't know how I'm going to get through it, how I'm going to survive an entire month without sleep. It was so loud last night. The foam earplugs seemed to make the noise louder and more muffled. My ear canals ache from the pressure of the earplugs, and I don't know how I'll be able to use them long-term. In total, I got about three hours of sleep.

I have never in my life heard something this loud. How do people live like this? My body feels like it's been battered around in a cement mixer, with chunks of dried cement rolling around in there with me. My entire psyche feels defeated and punished.

Depression is more than just "being down," as many people think. It is an inability to function, a weakness and fatigue that invade your body and mind, and a dark cloud that fogs your clarity. It's caused by any number of situations, either internal or external.

This night I feel the weight of the challenge ahead of me, and can see the specter of Depression sitting in the corner, waiting.

9.

Demands and Lies

AFTER BREAKFAST THE NEXT morning, I take my Nepal-English dictionary, and my notes from Sunjiya's Nepali lessons from our CGN orientation, and venture downstairs to the courtyard. Pradeep announced last night that he would be back here at 10:00 a.m. sharp, for the Nepali lessons he promised to Manesh and me during our initial meeting. He demanded that I be downstairs on time, and so I am.

There are a few red chairs out in the courtyard in a circle. Rosa is visiting with some people at the front gate, and Raju is sweeping. In Nepal, you sweep with either a stiff reed brush or a horsehair-style plant brush. Both brushes are handheld, with the reeds or plants gathered around a short wooden dowel and wrapped tightly with twine. It's back-breaking work to sweep a floor with one of these brushes. To be efficient at this task requires a certain flair and skill, and Raju is quite proficient.

At about 10:40 a.m., a few people venture into the courtyard. They eye me, suspicious, chat with Rosa and Raju, then take their chairs in the circle.

By 11:00 a.m., Mahti is seated with us, and Pradeep has wobbled in with his female sidekick, Sahdi.

Sahdi is young enough to be the youngest of Pradeep's daughters. Her traditional Nepali clothes are expensive, and her hair is henna-colored. She walks with the air of someone who expected to be a princess in this lifetime, but she loves me like a sister from the start.

It becomes apparent that this is a community meeting, and that it's a daily event. I'm witnessing more of how Nepalis lie to each other. Manesh and I were told that other elders come to the home during the day for activities. Wrong. This community meeting is the so-called activity.

During the meeting, Pradeep crosses his legs, places the tips of his fingers together in front of him, elbows resting on the arms of the chair, and gazes off with disinterest. As the community members discuss issues and debate topics, he never makes eye contact with any of them. When Rosa serves tea during the meeting, he makes her drag a chair over and leave it next to him. Then she has to put the tea on the chair. He never takes the tea directly from Rosa, or anyone serving him, and never looks at the server.

After the meeting breaks up, Raju stacks the chairs, leaving one next to me. I want to sit in the courtyard and work on my own Nepali lessons, but Mahti ushers me towards the stairs, motioning that it's nap time. I shake my head no, and point downward. I want to stay downstairs.

No, she's insistent. It's time to nap.

Really? Again, as with everything else thus far, I don't want to seem rude, so I venture back upstairs to my cell.

~

Two days later, I'm bored. My room is broiling hot, and there is nothing for me to do here. None of the elders who live here want or need my help.

I decide to venture back to CGN's headquarters, trying to find some place to hang out for a while. Perhaps I can get on their Wi-Fi, sit in the stairwell as the young kids do, and type away on my phone.

"Alisa!" Pradeep commands as I prepare to walk off the grounds. I stop and look at him. His community meeting has begun, and here he is with Sahdi and another woman I don't know. "Where you go?" His tone is sharp, accentuating his broken English.

"Out," I reply.

"Where?" he barks, still looking out at traffic.

"To the office."

He nods. I turn to leave. "When you come back to prita asam?" comes the next question. He is using his term for the elder care home. In fact, all of the people associated with this shrine and this elder care home refer to it by that name.

I pause, and shake my head in response to Pradeep's question. Do I have to know when I'm coming back? Do I have to have a schedule? Do I have to tell him? "I don't know," I say, then decide to make him happy with their requisite, "Radi, radi!" as I leave the grounds.

At CGN's offices, I slip off my shoes outside and switch into my yellow pool slippers, then stroll down the grimy hallway to greet Muna and Rekha, the two women who cook for us at CGN. When I greet them with a hearty, "Radi, radi!" they look at each other, confused, then back to me.

Am I saying it wrong? Sunjiya arrives and they speak to her, and I repeat the phrase, also confused. "Is this correct?" I ask, and Sunjiya's ever-present cheery smile fades.

"I do not know this phrase," she says.

"This is what they teach me at the prita asam," I explain, and her eyebrows rise, while Muna and Rekha continue to shake their heads.

"'Prita asam?'" Sunjiya asks. "Do you mean the ashram?"

Just a few days into this assignment and I begin to realize that the elder care home where I'm staying is quite different from the Nepal around it. No one at the home refers to it as an ashram, which is the proper Nepali word for it, and I never bother to ask anyone at the home why they call it a prita asam, or what the term means. It feels as if asking questions would get me more involved with this group, and I'm not so sure I want to get too close to these folks.

ॐ

It is still very early during my first week at the elder care home when I run upstairs mid-service to catch a break from the mosquitoes. I don't want to go

39

back downstairs. I'm the only one getting bitten, and while it amuses everyone else, it doesn't amuse me.

Within minutes Pradeep is at my door, bellowing my name. He pulled himself up the stairs on his painful, wobbly knees. He wants to know if I've eaten. I don't understand. I tell him I will eat at 8:00 p.m. I'm not sure what he's trying to ask me because this is the small talk that Nepalis go through before getting to their point.

Finally, he spits out, "You come back down."

It catches me off guard. I know that "please" and "thank you" are implied in tone and conjugation in Nepali, but this sounds bossy. Feeling as if I have no choice, I lock the door behind me and follow him back downstairs.

The reality is that Pradeep wants to show me off. It makes him look good that I'm here, even if I'm doing nothing. I am an American, and I'm staying with them, which impresses the folks who come to the services. Many have never met an American, and so Pradeep looks like a savvy negotiator and businessman for having me stay at this home. Plus, Pradeep gets money to house and feed me every day I'm here, although I'm not sure any of the congregants at the evening services are aware of this.

At the end of the service tonight, I watch as people crowd around the older man when he passes out the food offerings from the altar, and I glance towards the gate as the very young girl and her younger brother walk out into the dark streets again, alone. The girl is about eight or nine years old, and I imagine her brother must be four or five. It's clear they're dirt-poor. Every night that I've seen them, they've worn the same filthy clothes. She wears an old, faded, short-sleeved jersey-style top, with "The Amazing Spider-Man" printed on the front, along with a cartoon of Spider-Man himself. After every service, the girl takes her brother by the hand, and they leave. No one talks to them. They never get any of the offerings since the adults crowd them out.

There's no time to think about the children, though, and no time to ask anyone about them. Pradeep and Garima have arranged their chairs as usual so the regular participants can pay their respects to us as they depart, and

Garima is ordering me to sit between them. They are royalty, expecting their subjects to bow to them, and I'm included in this charade.

Once again, Pradeep reminds me to be downstairs again the next morning at 10:00 a.m., *sharp*. He slaps his palms across each other in the Nepali fashion of emphasizing his words. And as usual, I will sit in the courtyard at 10:00 a.m., *sharp*, with my notebook and notes and dictionary, and people will arrive closer to 11:00 a.m., and Pradeep will arrive, with Sahdi by his side, just past that.

10.

Mother Mahti

THAT NEXT NIGHT, PARTWAY through the service, a man asks if he can perform a song. Pradeep seems reluctant, but allows it. This man is in his late forties, has a striking head of hair, quite long by Nepali standards. He wears a short pendant around his neck, and very stylish Nepali clothes—almost Western styled. He is, in every sense of the phrase, an earthy artistic type.

When he takes to the harmonium, the man who normally plays the tabla seems lit up out of nowhere. This singer is a story teller. He pauses as he plays, sings to the audience of mostly women, gestures with his free right hand as his left continues to pump the back of the harmonium. Rosa and Raju come out to listen, arms folded, leaning against a wall, smiling. It seems that the world has paused because this performer is on the stage of our soul. He sings, he warbles, he gestures, he captivates. And while the noise continues outside the elder care home, inside we are all entranced.

All of us, it seems, except Pradeep.

As usual, Garima repositions the chairs so that I am between her and Pradeep, post-service. Tonight, we sit across from the storyteller.

As people begin paying their respects to Pradeep and Garima, this storyteller leans in. He doesn't speak English. I can understand, though, that he's talking to me about his performance earlier. Pradeep shakes his head, disgusted. "He want to tell his story," he gripes at me. He admonishes the singer in Nepali, saying to me that we've already heard his song. I stop Pradeep and say I would like to hear it again.

Once more, time stands still within the confines of this courtyard as the singer performs the story for me again. Those within earshot sink into the

43

closest chair, transfixed, and I find myself leaning forward, forward, almost so far that I could fall out of my chair and down to his feet.

~

A few days later, I'm disappointed to see Rosa and her family moving out. I knew this was coming. Pradeep had told Manesh and me that the family who lives here and cooks for us stays only a few weeks. Then they are asked to move out to give another family the opportunity to serve the elders. Rosa and Raju's friends come with a truck, and begin to pack the family's belongings into the back. The truck makes two trips. It seems they've been here much longer than a few weeks.

I am sad as they drive off, but even more so as Rosa gathers the last of her bags in her arms and walks towards me. We say our goodbyes. There is no hugging in Nepal, but I want to hug her. Then she's gone, out through the gate and away.

The couple who moves in to replace Rosa and Raju are very young. She is short and squat, and her name is Akriti. He is lean, stooping over at a young age from hard work, and I will never remember his name. Their young son is ill-mannered and doesn't once lift a finger to help the elders, the way Rosa and Raju's son would. I'm unimpressed. They aren't my Nepali didi—my Nepali sister—and her family.

~

I've learned that I had expectations for this trip, even after saying I didn't have any. I came here with the plan to work, volunteer, assist, and learn, and I understand that part of this process is sitting and observing. It's been a week, though, and I want to be of use. I would like to show Pradeep and others that I have value beyond just hanging out and making him look good.

This morning after the community meeting, I tell Pradeep that I need to do some work. I tell Mahti that I will trim her toenails. I've already brought everything downstairs. I sit on a mat on the ground in front of her, and Daya takes pictures as I trim toenails and check Mahti's feet for sores.

This, I realize, represents a significant cultural challenge for them. I'm sitting on the ground and *touching their feet* (but wearing non-latex gloves). The feet are the dirtiest part of the body, and to sit at someone's feet is to humble oneself, as if sitting at the feet of your teacher. But to *touch* someone's feet is to put yourself beneath them. For an honored guest to do all this is just unheard of.

When I'm done, everyone is quiet. Mahti, Daya, Akriti, Hajuraama are all holding their breath. Finally, Pradeep waves his hands in the air and announces in broken English, "This make me very happy. What you have done make my heart happy." The women finally smile and exhale in relief. I tell Pradeep, "I do this for you, for everyone here. I do this for the elders in the community." Even with Pradeep's happy heart at my actions, and my subsequent offer, nothing will ever happen.

Several days from now, I will learn that Mahti's husband recently passed away, and that her youngest daughter decided she wanted the house and the property for herself. Mahti and her oldest daughter, Daya, who is living with her at the elder care home, were chased from the house in the middle of the night. After months of arguing, the youngest daughter had decided to take a more violent approach. Mahti will say this youngest daughter has become involved with the Maoists, and it was those "friends" who helped force Mahti and Daya from their home.

Grabbing what few things they could manage, mother and daughter escaped to the home of friends. Somehow, they found their way here, to the safety of strangers. They will live here as they work their way through the legal battle with the youngest daughter. From time to time, they'll dress in their finest and walk to the government offices, disappearing for a day. As the month progresses, I will watch as Daya becomes increasingly frustrated with her mother after these trips, and I will see Mahti turn more and more inside herself, resigned to a truth I don't understand. I will watch Mahti turn to me, looking for someone to mother, and I will begin to understand her without being able to communicate in words.

જ

As I'm putting my nail care kit away in my room, Hajuraama appears at my door. I can't believe this ancient, stooped woman climbed up the extra flight of stairs. She wants me to come to their room, and I take my nail trimming kit along just in case. Once inside their room, I'm overpowered by the stench of urine, feces, and body odor.

Hajuraama gestures to her husband, seated at a small table. She wants me to trim his nails. I take a few quick photos of the conditions in their room. The last thing I want to do is sit on this rug, but I tell myself I can always wash my leggings. I came here to serve, not to pick and choose whom I serve this way.

I don't know what I can possibly do. It looks as if he hasn't been bathed in ages. Layers of dead, yellow skin are cracking on top of his feet. The brownish-yellow nails on the first and second toes on his left foot are so long they are curling down in front of the flesh, the quick underneath having grown up behind the length of his nails. I try to figure out how far I can trim before I hit the quick. I decide to file and chip away little by little so I don't cause him pain, but it seems anything I do hurts him. I keep working, checking with him until he says, "Pujyo." Enough.

He hurts too much from the little work I did on his left foot, so I can't touch his right foot, and those nails are just as bad. Maybe I can finish another day. That day, however, will never come.

I collect my kit and prepare to say my goodbyes, but now he's standing, taking my hands and touching them to his forehead. I start weeping. I'm trying to touch his hands to my forehead, but he's fighting me, won't have it. He's fighting back tears, too.

I go back to my room and close my door. I sit on the cement step along the back wall of my room, and take a few deep breaths. I can only do so much. I can't do it all.

46

࿓

Mahti checks on me later. I hear her shuffling feet outside my almost-closed door and glance up from where I'm trying to stay cool on the floor. She laughs a little, poking her head into the room, and then looks dismayed. One quick glance at my windows tells her what she needs to know. She swipes her hand down: Come here.

I push myself off the floor, slip on my sandals outside my room, and follow her down the hall to another room. She pushes at the door, but it doesn't give. One swift, strategic *bang* with the heel of her hand, and it opens. She looks in, looks around. Nope, not there.

Down to the next room. Another *bang* and another unstuck door. I walk in behind her and see a magnificent sight: a stack of window screens amidst grimy platform beds stacked against a wall. She smiles, nods, and I am laughing. I find one that will fit. Mahti nods some more, clasping her hands together in joy, and I grasp her hands and bring my forehead to meet them.

"Dhanyabad," I keep saying. *Thank you.*

11.

Sit and Stay

TIME IS A CONSTRUCT created by man to give us the impression that we are in control of something, when in reality we control nothing. We have created this illusion for ourselves that we make decisions, and that these decisions drive the direction of our lives. When something unexpected happens, however, it pulls the rug from beneath our feet, sending us flying into groundlessness, forward into fear and anxiety. This is life. It is unexpected. It is unplanned. It is.

Time isn't. It doesn't exist except in man's imagination. Still, I measure time here out of habit, or boredom, or perhaps desperation.

I have been in Nepal two weeks. That means in two more weeks I will have been here one month. Then I will think that time is flying by. Two weeks beyond that, I will be at the halfway point, in a desperate hurry to slow time down. After another two weeks, I will have been here two months with one month to go, and I will feel anxious that there isn't enough time left. That time will be moving too fast.

Every day, I work on being okay with being with myself. What I'm *not* okay with, though, is the boredom, which is what being with yourself is all about. You get bored and you get through it.

I've promised Manesh I will stick it out until the end of Dashain, and I still believe there's a reason I'm here, at this place, at this time. I must have patience.

I watch the days pass. One by one.

I'm restless. Sort of. It feels as if I'm being pushed to move. Maybe it's the noise that is driving me to move, to get away from it. Maybe it's the need to keep moving, so the depression that weighs on me doesn't take hold of me.

49

There is something I am supposed to do here. I don't know what, I don't know how, or why or where or when. I don't know who or what is placing this idea in my brain, but it is driving me to the brink of my sanity. Call it intuition, if you will, but I understand, somehow, that there is something I'm supposed to be doing here.

I should practice just sitting and staying and listening to this voice. I should wait for the opportunity to come to me. I shouldn't be running around in my mind. I shouldn't "should" myself, either.

I begin to stand in the doorway of my room, just observing life going on in the streets. I take my camera and look for interesting shots. I drag a red outdoor chair up to my lonely third floor balcony and set it near my room to drink my tea outside. I look for a rhythm to life here, for something that makes sense, and I see none. I look for patterns, for familiarity, and find nothing.

I am wallowing in my own private agony. I keep spiraling around the same questions. Why have I come home to Nepal? What is my purpose for being here? Why am I supposed to sit and stay at this elder care home?

ॐ

Because there's nothing to do here, I end up reading a lot on my phone app. Burning through data at an amazing speed, I am a regular visitor to Dil's services shop to buy more cell data. The concept of a services shop is new for me. You name it, he can do it for you. If he can't do it, he's got a guy who can do it. (Insert New York accent here: *"I got a guy…"*) He arranges for air and bus travel, treks and adventure tours; picks his hotel guests up at the airport and takes them back at the end of their trip; sells SIM cards and cell data—you name it.

I have no way of knowing that Dil will be the man who rescues me in a couple of weeks.

Dil is a small, but not slight, man. He is confident, honest, has good energy about him, and we recognize each other right away as brother and sister. We are old friends. He has a receding hairline, and his is hair is cropped close, still dark but with gray in it. His face is round, and he wears black frame glasses that compliment his face. One day he wears a black, Nepal t-shirt and jeans; another day he wears a black, Hard Rock Café Biloxi t-shirt and jeans. When I visit, he orders milk tea from the restaurant across the street, and we relax and chat. Each time, he invites me to join him and his partner, Puja, whom he promises he will marry someday, at their hotel. "Come any time you need to," he says.

~

It's gotten old. People gather and sing the same old, tired songs as the usual harmonium player plods along and the tabla player fights to keep awake, and every night people give money the way congregants do at any religious ceremony. How much these folks donate, I don't know, but between the donations and the rent these elder residents pay, it should be enough to keep us from running out of water at the taps once or twice a week.

It's a familiar routine already. The taps run dry, toilets won't flush, laundry gets stale, and several days go by before the water truck parks out in the road and pumps some water into our underground tank. In Nepal, buildings have a large underground reservoir for non-potable water. From there, the water is pumped up to a storage tank on the roof, where gravity feeds it to the taps and toilets. The continual lack of water is disrespectful to the people who live here, to the people who've entrusted their care to Pradeep.

It's not just the disrespect and the boredom that is driving me out of my mind. It's the combination of it all: The relentless traffic noise and the lack of sleep and the expectation that I will join every service. It's the expectation that I report to Pradeep and Garima and that they seem to own me, and the annoyance that if I arrive downstairs in the middle of the service, one of the regulars will chastise me and tell me to show up on time the next night.

Even when I bolt to upscale Thamel and to the fancy, uber-hip Western coffee shop, I know I'm not supposed to be there. I'm supposed to be *here*, stuck in orbit at this so-called elder care home.

I don't know that I really like upscale Thamel, anyway. Last week I watched as an elderly beggar walked along the side of the street ahead of me.

A young man standing in the doorway of his shop sneered at him, then cuffed the old man on the back of the head. He struck him hard enough to knock the man almost off balance. When the beggar looked up, his eyes asking why, the young man's lip curled, and he gestured with his head: "Keep moving."

I could have stopped the old man right there and given him all the money I had with me, telling the young shop owner, "This is the money I won't spend in your store because of your disrespect to this man." I could have done that, right then and right there.

But I didn't. I let it happen. I let it go.

I decided it wasn't my battle, I guess, and I don't like that. It's not who I am. It seems as if I've lost a bit of my humanity.

I *don't* need an escape. I *do* need to sit and stay and *be here now*. I need to sit with who I am and find the core of my being once again.

To drive home this point, the Universe or God or Fate intervenes with my restlessness and desire to keep bolting from this place: I tweak something in my left hip one night while Hindu dancing.

࿔

Tonight, I have come downstairs for the service like a dutiful child, ready to be put on display. Dashain, the fifteen-day holiday, has begun, and this evening's audience is twice the normal size. Most nights the ashram attracts about fifteen people. With Dashain, though, we'll have special evening services, with professional musicians performing, and the audience will swell to fifty or more people packed into the small courtyard amidst the temples and statue of Buddha.

Everyone is happy to see me. One young girl has me sit next to her. Her friend takes photos of us as the girl takes selfie after selfie with me for what feels like dozens of photos.

Soon I'm sitting with my sisters—Sahdi and Jhanchu—and we are laughing in the shrine room because the music is festive tonight. Jhanchu and I just met this evening, and she clasped my hands, both of us delighted to see each other again after not seeing one another this entire lifetime and never having met here before. We declared each other a sister. She has big teeth and a bright smile and wants me to sit with her on the floor of the shrine room.

I feel myself wanting to cling to her. We are sisters from before and sisters now, but our paths were only meant to cross for this important moment in the vacuum of time.

The priest is here leading the service, and Garima sits on the floor of the shrine room with us. The priest is shorter than me, lean, and very much a mischievous pixie. His eyes always twinkle when he spots me on the temple grounds. His hair is short all around, with the exception of a six-inch-long ponytail high on the back of his head. Also with us tonight is the Acharya for these temple grounds. I'm familiar with the role of an Acharya from my Buddhist studies. This is a man (or, in Buddhism, it could also be a woman) who achieves a certain level of study, and then is assigned an area or group of congregations as a spiritual leader.

The music is amazing tonight. Our usual tabla player is going to town, with new harmonium players and singers rotating through. I find myself moving to the beat. Jhanchu, seeing this, knows I can't resist the God in the music. She jumps up to dance, spins, and reaches a hand out to me. I'm shaking my head. Sahdi is nudging me from behind. Other women are calling for me to dance. The priest turns, sees me being prodded, and his face lights up. He starts dancing, gesturing to me, luring me up and out of my seat, and Jhanchu is calling to me and shimmying. Despite my efforts to keep my tush glued to the floor, I find myself up and joining them.

The crowd goes wild, as they say in sports.

Sahdi has her phone up, recording every moment. People are clapping to the beat. The usual women outside in the courtyard are elated, leaning into each other and pointing, excited. And I'm nowhere to be found.

I'm lost in the music. Small steps, delicate hip shimmies, arms moving, mudras—my hand gestures—are evolving from one to the other. Sahdi holds the phone up higher, moves to get a better angle. I turn my backside to her and wag it a little. Everyone howls in joy. I am in heaven.

And then I feel the snap.

I pause, put my hand on my left hip. I dance a little more, favoring my left hip, but beg off any more dancing and sit down.

Jhanchu wants to know why I'm sitting. Sahdi prods me. I gesture to my hip, tell them "duksnu"—"pain"—and shake my head. I have to be forceful. They can't understand why I can't or won't dance. But they see the look on my face, and they know I'm not faking it.

My first thought, as the festivities proceed and I laugh and cheer, is how can I immediately get my hands on some ibuprofen?

Our Acharya is on the tabla now, and Jhanchu's husband is on the harmonium. Blind from birth, Jhanchu's husband is a self-taught harmonium player and has won awards. The Acharya is tall and handsome in a boy-next-door way, and his clothing is expensive. Both he and Jhanchu's husband together are polished performers, and we are all alive with their music.

The priest is spinning, and we are clapping. Jhanchu's husband and our Acharya are keeping up with each other. The music is tight, the priest is spinning faster and faster, until everything—the music, the dancing, the clapping, the laughter—falls apart into more laughter, and the priest is panting and clapping in appreciation of everyone's skills.

My hip will stiffen, and the pain will start tonight. I'm going to have to be as immobile as possible for at least a week, perhaps two. I check what movement hurts, what doesn't.

At the end of the service, I stand with everyone for the last song. Then, as if I'm in a one-woman receiving line, people begin coming up to me. Am I really hurt? Yes, yes, really hurt. My left hip. "Khomann duksnu," I say—"hip pain."

Underneath my smile, I'm despondent. This means no more venturing away from the elder care home for space. No more exercising in my room. No more escaping.

Now I really have to sit and stay.

☙

The next evening, I still need ibuprofen, but have no way to walk up the street to the "medical store," and there's no one to go for me.

But Mahti knows much without saying much. Earlier I had hobbled down the stairs to find Daya, Mahti, and Akriti chatting in the hallway outside the kitchen. I held out a note to Daya with the word "ibuprofen" on it, along with a few hundred rupees, which is far more than the pills would cost here. In my dodgy Nepali, I asked if she could go to the medical store.

Recoiling in disgust, she shook her head no. She would not walk one block to help me. Perhaps in disbelief, I tried again but again got the same response, except that this time she looked to Akriti as if she would share Daya's horror at my request.

Despondent, I dragged myself back up the stairs, one at a time, back to my room, hoping to figure something out.

Now the guests have started to arrive for the evening's service. As I lie in my bed, I tell myself I won't go down tonight. I don't want to put my hip through all these stairs.

A gentle knock at the door, and I rise to see Mahti poke her head in. She gestures. One swift and stern hand swipe down. *Come here.*

Before I can rise, she's gone. I grab my note and money and head to the door, and she's nowhere to be seen. Down to the second floor, no, she's not here, either. Down to the ground level, where she is waiting outside the shrine room. One more quick swipe of her hand, and I hobble to her.

Mahti stabs her finger into the shrine room, and suddenly Sahdi sees me and is rushing over. Am I all right? How is my hip? I tell her that I need someone to go to the medical store and buy some ibuprofen. She barks out orders. A man rushes over, and I explain everything to him in English. He understands and leaves before I can even thank him. Within minutes I have my saving grace: bright, pink round, magic pills of four hundred milligrams ibuprofen. I search for Mahti to thank her, but she's not around.

12.

Pradeep, the Bully

STUCK IN MY NINE-BY-THIRTEEN-FOOT sweltering room, I meditate even more than before, trying to rise above the noise. I work on the Buddhist practice of putting myself in other people's shoes, and on finding grace with Pradeep. I work on observing everything and not being irritable.

My issues with Pradeep go beyond cultural dissonance. It's not just his attitude or the bossiness. There's something with which I continue to struggle. I know I can't take responsibility for his actions and his behavior. I can only take responsibility for *my reactions* to his behavior. So then I look to myself without blame.

It is me, not enjoying the requirement to treat him like royalty, and not enjoying the questioning when I start to walk off the temple grounds, having to report where I'm going and when I'm coming back.

It is me, not wanting to be put on display, and not wanting to attend every evening service, without fail, and on time. I'm annoyed at the expectation these folks have that I will attain perfect attendance at their service while I'm here. Organized religion and I parted ways many years ago.

Plus, I cannot stomach the thought of being used by Pradeep. He's using me to make himself look good, and he has no qualms about forcing these elders to live in a toxic environment where the water is always running out, while he lives in his nice apartment up the street.

৵

Before Dashain started, Manesh moderated a meeting with Pradeep, Sahdi, and me. During that meeting, and all the meetings after it, Pradeep spoke only Nepali, forcing Manesh to translate everything. Not once did Pradeep speak English, or use the unique dialect found here at the elder care home.

When Manesh told Pradeep that I was willing to find grants so they could fix the toilets in the facility, Pradeep fumbled through his pants pocket until he found a random slip. He waved it in the air without showing us, then told Manesh, with great pride, that he had a list of everything wrong with every toilet and had already hired someone to fix them. He didn't need my help.

It was a lie, of course, and I'm certain Manesh knew it.

Manesh next told Pradeep that I could help create a brochure for the facility, and Pradeep seemed pleased with this news. I explained, through Manesh, that this brochure would advertise the facility to others, once the toilets were repaired. Manesh translated Pradeep's reply. "We opened this elder care home with our heart and no money," Pradeep claimed in a soft voice, patting his hand across his chest. "We did not have a thought to these things," he said, meaning that they never thought about making brochures.

Another lie. One year from now, I will learn that he did not open this elder care home. Others did.

At that meeting, it was decided that Pradeep will have his English-speaking friend translate for us, and I will write and design the brochure.

One week later, nothing has happened.

Only Sahdi and Pradeep have shown up for my so-called Nepali lesson this morning. I ask Pradeep if his friend is still going to help us with the brochure. He was supposed to be here a few days ago but never showed up. Since Manesh isn't around, we are conversing in English. Pradeep replies that his friend had to leave town, and that he's too busy to help anyway.

As I text a Nepali acquaintance on my phone, I ask Pradeep if there are students who can help. A friend of mine, Suzie, who spent three years in Nepal with the Peace Corps, is introducing me via email to a woman she used to know. We are planning to meet for coffee.

Pradeep asks who I'm texting. I tell him I'm meeting a Nepali friend today.

"She speak English?" he asks.

I say, yes, she's a Nepali woman who speaks English.

He tells me to text her to "come here *now*." I say, "Excuse me?" He repeats it, firm. "You tell her come here *now*," he says, stabbing his index finger downward, emphasizing his demand. "I am here now, she come here *now*." Pradeep's demand is that this woman—whom he doesn't know—should drop everything and rush to the elder care home to help with the brochure.

I glance at Sahdi, who appears to be holding her breath. Pradeep waits. We all sit, with nothing to say, until Sahdi breaks the silence, asking about Pradeep's nieces. But only a few minutes pass before Pradeep is back on his demands. "You text her?" he asks. "She come?"

I look at him evenly. "No, I didn't."

Pradeep looks stunned. "No?" he asks.

"No," I reply. "It is not her responsibility."

I can't tell if Pradeep is silent because he's never had a woman refuse to jump at his command, or if he's silent because he's never been told no by anyone. I do know he's dumbfounded.

My refusal to text this woman has annoyed him. I glance up to see him look away, angry, his foot circling in the air.

꙰

This evening, my meditation practice revolves around everything having a purpose, even though it might not be the intended purpose we have devised. As much as I ask myself why I'm here, tonight I let my mind quiet, and this is when the correct question arises: *What if I'm not here to just do elder care?* After all, to insist that I'm here to do elder care is to force life to happen instead of letting life flow.

Perhaps it's time to let go of the rocks in the stream and flow with the water.

13.

Dakshinkali

DASHAIN IS FULL OF special days, and today is one of them. Garima is taking me on a bus ride with thirty other women, most of whom attend services at the shrine. All I know is we are going to visit a temple.

I've decided to wear the beautiful red kurta that Rekha helped me purchase on one of my first days in Nepal. A kurta is the traditional long tunic-styled top for women, with slits up each side from the hem to the hips. Rekha works at CGN, along with Muna, cooking and cleaning for everyone at CGN's offices. One day during orientation, after her work was done, Rekha had taken me to a store where she felt we could find the best options. When I returned to the same store the next day with two other volunteers, the shop owner refused to let us in. She apparently didn't like the fact that Rekha had negotiated the price of my kurta down from one thousand rupees to eight hundred rupees.

Now, as I wait for this temple trip to begin, the short bus fills up with women sitting everywhere they can, including on the carpeted hump next to the driver. Soon enough they are singing and clapping. They repeat variations of *"Hare Krishna," "Hare hare,"* and *"Krishna Krishna."* The song seems to go on forever. When it does end, there is silence for only a few moments before another woman picks up a similar refrain and tune.

We turn right off the main road and cross a bridge, turning left along the waterfront, and head into what I will later call No Man's Land. Outside the bus window, I see tarps and bags strung up to create lean-tos, forming a loose, unstructured, tent city. A deep layer of rotting garbage surrounds the structures. Young men and old, bean-pole thin, pick through the garbage or sit by the side of the road, their clothes thick with layers of dust, grime, and

61

exhaust fumes. The water I saw when we first crossed the bridge has changed from brown liquid to muddy liquid to thick, stagnant mud.

Ninety minutes into the rocky, nerve-wracking, and dangerous drive, we come to a stop in a wide dirt area. As we start walking, Garima turns me to face the bus. "Alisa," she commands, "remember we are bus number four-seven-seven." Nepali numbers are nothing like Arabic numbers, and I try not to laugh. "Four-seven-seven," she intones again, and I opt to just take a picture of the curlicued figures. "You come back here when you want," she continues. "You are not allowed inside the temple. You are not Hindu." She wags her finger in my face as if reprimanding me for not being one of them.

For a bunch of older women with bad backs and arthritic knees, these ladies really can move, and I struggle to keep up with them on my injured hip. We trek up a long road, and then I'm looking at a seemingly never-ending set of stairs, down and down some more. Religious pilgrims are making the trip back up the stairs, some carrying children too tired to walk anymore, others carrying baskets or bags that held offerings for the goddess Kali. Each one is wearing a tika, a red or orange dot on the forehead symbolic of religious devotion for many Hindus. For others, the dot is considered a blessing that improves concentration, being positioned on the Third Eye, or sixth chakra.

Vendors sit on the side of the steps, cooking food for sale to those passing by, or selling fruits and vegetables. A few amputees beg for any type of help the pilgrims might be willing to give.

We are still making our way down the never-ending stairs, when we pass a wall of brass bells on our right. Thousands of them, in every shape and size, hang from racks lining the stone wall. They are strung up by chains, by yarn, or fabric, and most just hang off each other. I ring random bells on the way down, following the example of other women around me. It feels like the right, respectful thing to do.

Down below, to my left, I see the full impact of this temple: Sprawling across two trickling streams of mud are stairs, platforms, and buildings. Across from us are even more stairs leading up and away to the other entrance, with another mass of worshippers heading down. Joining with the people from this side, they are two crowds of tired pilgrims trying to merge into one thin stream of life.

Intricate brass statues of beastly looking dogs line each side of the stone gates which lead into an area called the statuary. People enter the cramped statuary from one side, and shuffle their way through to make offerings to the statue of Kali so their wishes will be granted. From there, they head past a row of boxes angled outwards. I see women touching something in the boxes and then touching their foreheads—blessing themselves? With what? Stuff is hanging from everywhere—decorations, balls of orange fabric strung together, strips of red fabric decorated and trimmed with gold thread. Marigold petals rest on any flat surface. Orange, yellow, and red tika paint seems to have fallen from the sky. On the outside of the statuary gates, men are seated on mats. Are they giving blessings? How someone becomes qualified to give blessings to strangers is beyond my grasp right now.

It is a controlled chaos of people and layers of stuff.

Farther along this walkway is a plaza with more men sitting on mats giving blessings for a small fee. Through a massive haze, I see people burning incense along the curved railings. As I turn to the stairs leading into an open structure, a boy about ten years old comes down the steps with his father's arm draped around his shoulder. His father is beaming with pride. The boy is holding a limp chicken resting across his forearms, the chicken's head in his right hand. Many Hindus make animal sacrifices to Kali in order to obtain favor with her. Blood must be spilled, these people believe. Traditions must be upheld, they think. This is the way it is done, the way it has always been done.

I ascend the steps of the large, open-sided building. Even if the room weren't quite so shadowed, I couldn't say if the floor was stone or cement because all I can see are blood stains. The stench overpowers me, and I have a sudden need to get out of there.

I walk back down the steps and out into the small, circular plaza, where incense burns everywhere. The air is choked with smoke. All of this is cut into the sides of the hills, and I am speechless. It is sensory overload—where to look, how to take it all in, how to comprehend all that I'm seeing. The incense plaza overlooks the muddy stream, which is drying up. Children play in the rock-bottomed, ankle-deep water; adults bathe in it and drink it from their hands.

As I start to walk down the third side of this sacrificial building, I'm stopped by a young man who asks in English if I can take a picture of him and the three young women on the bench under the railing. They are volunteers for the temple for Dashain. It is a strange honor to snap photos of them on his phone as the girls preen and pose, except for one girl, who simply smiles at the camera. She is the one with whom this young man is infatuated, it seems. As crowded as this place is, he chose me to capture this moment for him.

When the photo session is done, I ask him why this place is special, and he gives me the straight answer: This is Dakshinkali, where devout Hindus come to worship Kali, the most bloodthirsty goddess in their religion. They believe that if they worship her, she will grant them their wishes.

Since that isn't quite the answer I'm looking for, I ask again: "But why *this* place? What makes this place so special?" The young women around him giggle. He starts to explain the beauty of the valley and the river, which is long and muddy, and scattered with garbage, so I rephrase my question. "But why not someplace else? Why not build a temple to Kali someplace else?"

"Ah," he says. "So the goddess Kali appears to King Malla a long time ago and tells him to build a temple to her here on this spot for sacrifices, and she will be happy. He had a dream, but when he wakes, he realizes it is not a dream but that she really was there. She was appearing to him." The young women are nodding in agreement as he talks. "So he went to someone and said that a temple was needed here. There was already a statue here, so they build the temple also."

"There was a statue here already?"

"Yes," he says.

"And do you know why there was a statue here already?" I am trying to understand the full history of this place. It seems a random spot to just place a statue.

The four laugh, a bit uncomfortable. No, they don't know.

As with any nine-hundred-year-old story told and retold through history, a lot can get lost in translation, and much more than that can be lost all together. Which king actually had the visit from Kali isn't clear, since the Malla Dynasty lasted almost six hundred years.

Known as a bloodthirsty goddess in the Hindu religion, Kali (translated as "the black one" and also "she who is death") is portrayed as a vicious-looking warrior with a long, red tongue hanging out, from which the blood of her enemies drips. She has ten arms and wears a necklace of bloody, severed heads. Seven arms hang from a belt around her waist, cut from the demons she's destroyed, and she often appears standing, victorious, with one foot on the body of a slain foe. Another interpretation is that the body beneath her foot is that of Shiva, her consort, who hid among the dead as she celebrated her victory over the demon Raktabija. Overwhelmed with her celebration, it is said Kali was calmed when her foot touched the body of her beloved lord.

Along with being bloodthirsty and demanding, Kali is also regarded as a protective mother figure, and a dispeller of ignorance. She is associated with the death of ignorance that comes with the belief, "I am the body." The skulls and arms adorning her torso are said to be a reminder to devotees that their bodies are limited and not who they are.

Hindus believe that if they sacrifice animals to Kali, or make offerings of fruit, flowers, and garlands to her, she will fulfill their wishes and grant them protection from evil and liberation from ego.

As I watch the scene around me, I recall my childhood days and how busy our Greek Orthodox Church was on Christmas and Easter, how it overflowed with people who came because that's what they were supposed to do. We used to call them "C & E Christians." I frequently wondered why I was even there, why my parents felt the need to go through this routine. Regardless of our religion or spiritual beliefs, we humans do things out of tradition, because we've always done them that way. Because that's what we are taught. We follow tradition because where would we be without it?

ॐ

By now, the young man at Dakshinkali has taken a liking to me and decides he will let me closer, deep into the heart of forbidden territory for non-Hindus. He tells me to follow him. As we walk, one of the women I came with stops me at the top of the stairs leading to the plaza in front of the statuary. I am not even allowed to stand on the top step, she says, but the young man turns around to find me and calls me down. Once in the small plaza, I nod as he tells me I am not allowed through the gates to the statuary.

Armed guards patrol this area. There is so much to take pictures of and too much to photograph. I start with the three intricate bronze statues which line the gates, fierce dogs with the manes of lions, sharp teeth and long tongues, all wearing elaborate battle armor. As I snap a few photos, I realize the statues are covered not just in orange flower petals and tika paint, but blood as well. I look down. I am standing in blood. The ground is awash in it.

જ

It isn't until I finally make it back to the bus that I realize how anxious I was to get away from the temple. I sit in the quiet, feeling the tension of all the activity leave my body, and let my aching hip relax a bit.

As it turns out, I am mistaken in thinking we're just going to this one major temple. No, I have a long day of temple visits ahead of me.

About two hours later, we arrive at the next temple. This is the quintessential pagoda-style temple seen in travel guides. An ornate wooden structure rises before us at the end of a stone walkway, raised above a brick courtyard. To our right, small shrines; to our left, an old building with pillars lining the front.

The volume of carved wood details on this temple is hard to fathom. The core of this massive structure is brick and mortar, but two-thirds of this three-story building is wood. This is Tiger Temple.

The gates are closed to the inner sanctum, and even if they weren't, only Nepalis are allowed in. One sign uses the old terminology: "Entrance only for Nepalese." The other sign uses the new terminology: "Entrance only Nepalis," and, for some reason, that sign is also written in Nepali. Never mind if you're Indian and Hindu, or American and Hindu, you can't get in.

I start shooting photos of everything and make my way around the left side of the temple, where a separate shrine is set up. Since I am in observation mode, I'm not attached to what I'm seeing. Turning to one of the young girls in our group, I ask what is hanging around the shrine. She cringes, embarrassed. "Those are skull pieces of animals who have been sacrificed here."

For a long moment, I stare at the sections of skull and horns and ask myself, "Why?" Once again, I arrive at a familiar answer: Because it is the old way, the way it has always been done. Because they don't question it.

We are all walking clockwise around the temple, and on the back side, several women climb onto the stoop and make their way to the next corner and around the side. They are all hushed. Garima calls to me in a whisper full of reverence, tells me I am to witness the eyes of God.

We make our way along the stoop as the women, one by one, look into the temple through a small window behind a protective grate. They say their prayers to Krishna and bless themselves, touching their forehead and heart three times. Thumb and first and middle finger on their right hand. I think of the countless times I made a similar gesture—thumb and first and middle finger on my right hand touching my forehead, then heart, then right shoulder to left shoulder as I crossed myself as an Orthodox Christian.

When it's my turn, Garima whispers, "Through there, the eyes of God. No pictures," wagging her finger at me again. "This is holy."

No photos is no problem.

I peer through the grate and the little window.

"Do you see?" Garima whispers.

I don't. I don't know what I'm supposed to be looking at.

"In back," she says. "Look to the back."

So I look to the wall across from me in what appears to be the inner sanctum of the temple. I mutter an audible, "Oh."

A stylized set of Buddha's eyes has been painted on the wall above an ornate and well-decorated chair. On a stand next to the chair is a bottle of Mountain Dew.

I step back. "Did you see?" Garima asks, breathless. I nod.

Each woman steps away from her experience with the eyes of God, and each seems transported, feet barely touching the ground.

As we visit one temple after another, I begin to wonder to myself what the point of it all truly is. Religious leaders tell us what to do so that we don't think for ourselves. We are held back by not knowing better, held back by fear, held as indentured servants.

14.

Sewage

AT 4:45 A.M., SEVEN or eight young adults march through the streets, beating drums, blowing horns, and clanging cymbals. They aren't moving very fast, and they aren't playing anything in particular. This is the second time they've done this, and it won't be the last. After breakfast, I ask Daya what the noise was all about. She wrinkles her nose in disgust, shudders a bit, and just says, "Politics."

It will be at least one more month before I understand what this means, and the emotional turmoil it involves.

Still struggling with the compulsion to do something, this morning I decided to focus on what I can do, out of everything that needs to be done, in Hajuraama and Hajurbaa's room. Now their front curtains are washed and hanging out to dry on the railing outside my door.

Their daughter showed up as I was preparing to take down the last curtain from the front window, and she made a half-hearted and useless attempt to help me. I smiled and restrained the Chicago in me, which wanted to grab her by the neck and put her up against the wall with her feet flailing for the floor, her expensive little shoes wiggling beneath her. She looked a bit sheepish as Hajuraama explained what I was doing.

How can anyone think it's acceptable to allow their parents to live in such disgusting filth? The room is coated with urine and grime, and I understand dealing with stubborn parents, but there comes a point where the child becomes the parent and puts her foot down: *You are not going to live this way. This is what's best for your health. Trust me.*

"We are all doing the best we can," I reminded myself as I washed and rinsed and washed and rinsed, each one of the three curtains requiring more than a half an hour's work, until the water ran clear in my bucket. I reflected on my disgust for the daughter. As I acknowledged my ugly feelings and judgment towards a woman who would let her parents live in such filth while she herself goes around in the finest clothes and shoes, I considered all the possibilities. Perhaps she can't get here often. Perhaps she's given in to their previous resistance to receiving help. Maybe she feels paralyzed and unsure of how to help.

I glance up from my seat on the cement step in the back of my room, where I'm taking a break, and then head outside to move the curtains along the railing, chasing the sun.

One year from now, Hajuraama and Hajurbaa won't be living here at the elder care home.

༄

When tonight's service ends, I head back upstairs and stand in my doorway. I watch people passing by on the street as I wait to be called down for dinner. A man walks past with a tall pole laden with specialty balloons for children. Another man pauses by the gate, smokes a cigarette. A few people glance in at the shrine room as they walk past, blessing themselves. I watch for a while, then retreat into my room.

Earlier this evening, a new man appeared at the service. He was just taller than me, lean, a little stooped. His skin was dark, his fingernails dirty, and with him came a cloud of darkness. This man marched across the cement bricks of the courtyard, then stood before the shrine room, palms touching in front of him, eyes upward, engaged in intense pious concentration.

After blessing himself, he bee-lined for Pradeep and held out his hand, palm up, and said something. He was standing sideways to Pradeep, as if he didn't want his back to the audience, as if he understood that you don't turn your back on others for safety reasons.

When Pradeep wouldn't look at him, this man's tone became sharp. Getting no response, he gestured with his fingers, "Give me the money," and his tone became more forceful. He shifted his weight to his other leg and turned to face Pradeep, leaning towards him a bit.

I felt Sahdi, next to me, withdraw into herself. She kept her eyes down, staring at her hands in her lap.

Without looking at this man, Pradeep relented. He reached into his pocket, peeled off a couple of bills, and held them out. The man snatched the money from Pradeep's fingers, and then held out his hand for more. A short, heated discussion ensued before Pradeep gave in again, handing the man a few more bills.

I try to rest before dinner but hear a rustling at the door. Only Mahti would be so hesitant. The door cracks a bit and I jump up. I welcome her to sit on the edge of my bed, but she says no, no. Points to her hip. I show her the sheet of bright pink pills that I'm taking. She nods. It is good. I bow, touch her hands to my forehead, bow again, she bows to me. I am forever grateful to this woman. A woman who snoops in abandoned rooms, who helped me to find a screen for my window, who sees a need and finds a way to fix it. A woman with a sense of humor—last night turning, stooping and pointing over her shoulder, offering to carry me down to dinner. Mahti is a mother in the truest sense of the word. She turns to go, and with a gesture tells me to nap. We wave our goodbyes as she closes my door behind her.

ॐ

The next day, both jars of drinking water are empty in the kitchen, so there's nothing with which to make tea or to cook, and we have run out of water at the taps yet again. I ferry a bucket of water from the sewer up to my toilet to try and flush it all down. A second bucket to the room down the hall to flush that toilet. Fighting sewage with sewage. The same greasy, heavy water filled with silver specks and black grime that Akriti and her husband use to wash up and to wash dishes whenever we run out of water at the taps.

71

15.

The Weight of Darkness

I AWAKE AT 5:00 a.m., roused by the sound of joyous birds in the fig tree and very little traffic on the roads. I begin my personal chores, washing the night's grime off the chrome railing on my balcony, then sweeping my room with the handheld reed brush I've claimed as my own. As I sweep my carpet, I meditate on each stroke and how I feel. It is backbreaking work. I'm tired of cleaning every morning. Why keep doing this? I sweep away, but a kind of madness remains. I will soon turn into the mad woman across the street who yells, upset at the world, then cackles viciously to an inside joke.

When my bright, royal blue carpet is somewhat less dusty, I sweep the balcony clean. Next, I do a bit of laundry in my bucket, using the bidet sprayer in my toilet closet. Since our reservoir was filled yesterday, I want to take advantage of having water while I can.

At 7:14 a.m., the birds have quieted, traffic has picked up, and it's raining lightly on my wash hanging over the railing outside.

I'm losing myself. I don't know this place, this home, and my home in the US is vanishing from my memory. Closing my eyes, I search for the feel of dirt in my hands as I work in the garden, ache for the sound of Tristan's whinnies, carried on the wind from a half mile west as he waits for Sadie to reply from a half mile east. I try to remember the sound of our own horses' whinnies and hoof-pounding, late-night races, and fight to recall the sound of a raven's wings slicing the air above me, the gentle croaks of frogs at night, and coyote choruses echoing through the valley and bouncing back from the hills.

All of it, gone. And with it, my sense of self.

I try to write; it feels useless. There is so little meaning in language. Still, I write, because I'm lonely. I write because I have no one to share this with. I write because I think what I have to say is important.

So, what should I write about? My boredom? My fear that time is dragging by and, at the same time, slipping through my fingers? Perhaps I should write about lying in my room on the floor, crying after scrubbing Hajuraama and Hajurbaa's disgusting bathroom? How Hajuraama and I both wept when I was done? How we kept touching our foreheads to each other's hands? How it took me ninety minutes to scrub, top to bottom, a bathroom the size of a large bathroom stall?

My whining is nothing anyone else wants to hear. I am homesick, angry, frustrated, absurdly tired, hungry, isolated, lonely, unfulfilled, and desperate. Who should care? After all, I asked for this. I signed up for this "adventure" as everyone else calls it.

I am not me. I am not the old me. Or perhaps I am who I should be. I question fate, God, karma. What lesson am I to learn by being injured and stuck here, on these grounds, with no outlet of any kind? Nothing. Patience? I don't believe it any more. I don't believe there's a reason for anything.

And if there is a reason for this, then it has backfired. I have lost my faith, and lost my belief in anything.

৵

It seems as if there's a heaviness, a bottomless depression, and a darkness all rolled into one feeling, and it's all pressing down on me. In my journal, I write that "it feels as if a deep sadness has permeated the earth here, and saturated the air above the bricks in the courtyard." During my first week, I'd emailed my shaman back home, asking for her help in clearing these energies—for lack of a better word—that surround me. She'd replied in all caps, "WHERE ARE YOU? ALL I SEE IS DARKNESS."

I am stuck in my tiny room, which is crowded by a pressing, invisible hunger and ache, and a sense of futility has taken custody of my soul.

࿇

All week long, I hear the sounds of the goats screaming for their lives. I hear it in my room and as I walk through the streets. The screaming echoes in my sleep. I have not been able to get away from the horror that these animals endure in their slow, painful, and undignified death. As I was planning this trip, I tried to prepare myself for the mass sacrifices made during Dashain, but there simply isn't a way to fully prepare for this experience.

I am wringing out my wash and preparing to hang it on the railing, when I happen to glance down at the cluttered walkway between our building and the building next door. There I see a woman and her young child standing in front of a man who is manhandling a goat's body as its limbs shudder the last of its life into a beat-up blue bucket. I turn away, disgusted. I go back into my room, light incense, and pray for the animals' souls to leave their bodies before the knife slits through their fur, through their skin. I apologize to the goats, apologize that humans have to be such assholes.

The end is not quick and painless for these animals. They fight for their lives. They scream, just as humans do, and their screams sound just like human screams. They are treated to final days and moments of sheer terror as their bodies are mistreated and their blood is spilled.

This is a relatively new practice, I tell myself. The native populations of the Kathmandu Valley didn't practice animal sacrifice. My gut doesn't care what happened hundreds of years ago, though. I'm still disgusted.

I sit with this emotional response for a long time, trying to be able to observe the situation without reaction, but I am unsuccessful in my endeavor.

࿇

I've been lying on my bed, listening, focusing on being in the now and not thinking. On leaving the service behind when I climb the stairs to my room. Still smiling from the sound of the conch shell, which the priest blew tonight, I decide to read before dinner.

Three pages in, it starts.

It comes on fast, as it always does. Feeling trapped, desperate to get out of my skin, I fight the urge to jump off something just to feel grounded again.

I sit up in my gauze tent of mosquito netting, breathing hard, feeling like a caged animal.

The walls are closing in, everything around the edge of my vision is dark and getting darker, ringing screaming in my ears.

I pull up the netting and throw my legs over the edge of the bed, fingers wrapped around the cotton batting that separates me from the wood panel below. Rocking and breathing hard, I hear myself whimper, "Oh my God oh my God oh my God." I groan, feel every fiber of my being tense and aching.

Get up, do something, drink something. You always panic when you're overheating. I force myself to stand, wobble a bit, then stagger over to the cement step along my back wall and sit. I jiggle my water bottle. I have just a little bit left.

"Go get more," the voice inside my head screams. Go. Get out. Go somewhere.

I will myself to move, to slip my sandals on outside the doorway and creep my way down the dim marble stairs, clinging to the railing to steady myself.

Akriti turns from where she's preparing dinner as I walk in. "Pahni," I say with a forced smile, as I turn and reach for the massive jug of water resting on the floor. She watches to make sure I have it all under control. I force another smile as I leave. She smiles back.

I wobble on the landing as I head back up to my room. I concentrate on breathing. My head feels as if it's going to explode, and part of me wants to throw myself over the railing to make it stop.

Back to the cement step in my room. I mix some electrolyte drink in my water bottle and chug it down. "Sit on your bed. Write this down. It will calm you."

On the edge of my periphery, the darkness waits. Patiently.

I'm ready to cry, but there's nothing to cry about. I'm ready to run, but there's nothing to run to or run from. Everything is the same, and yet it's all new. I don't understand any of it.

I'm trying to live in the now, but there's too much "now," and I'm drowning.

16.

The Angry Pakistani

EARLIER THIS WEEK, THE angry man who had shaken down Pradeep for money made an appearance during the daily community meeting. Sahdi was helping me try to learn their dialect, when this man marched in and sat down in an empty chair without greeting anyone. The dark cloud surrounding him threatened to choke us all.

At one point, as Sahdi and I were laughing over my verb conjugation, this man leaned forward and said, "You listen to me. I have the answer." His tone was aggressive. Demanding. Coming from someone else, maybe, his exact words would not have caused the hair on the back of my neck to stand on end, would not have brought a flash of anger to my face.

Before I knew it, I spat out, "Well, *these* are my teachers." I gestured to Sahdi and Pradeep. "I listen to *them*," I said. My stare was even as I met this man's glare. I remained dispassionate. A thought flashed across my brain. *This might not go well.*

A long few seconds passed. I heard Pradeep chuckle, and I could tell that Sahdi was fighting back a smirk. The noise of the city surrounded us – horns, screeching brakes, rattling trucks, barking dogs.

Then the man slapped his thighs, stood, and approached Pradeep, hand extended as before. I was still staring at him, and he was staring back at me, not hiding his anger. "We have business now," he said, waving his hand, dismissing me. "You do not pay attention. This is not your business."

Pradeep was firm that day, though, and refused to pay him anything, even as the man became more enraged at being refused. Instead, Pradeep gazed off to the side, unaffected.

The man gestured one last time, then stepped back. In a flash he turned to me and pointed, barked out something I couldn't understand.

Now this man has returned to the temple grounds during tonight's service.

I am sitting in the back with Pradeep and Sahdi, and the scattered red chairs are almost all filled with regular guests and infrequent visitors. The lean old men in their topis—their slim caps—line the wall outside the downstairs room that's being used as storage. These lovely men all sit the same way, with long, lanky legs all crossed right over left, arms folded across their chests. As usual, they were the first to greet me with large, toothy smiles when I came down the stairs for the service, and their smiles always pick up my spirits, even on my crankiest nights.

The Acharya is with us tonight, playing the harmonium again, and the music is alive and vibrant. He infuses life into the service, and people flock from all over, excited to be a part of the evening's festivities. Garima is perched on a stack of cushions on the floor near the Acharya. She plays a small tambourine, and another woman nearby is chiming a small bell. Four or five women sit cross-legged on cushions along the gate, their backs to the audience in the courtyard.

The shrine room lights are sparkling, incense is burning, and our priest is performing the service. Here in the courtyard, we are all tapping our toes, moving our feet, bouncing our heads, keeping beat with the music.

A cloud of darkness moves in, straight up the walkway between the rows of chairs, right to the edge of the shrine room. The angry man stands before the step in his usual deep prayer. Praying for what? Forgiveness? Strength? To be free of sin? Or is he praying for blessings, or to be liberated from his lot in life?

He blesses himself three times and then turns to make his way back to Pradeep, but Pradeep is already standing, preparing to keep himself away from this man. The confrontation is short. Pradeep holds out his empty hands. No money will be given this evening, possibly not ever again, from what I can see. The man begins to get loud, but I doubt he'll get physical with Pradeep. That's not the Nepali way, it seems. The musicians are nearing the end of their song. The tempo picks up.

When Pradeep walks away, pulling himself up the stairs to the kitchen, the man turns and walks towards us. Sahdi is already standing and walking away, making her way to the stairs as well.

It's my turn now. The music has reached its long, frenetic ending, the audience is clapping in appreciation of how well the Acharya can keep up the pace, and how well the tabla player can keep up with the Acharya. The priest is spinning and spinning, and it seems the heavens have joined in the festive sounds.

As the music comes to a sudden halt, the man begins to yell at me.

"You are American, yes?"

I hold out my hands as if to say that I have no battle with him, and I stand up, as the first move to separate myself from him.

"You need to watch out. Your government needs to watch out."

I am turned to the side to let his ranting negativity pass me by. I wave my hands a little. "I don't understand," I say.

"America needs to understand. I am Pakistani. Do you understand me?"

I am stepping away from him now, being careful on my bad knee and my injured hip, shuffling my way around the chairs.

He steps towards me, jabbing his finger in my direction. "There can be no India without Pakistan," he yells. "America needs to be careful. There will be war. *You do not want war.*"

Most of the audience has turned their attention to us. The men in their topis uncross their legs and lean forward, watching. Several of the women from the shrine room turn around as the man continues to yell.

I head towards the shrine room.

"You stop!" he screams.

More people turn in their chairs to check out the confrontation. My refusal to engage with him or even look at him enrages the man even more, and his voice gets louder, more shrill, as he yells words that don't register in my ears. He is not coming after me, though, and as I get closer to the shrine room, he loses his target for his rage.

He leaves.

I am at the edge of the shrine room now, slipping off my sandals and preparing to bless myself before stepping inside. The Acharya starts his next song, watching me to be sure I'm okay. The priest turns, looks at me. *Are you okay?* I smile, touch the floor to the shrine room and then to my forehead, blessing myself — forehead, heart, three times—and step inside. Taking a deep breath, I let the twinkling lights, the candles, the incense, the cymbals, the music, sweep away the man's anger.

ॐ

In a few days, I will meet a man named Saami at the coffee shop and we will become fast friends. I will tell him about the exchange with this angry man and ask if he knows what it was about. I will ask him because he is from Bangladesh, and because he strikes me as the one expert on this region that is as knowledgeable as I can hope to find: He was a young boy when a civil war split Pakistan apart in 1971. Driven by a strong Bengali sense of nationalism, and a desire for self-governance separate from Pakistan, the Bengalis achieved their end goal of a sovereign state when their country of Bangladesh was officially recognized by the UN in 1972.

It won't surprise me that Saami will almost shrug at my question about this angry man. Saami will smile and say this man was angry "over nothing new." He will tell me, "America is doing its usual thing: You are selling weapons to India and weapons to Pakistan and backing both horses in the war. You make money off instability in the world." Of course, there is no actual war happening now between Pakistan and India, but there is always a battle simmering below the surface of the two countries' relationship, and the West will make money any way it can.

At that moment outside the shrine room, in that evening's events, I understood that being an American overseas made me a target in ways I hadn't expected, and could never have predicted. A piece of innocence inside of me was exposed that night and made raw.

17.

All Weapons on Us

YESTERDAY, I DECIDED NOT to fight the restlessness that had settled on me. I gathered my things and managed to limp my way through the long walk to the coffee shop in upscale Thamel. After hobbling into the shop, I collapsed into the nearest empty leather seat along the windows and absently rubbed my aching hip. To my right, across the aisle, sat a gathering of non-Nepali guests.

Within moments, the woman from that group approached me to ask about my hip. This was Anna, from Cuba. She was beautiful and petite, and clearly not Nepali. Early in our conversation, she asked what I'm doing here, and I gave her the short version: I'm doing elder care through an NGO, but I don't like where I'm staying. She asked where I am, and I told her. Anna gasped, "Oh, those people are the worst!" She leaned over me, called to her friend, Howard, told him where I'm staying. He shook his head and said, "Those people are bad news." Howard is from the Bronx, and has lived in Nepal for fifteen years. Anna has been here for twelve years.

Seated across from Howard was Toon, from the Netherlands. Tall and blond, he towered over everyone even while seated. Anna's eleven-year-old daughter, Aleja, who is half-Nepali, lounged in another chair, focused on her iPad.

Anna surprised me by saying, "We need to get you out of that place tomorrow night." She had made it final and without question. "You'll come to dinner with us at Howard's place." I surprised myself by accepting the invitation, and even more so by not asking why tomorrow night was such an important night. I just figured I'd find out tomorrow.

~

The next afternoon, Toon and I are to meet Anna outside the coffee shop at 3:00 p.m. Before leaving the temple grounds, I stop in the kitchen to tell Akriti that I won't be back tonight, that I am going out with friends. Her brows furrow.

Pradeep's nieces have washed their car in the temple courtyard, and decorated it with paper flowers and marigold strands. They park it close to the gates of the shrine room, then hop out to take selfies with Pradeep. As I walk past, observing all this, two motorcyclists pull into the courtyard, their bikes similarly spotless and decorated. They talk to Pradeep and he gestures, yes, of course. The young men pull their bikes up behind the car.

Every day during Dashain brings something new. Perhaps this is the evening they bless their cars, I think as I walk up the street, weaving my way through countless other vehicles, also recently washed and decorated.

~

As we wait on the sidewalk outside the coffee shop for our ride, Toon and I talk about what we're both doing here in Nepal. He's providing funds and building materials to a small village in the mountains so they can build a school that will be able to house and teach ten children. The villagers can decide how to construct and run the school, with one exception: Toon's rule is that at least five of the ten children must be girls. The village has agreed without question. In a few days, he'll board a small plane to travel two hours northwest by air, then take to the ground and trek for two days. He also just met Howard and Anna yesterday.

A white compact four-door car slides up to the sidewalk in front of us, driven by a woman we haven't yet met. Anna gets out of the passenger seat, apologizing that they're late, then gives Toon the front seat so he can stretch his long legs. Anna, Aleja, and I pile into the back. Demi, the driver, is an acquaintance of Anna's. She slips into traffic, and drives like a pro. She tells me she's lived in Kathmandu almost seven years.

Just a few short minutes after we pull away from the curb, Demi announces she has to drop something off at Singhadurbar Palace. Anna tells her that it's closed for Dashain, and reminds her that all government offices are shut down. Somehow, this bit of news comes as a surprise to Demi.

Even as Anna is insisting, over Demi's arguing, that the palace is closed, we speed around one last roundabout and come to a sudden halt in front of the gates of the palace. Six guards on duty, each one having a firm grip on his own large semi-automatic weapon, suddenly snap to attention. Two of the guards hold up a hand to stop her from getting any closer to the gates. One of them starts to approach the passenger side, while the other is heading towards the driver's side. They aren't moving very fast, but Demi is: She jumps from the driver's seat and walks up to the second guard to explain that she's on business from the Greek Embassy, and that she has to deliver something directly to the minister.

Two more guards snap to attention and move to new positions on alert as Demi turns to walk to the back of the car, but then turns around again to walk back towards the second guard. Both the first two guards are trying to reason with her while she continues to talk over them.

Anna leans across Aleja and yells out my window for Demi to get back in the car, and I also do my best to get Demi's attention, but Demi isn't hearing anything any of us are saying—not even the guards. None of us, it seems, will be able to get her under control.

She moves again towards the trunk and I watch as the two remaining guards nearest to the gates move into a new position. Now all six are loosely fanned out around the car. I scan the guards' hands, noting that each of their right first fingers are now on their gun's trigger. Now we have the full attention of all six guards, and have all six weapons pointed in our general direction.

"Oh, my God," Anna moans. "She is going to get us all killed."

In the front seat, Toon is frozen. I can't imagine what he's thinking. My mind is racing. Anna has thrown her head against the back headrest, and is muttering to herself in Cuban Spanish. Next to me, Aleja sits wide-eyed and silent, staring at the front dashboard, too afraid to look up.

The arguing continues in broken English with Demi telling them, in a heavy Greek accent, that they *must* let her inside the palace, and the guards replying, with heavy Nepali accents, that she is *not* going in there.

I am resigned to our fate, as my head fills with visions of us being ordered to lie on the ground with our hands behind our heads. I've heard enough stories about Westerners traveling in foreign countries, and I'm convinced we're going to be those innocent bystanders who get dragged into something from which they can never get out.

It seems that none of the guards are convinced yet that Demi is harmless. She's opened the trunk and is now holding a large manila envelope and is gesturing and repeating that it's her responsibility to put this "package" in the hands of the minister, although she hasn't said which minister of what, and saying that she can't just leave this package with these men. "She's nuts," Anna groans. How and why these guards didn't open fire on her as soon as she opened the trunk is beyond me.

For someone who's lived here seven years, Demi is shockingly clueless about her behavior. Nepal is just ten years out of civil war, and the Nepali people are still nerve-racked from the experience. In fact, the violence has never quite ended here, and these guards look as if they are always ready for the next battle to begin.

Demi makes one more demand that her package needs to be delivered by tomorrow, but the guards have run out of patience with her. One guard takes two hard steps towards Demi, points at her, and in a loud voice, yells that the palace is *closed*, and that she either leaves the package with them or that she returns after Dashain.

In the moment of silence that strikes, I swear I feel my heart stop in anticipation.

Demi throws up her hands in defeat, and the guards flinch ever so slightly. Muttering to herself about her responsibilities and her work at the Greek Embassy, she returns to the trunk, drops the envelope back in, and slams down the lid. Now muttering in Greek, she storms back to the driver's seat and slams her door so hard I'm surprised the rolled-down window doesn't shatter.

I don't think any of us breathes a sigh of relief until we are back out on the road adding our own brand of chaos to the traffic.

࿐

In true Nepali fashion, we are able to leave our palace escapade behind and move on to enjoy dinner at Howard's apartment. Never mind that Demi could have gotten us all killed—we don't even discuss that amongst ourselves in private. We're here to enjoy dinner, and so we do.

The feast is abundant. Seasoned rice, stewed chicken, a massive salad, bread, fruit. The wine flows but I abstain. I feel guilty that I haven't brought enough money to help pay for all of this. We pose for a group selfie, clustered together, a UN gathering of sorts. Nepal, Greece, Cuba, the US, Netherlands.

Howard's employee Naresh has joined us, and is sitting next to me. I ask if there will be much more slaughtering this week. He shakes his head no, tonight is it. Anna calls to me from her end of the table, telling me tonight is the night during Dashain when the mass slaughtering is done. This is the night when upwards of twenty thousand water buffalo, along with countless goats, are ritually sacrificed across Kathmandu. Anna tells me that they are slaughtering a goat at the temple where I am staying. Gesturing with her plastic fork, eyebrows raised, she says, "This is why we bring you here tonight."

Now I know why decorated cars and motorcycles were being brought into the courtyard before I left the elder care home. The blood of sacrificed goats is poured on the vehicles as a way to thank them for their service during the year, and for keeping the riders, drivers, and passengers safe. It's a way of blessing the vehicles.

After some cleanup and leaving most of it for the morning, after Demi, Anna and Aleja leave, it is just Toon, Howard and me. We talk late into the night, and then Howard gives me his bedroom for the night, while he crashes on the couch and Toon on the spare bed in the front room.

85

Howard has a real, Western mattress. I'm so comfortable I don't know what to do with myself. I sleep with the window open, and it's peaceful here during the night, with just a few insects muttering to themselves and to each other, and no screens and no mosquitoes. I doze a little, but for most of the night, I just lie there, listening to the quiet.

ॐ

When I return to the elder care home the next afternoon, the atmosphere is subdued. Yes, I left them last night to go out with friends and missed an important ceremony. I glance at the splash of darkened red on the courtyard bricks, and keep walking.

I'm happy and I guess it shows. Mahti greets me with a smile as I head up the stairs to my room, and gestures to her face, puts her hands together as if I should nap. I tell her yes, I'm tired. She is the only one who speaks to me tonight.

My room is stuffy but cool. I drop everything and don't bother changing my clothes, instead just collapsing into bed and sleeping through the afternoon and most of the service. No one comes to get me. They couldn't get me to budge from my room if they tried.

18.

The Homeless Man

I REALIZE I'M TIRED of a lot of things, not the least of which is being unsure of who I am anymore. If I can't live my values here the same way I do in the US, then who am I?

That day in Thamel continues to pick at my conscience. Why didn't I stand up for the old man? Why didn't I berate the young shop owner after he cuffed the old man on the back of his head?

I don't want regrets. Standing up for what's right when it comes to being a decent human being shouldn't be something I have to debate with myself.

This morning, the debate is going to end.

I've seen the old man in black sitting in the doorway across the street before, and each time during the last few weeks I've wanted to go over and help him, but each time I was frozen and unable to act.

Before I left the US, people called me "brave." Who does this? Who packs up and goes to the other side of the world for three months without knowing a soul? Other people do. Not me. This is what other people do.

But apparently, I am one of those other people, because I'm here. *I did this.* So now I can go across the street to help a stranger—I can do this. There's nothing to it.

And yet, I'm still shaking with nerves.

I grab my phone and my day pack, already set with everything I need, and head out. Somehow, my brain has presumed this man to be homeless. He walks this route almost daily and sits in the same doorway, looking lost and alone. It seems easy to assume that he's homeless based on his appearance and behavior, but there is something else, something intangible, that speaks to me as well. There is something in the way he moves and in the way he sits. Perhaps it's just that I've learned to see what others may not see in people who have no home. I was homeless for four months a few years before this trip. That experience changed me. No older person should have to live on the streets.

There's a sudden break in traffic as I beeline across the six lanes. I don't even have to look left or right. I just know there's a massive gap in chaos as I focus on the man in black. My heart is racing and I'm terrified for no reason whatsoever, but there is no stopping, no turning back. There is only forward.

He sees me coming and doesn't look interested. I take the large step up onto the curb and sit with him, and now he looks a little nervous. He has just a scruff of stubble on his face and his knees are pulled up to his chest today.

I don't know how he does it in this heat. His black quilted jacket looks hot, and it's zipped all the way up. He wears his black topi again today, the traditional round cap that's folded into a point in front and in back. Also in this heat, he's wearing black corduroys with pale blue socks and ancient black work shoes. Even though he's older, and older people are always colder than younger folks, he is dressed in a way I don't see any other older people dress. Maybe these are some of his only clothes. Now that I'm sitting with him, I count twelve or thirteen rings on his fingers, and several malas on his right wrist—bracelets made of round, polished stone beads.

But the most striking feature I see is his eyes. He has kind eyes set in a face wrinkled from years of living a hard life.

When I pull the bottle of water out of my bag, asking, "Pahni?" he clasps his hands together and looks up to the heavens in gratitude. "Thank you," he replies in English. He is shaking his head in disbelief as he cracks open the plastic, removes the cap, and takes a long drink. He places one hand over his heart, looks at me. He tells me he is an orphan, though I'm not sure how he's using that word. Does he really have no family? Has his family put him into the streets? Next, he says he was praying for water.

I ask him if I can take a picture. At first, he says yes, but as soon as I hold up my phone he asks if I'm a journalist. At CGN, Sunjiya explained to us that the concept of volunteers from other countries is still foreign to a lot of the locals. If we're asked what we we're doing here, she said we should tell people we are social workers. When I tell this man I'm a social worker, he nods and understands.

I then make a rather immoral decision: I start a video recording without asking his permission. I want to capture his words, his gestures. I don't want to lose any part of him to my faulty memory. Meeting him like this, on the street, I'm convinced I've found my reason for being stuck at this elder care home: I need to document the plight of homeless elders in Nepal. I need to tell the world that all is not well in Shangri-La.

We have to shout over the traffic noise to hear each other speak. He cups his hand to his ear as I ask him about what he just said, about being an orphan.

He looks away, holds his hands out, shakes his head. We are speaking English, but between the noise of traffic and his heavy accent, I have trouble making out what he is saying.

"I get no help from nobody," he says. "I am not happy. Just then you came from there so this—" here he holds his hands up to the heavens again, "—is the honor of God that you came here with a bottle of water."

I have a package of CocoCrunchies left over from breakfast—light, coconut-flavored wafer cookies—and he accepts when I offer them to him. As I dig in my bag for more, he says, "Enough, enough." I offer him an apple, which he declines.

When I ask if he has any family, he says again that he is an orphan. He wants to know how I knew he was there. I point to the building across the street, tell him I am staying there, and that I saw him from my room. He asks how I knew he wanted water. I tell him that it's hot and that everyone needs clean water to drink.

As we talk, people jostle past each other on the sidewalk. One man looks down at us in disgust, makes a noise in his throat as if he's going to spit. He turns his head to the side a bit, away from us, and spits while still staring at me. I get the feeling I'm supposed to know he'd spit on me if he could get away with it.

At one point the man in black interrupts our conversation, saying, "Excuse me, excuse me," and rushes off. I watch him hurry down the sidewalk to a woman carrying an infant, who is trying to cross the street. He holds out his hand to the cars flying down the hill, steps right out into traffic to help her cross the street, then jogs back up to rejoin me. The woman never thanks him, never acknowledges him.

He sits back down and says again that he "gets no help from no one." He tells me he helps people every day, and no one repays him.

A few young men are passing us now, and two of them slow when they see us talking. Sneers spread across their faces. One young man makes a quick, subtle move, as if he's going to hit the old man, keeping his eyes on me the whole time, looking for a reaction. The homeless man doesn't see, and I ignore the young man.

The man in black asks me where I'm from, and I tell him. He wants to know all about me: How long will I stay here? I tell him one more week here, and then I move to another elder care home. How long will I stay in Nepal? Three months in all. Do I have family? Yes, a husband and sisters and their husbands and my sister's son.

He nods. Family is good, he says.

I don't get the sense that he's Hindu. I ask if he's Muslim or Buddhist. He pauses, places a hand over his heart, looks away for a moment. He says, "My religion is humanity. My religion is humanity."

స

I sit on my balcony, watching him for the remainder of his stay in the doorway. He drinks some more from the bottle, moves up to another doorway, pulls open the package of biscuits as he sits. He crosses his legs, takes one biscuit at a time from the package, savoring each one with slow, thoughtful bites.

After a short while, he stands, brushes off his slacks, and tucks the biscuit wrapper into his pocket instead of dropping it on the ground as many Nepalis would do. He looks one way and then the other. Head down, hands in pockets, bottle tucked under one arm, he walks up the steep hill and disappears from sight.

It won't be our last visit together in the coming months, and each time we meet, it will be like sitting with an old friend. And each time he will ask the same questions of me, although he remembers my face and my kindness.

᷍

Back in 1994, Nepal started a social security program to benefit the disabled, widows older than sixty, and any other elderly person over seventy-five. The beneficiaries are disproportionately women over men, since women here outlive men. (I should point out that up until the 1960s, widows were expected to accept being burned alive on their husband's funeral pyres. A woman's life wasn't valuable without her husband.)

When the cost to continue this benefits program became overwhelming for the government, the decision was made to place an income tax on Nepali workers. This tax supports elders by providing a stipend of two thousand rupees per month, which is not nearly enough to pay for rent and food for an entire month in the expensive city of Kathmandu. One meal of noodles alone can run a person one hundred and fifty rupees.

In the past few years, a disturbing new trend has emerged. Adult children have begun to put their elderly parents out into the streets. "I can't afford to feed you anymore," and "You're getting a payment from the government now, so you can support yourself," have become familiar refrains across Kathmandu and the valley as elderly parents are forced to figure out how to survive on their own. Tourists see them everywhere but don't know what they're seeing. The little old man selling his wares in Thamel was just trying to make enough to eat for the day when the young shop owner cuffed him on the back of the head. That little old man was likely homeless, or living in very filthy, unstable conditions.

Maybe the man in black's children have done this as well. Maybe they have put him out into the streets, and this is why he feels he's an orphan.

Homeless people are all around us, every day. We just don't see them all the time. We focus on the ones who look filthy, who have no access to showers or clean clothes. Many, however, don't look homeless. And for tourists in Nepal, well, they're focused on being tourists, so they're not paying attention.

I refuse to be a tourist.

Now I know why I was forced to sit and stay at this so-called elder care home. It was so I could find what I really wanted to do here.

Why not me?

I grab my day pack again and my satchel, lock the door to my room behind me, and head up the road to the little sundry shop that I've frequented a few times each week. I chat in casual Nepali with the shop owner as I buy five more one-liter bottles of water and several more packages of biscuits.

This... *this* I can do.

৯৹

The next morning, I sit on the floor of the shrine room, meditating, as the little pixie of a priest sits near me, chanting into a microphone hooked up to all of the speakers. His hair shorn except for the short ponytail high on the back of his head, he rocks forward and back as he reads. When he's done, I stand to leave, but he stops me and puts a special tika on my forehead in red, orange, and white paint. Then he blesses me, tapping me on each shoulder twice with his holy book. I need this blessing this morning. Afterward I feel stronger. Brave.

Minutes later I am on the floor in my room with my map, when Akriti arrives with breakfast. As I study the map, searching for the area we passed on the bus the day we went to Dakshinkali, I tell myself it's not far. I've walked a similar distance since my hip injury, and I know I can do this. I don't know what I'll find when I get there or what will happen, but whatever happens, happens.

Since I don't know what stores I'll find along the way, I've loaded my backpack with bottles of water, apples, and biscuits. I hoist the pack onto my back, tighten the straps around my hips to try and alleviate some pressure on my bent spine, and start the long walk.

I enter unfamiliar territory, but it's comfortable. New shops, new faces, new fruit and vegetable vendors. It's hot, the bag is heavy, and I'm sweating. I'm taking my time. There is no rush.

Ahead of me is a river that is no longer a river. Filled with construction debris and garbage and smelling like the sewage that is dumped into it every day, it has died a slow and agonizing death, choked by the locals who once bathed in it, fished from it, and revered it as a water source.

I stay to this side of the river and keep walking. There are no Westerners here. Not many locals, either. A little foot traffic on the other side of the four-lane street, but not on this side, and very few cars or motorcycles on the road.

I am entering No Man's Land.

A young Nepali woman heading towards me chooses to walk in the street instead of passing me on the sidewalk. I've left her plenty of room, but for some reason she doesn't want to get too close to me. I hear chatter from the other side of the street and glance over to see a few men, a bit younger than me, talking loudly and watching me. It's clear that this isn't an area many locals walk through or visit, and that the sight of a Westerner here is an aberration. Maybe it's not safe for me to be here. Maybe they think I can't be trusted. Maybe I look like an easy target and one of them, or someone else, will try to mug me. None of this is occurring to me in these long moments. I don't consider my safety until after I return to my room and have time to think about what might have happened.

I don't want to give up. I don't want to walk all this way only to turn around and go back without doing anything. I'm here, *now*. I want to do something, *now*.

I've passed a few tents and shelters along the river already. A bit farther, and there is a small police station. At some point I stop being wary of looking as if I'm trying to figure out where to go. I decide I'm tough enough to handle this situation. Now, seeing the police station, I'm feeling more confident in my decision to come here. Turning around, I head back and pick my way down the dirt and garbage to the last row of tents.

"Home" for these folks means old and ratty shelters constructed of tarps, held up by poles, propped on frames of sticks tied together, and held down at the base with twine wrapped around either large rocks or metal stakes. Everything is faded, worn, and disintegrating from the sun, wind, and dirt. Yellow tarps stretch over older blue tarps. I glance into a large yellow shelter to see some blankets, a small stool, and a bucket. Nothing to cook on.

When I turn around, I see four young men sitting under another tarp behind me. One smiles and waves me over, but I don't move at first. I ask him who lives in this yellow tent. He gestures to the two young men sitting closest to me, saying, "They do." I ask him again. It's involuntary. Apparently, I can't believe that these two young men are homeless. He says again, "They do."

As I approach, the young man who spoke to me moves off his stool and motions for me to sit. I take my bag off and set it on the ground in front of me, then hand out the bottles of water, even to the two young men who are not homeless.

Despite the weather, the two young men who are visiting their homeless friends are dressed in long pants, long sleeved shirts, and jackets. The youth who invited me over has on a black jacket, fresh and clean, and a black backpack; his friend has on a crisp white-and-red, plaid shirt and a light-blue jacket, also fresh and clean. His pinstripe pants don't seem very dirty at all. I've noticed that many Nepalis seem to dress for cooler weather despite the fact that it's ninety-plus degrees during the day. The heat just doesn't faze them.

It appears the two young homeless men don't speak English, or aren't up to talking. I ask how long they've been homeless, and they look to the young man who invited me in. He answers for them: six months. In careful, broken English, he says they cannot do anything, so they live here.

I ask, "No work?"

He replies, "No work."

One of the homeless youths has on a faded Adidas t-shirt, black shorts, and gray sandals. He has a bit of razor stubble and a modest haircut. The other homeless youth wears a bit of a soul patch on his chin with fashionably long sideburns, and wears a gray t-shirt and blue jeans with the same gray rubber sandals as his friend.

They are sitting on bits of wood piled high enough to keep them off the ground. I snap a photo, take a short video. I ask if the water helps, and the young man who welcomed me over translates for me. The others smile, nod, tell me yes, water is good, it helps. I ask if they want an apple, but I try to say it in Nepali and can never get the smoothness of it: *syoo*. One quick syllable. They don't know what I'm talking about. I reach in my bag and hand the young man in gray an apple, and they chuckle. Ah. They correct my pronunciation. Most of the food I have goes next: the second apple, a package of biscuits, plus the bag of packaged food that a young family gave me the other night at the elder care home. They had come to give food to the elders on their young child's birthday, and I was included in the gifts.

As I pack up my phone, I tell the young man I will try to come back. He translates for them, and they smile and nod.

While I'm climbing back up the bank to the sidewalk, I hear laughter from the shelter, and I wonder if I've been had. I question how homeless these kids looked. And how would I know what homeless looks like out here? Homeless in the US is hard to see as well. When I lived out of my car, no one had a clue. My clothes were always clean, and I was always showered because I worked at a gym, and so what if these kids' clothes weren't filthy? And, okay, so maybe I *was* had. Maybe they were simply a group of kids just hanging out—and if so, that's their karma.

But no, as I walk, as I think back on it, no—there's no question in my mind. *I just know*. I know from the quick response that the first young man had to my question of who lived in the yellow shelter. I know from their responses as I talked to them. I know because they weren't doing anything illicit when I walked up. And I know because the first young man offered his seat to me when I approached.

Within a mile or so, I pass a man sleeping on the sidewalk. His clothes are filthy, and he's lying on a burlap sack, using a black backpack as a pillow.

My last bottle of water is for him. I don't want to wake him, but I don't know where to leave it for him. I try to rest the bottle in the crook of his arm, and wake him in the process. He stirs and in one swift movement sees the bottle, sits up smiling, and cracks it open. All at once. He takes a long drink and smiles some more, nodding his head in thanks as I hand him a package of biscuits.

My favorite sundry shop is closed for Dashain. I re-route and find another shop, buy three more bottles of water.

Later, in my room, I'll watch the video I took of the young men. I'll see the looks in the eyes of the homeless youths. A mix of wonder and gratitude. I'll stare at the photo for a long time. Stare back into the eyes of the young man in the Adidas t-shirt.

19.

The Lost Girl

FOR SEVERAL WEEKS, I'VE watched as the two dirt-poor children come to the service and leave without food, walking hand-in-hand into the dark streets alone. At the end of each service, someone takes the offerings from the altar and passes them around to the other attendees, and the adults close ranks, crowding out these kids. I never eat any of this food, and I never consider taking some and giving it to the kids. It's always just a few scraps of fried treats. Not enough to fill a hungry belly.

Dashain is a holiday full of separate holidays, each day celebrating or honoring something or someone. Every day seems to bring some new surprise from a guest. Early one morning, a young man arrives at the elder care home, and I am called downstairs to join Hajuraama, Mahti, Daya, and a few other local women. We are all seated in a circle. The young man takes out a package from his satchel, hands it to the oldest woman present, then takes out another package and hands it to the next oldest, and so on. I am second to last, being older than Daya by a few years.

The other women have not opened their packages. They simply received the wrapped gifts with gratitude. It isn't until I retreat to my room and unwrap the package that I see his Dashain offering to us: He has given us each a new sari. I am ridiculously overjoyed.

On another day many people show up from the community and gather in the courtyard. In the center of the circle, yet another stranger hands each of us a box of packaged sweets and a brown paper sandwich bag full of other foods. I am surprised to see the little girl and her infant brother sharing a red chair across from me. Upon receiving my box and bag of food, I open the bag and gobble down the hard-boiled egg inside. Then, finding fault with my behavior, I step over to the children and give them the rest of it all—both the paper bag of food and the box of sweets. As the little boy's eyes widen in surprise, his sister grabs the items from me and stuffs them behind her on the chair. She glances around as if to spy someone wanting to take them from her.

When these two kids don't show up for Children's Day—where the mothers wash their children's feet, and then the kids get gifts—I am certain they weren't invited. I'm sure they're Hindu. Maybe they're not Nepali? My contribution for Children's Day is sheets of stickers for the kids in attendance, which they all enjoy. After the celebration, we all line up for photos, and I tower over the mothers as we stand behind their children.

A few nights later, I spot the little girl and her brother in the first row of the audience, and race back up the stairs to my room as fast as my hip will let me, returning with a big stack of stickers. As I fan the sheets in front of them, their eyes grow wide. They look at each other, look at me, and eye the stickers. The little boy chooses one sheet. I say, "Dui,"—two—telling him to select another sheet. He looks up at me with his big eyes, then cautiously, as if it might be a trick, takes another sheet. I think for a moment. How can I just offer two sheets to the little girl, then walk away from here still having stickers in my hands? I smile, then hand the rest of the stack to the girl.

For the rest of the service, they compare the stickers, roll the sheets, and turn to look at me over the back of their chairs, shy. I can't stop smiling at them. I adore the little girl, and she seems to adore me, but she especially loves my camera. Any night I have it with me at the service, which is often, I can snap off twenty photos of her without her hesitating. She poses for me, crowds out her brother with an elbow or a shoulder, and eats up the attention.

ༀ

During the second week of my monthlong stay, I started to teach occasional, basic exercise classes for some of the women who come to the evening service. We worked out in the shade of the shrine room, early in the afternoon, with the various therapy bands I've brought, and these ladies loved strength training. They wanted more and more, so I added different exercises. Since it was still not enough for them, I then added a long stretching section to the end of each class.

As we are finishing up our stretches one day, an ancient woman appears at the edge of the shrine room. She peers at me, then at the others. My class participants don't acknowledge her. They just exchange glances with each other when they see her.

When Akriti comes downstairs to check on us, she greets this woman and asks her in Nepali what she needs.

She is here to see the American, Akriti says. The four women in my class look at me, and one of them repeats the statement, as if I hadn't heard: "She is here to see the American," she says. The others seem to know what this means. I don't. I interpret it to mean that she wants to join the class, so I encourage her to come in to the shrine room as we finish our stretches. Akriti retrieves a plastic chair for her, but the ancient woman doesn't want to sit in it. Instead, she sits on the filthy, blue, stuffed chair, perched on the edge, hands folded in her lap. She wears an old yellow print kurta and worn out sandals. Her gray hair is back in a braid. Hers has been a hard life. It is written in the creases on her face, in the sadness of her eyes.

When we are finished, I ask one of the attendees to see what our guest wants. The class member doesn't seem pleased at my request.

The old woman's response is translated for me: She is here to talk to me about her granddaughter. I'm still unclear on what's happening. As the old woman talks, she keeps a respectful distance from us. Her body language is humble, as if she has known from childhood that she isn't worthy of being in our presence.

One class participant looks at me, almost holding her breath, as she translates again. This woman wants me to take her eight-year-old granddaughter with me to America. I tell her I can't. I tell her I can't afford to take care of a child. She pleads with me more, and her responses are translated. She will be lost if she stays, the woman tells me. She will be lost, she repeats.

My heart is aching, but I stay strong. *I'm sorry*, I tell her. *I'm sorry. I can't afford it. I'm sorry.* My gut hurts and my chest is tightening. *I'm sorry.*

But she will be lost if she stays, the old woman says again, almost in tears now. Lost.

The women from my class are watching me. I look firm in my position, but my heart is wrenching, and my stomach twisting in agony. I would love to help every girl, every elder here, but I don't know how. All I can think about right now is that I have no job to go back to, and I don't know how I'm even going to pay my share of the bills when I get home. I can't possibly take care of a child.

After my return to the US, I will tell this story to a friend. That's when I'll finally realize the granddaughter this woman spoke of may have been the young girl who came to the services almost every night with her little brother. It's then that I realize I would have moved heaven and earth to help this old woman somehow.

Now, though, I haven't put the two together yet. I haven't considered that the ancient woman was this little girl's grandmother. The little girl is not yet lost.

≈

It's been more than a week since the old woman's visit. Tonight, as it turns out, is one of my last nights at the so-called elder care home. I just don't know it yet. I only know that I arrived late to the service, as usual, and that now I am watching as the adults once again crowd out the little girl and her brother while the offering is being passed around. As I see the children start to leave, my first thought is that I need to know where they live. I need to know how I can help.

One of the regulars is lecturing me, standing before my chair. I'm watching the children, and lean forward, about to go after them.

"They go home alone?" I ask.

"Yes," says this man.

"In the dark?" I ask.

In broken English, he tells me not to worry about them, then steps to the side to block my view of the gate and to keep me from standing. He points his finger at me, and barks out orders.

"You come each night late. Tomorrow you come *five o'clock*." He slaps his palms across each other for emphasis.

I look at him, startled. "No," I say, much to his surprise.

He stops. "No?"

I am done with being bossed around at this place. "No," I repeat.

He doesn't know what to say. I shrug, a defiant and distinctly indifferent gesture, and one that is borderline rude in Nepal. I am dismissive of him.

"I come when I come," I say, stunning the man into silence.

It's too late. The kids are gone, out into the darkness. I retreat to my room to stew and worry.

&

In a little more than a year from now, I'll return to Kathmandu in an attempt to find the kids. The elder care home will have changed. It will feel as if the gates of Hell have opened in the courtyard, and I will discover how easily the people here would sell children. Right there, on the temple grounds.

I will never see the girl again. She will be lost, forever.

20.

Rolling Downhill

JUST THIS AFTERNOON, AFTER a short email exchange with Manesh, I got the ball rolling towards my freedom from this place. We will meet at 3:00 p.m., Tuesday at his office. Earlier he had asked if I could stick it out until the end of Dashain, and I had said yes. Dashain is ending, and so, I've declared to him, has my commitment. As I kept reminding myself this past month, there really wasn't anything else CGN had to offer me. Now I don't care. I will figure it out.

Even though I enjoy Garima's company and believe she has a good heart, and even though I wish I could get to know Mahti better, I have endured nearly four weeks of what feels like harassment from others.

Akriti barges into my room without notice, instead of being gracious the way Rosa, our first cook, used to behave. She has asked if she could have my bottle of shampoo and one of my scarves, and has told me more than once that I'm going to take her son back to America with me.

During one evening service, I listened as Pradeep ordered Sahdi upstairs to ensure my room was locked, even though he could see that my room keys were attached to my water bottle. I was sitting right next to Pradeep during the exchange, but that didn't seem to bother him.

There was another service when I was told by one of the regulars to go back up to my room and get a monetary offering for the shrine, even though I'm a guest and not a Hindu.

And of course there are all the times I've been scolded by the regulars for not coming down on time each night, and the times I've been chased back downstairs by someone when I ran up to my room for a break from the mosquitoes.

While I recognize there is a distinct cultural difference at play here, I also recognize that bullying is not a quality endemic to all Nepalis. It's just the folks here, at this place.

More than anything, though, I am tired of being here with nothing to do. Take the brochure, for example. Nothing has happened with it. It hasn't even been mentioned since the day Pradeep insisted my English-speaking Nepali friend come to the temple grounds to translate for him. I realize there is the *very* slight possibility that Pradeep really does want my help with this but that he's just been busy. For some stupid reason, I need to know that he doesn't want me staying here just because he gets money for it—money that he seems to be pocketing. I need to know if he wants my help or if he just wants the money.

I was sitting in the courtyard earlier this evening with Pradeep and the friend of his friend who speaks English, and who was going to translate for the brochure. Seizing the opportunity, I asked Pradeep's friend to ask Pradeep if he still wanted my help with his brochure.

Pradeep responded, indifferent, without looking at me.

He replied, "Ask me again in two weeks, and I will think about it then."

"Well," I replied, "I can always come back, I guess."

Pradeep was jolted with alarm when my response was translated. I replied that I am leaving next week, and was only staying here one month. I said I am not needed here.

Raising his voice, he stabbed the air with his finger, accusing me. *You said you were going to be here three months.* For just a brief moment, Pradeep looked right at me.

"No," I replied, staying calm. I said I was staying in *Nepal* for three months. I never said I was staying *here* for three months. I have, in fact, told many people who've come to the evening services that I'm only staying until the end of Dashain.

I told Pradeep that I go where I'm needed, and I'm not needed here. I told him I'm in Nepal to work, and there is no work for me here.

Pradeep's anger continued to be translated, and as anger began to rise in me as well, his friend became more subdued. He had found himself in the middle of a sudden, heated exchange.

In spite of the fact that he says he talks to Manesh "all the time," Pradeep can't even remember Manesh's name. He demanded that I give him my "manager's" phone number. I held out my phone so he could read the number off my screen.

After an animated conversation with Manesh, Pradeep snapped his phone closed with a self-satisfied grin. He claimed that Manesh said I will be leaving for one week, and then returning here. I was pretty sure Pradeep was lying, but Manesh may have told him what needed to be said to keep him happy for this week. Nepalis lie to each other all the time. Still, seeing the smug look on Pradeep's face had my blood boiling.

I stared at his friend, who was recoiling from the escalating discussion.

I reached out and patted Pradeep's arm, saying, "Unfortunately for you, it's not your decision."

I turned back to his friend. "Translate *that*," I ordered.

Pradeep's face grew red. He looked as if he might stroke out.

My breathing was still heavy with anger when his friend asked me where I will go. He wasn't acting as translator; this was *his* question, and it felt very much as if he knew Pradeep wasn't paying attention to us at that moment.

"To my next assignment," I replied.

He asked where.

"I don't have to tell you. *I don't report to you*," I snapped. I was out of control. I hadn't felt like that in years, and I don't like being that angry.

His friend replied in gentle, fluent English, "I am asking because I have another friend who runs an elder care home. I thought if you were looking for a place to work, I could talk to him."

I looked at the man and felt myself soften with relief. I realized this man is *nice*. He's not like the others here. I said I may take him up on his offer, but that I'm talking to two other places. I was lying. There is only one elder care home, out in Pharping, that's interested in me.

Look at me. I've started lying like a Nepali.

I didn't feel like staying for the rest of the service, and if I had my way, I'd be leaving tonight.

Now that I'm back in my room, my mind is reeling.

I've announced that I'm leaving. With the way things work in Nepal, Manesh may have not wanted them to know, which is why he may have lied to Pradeep about my being gone just for one week.

I am not called down for dinner tonight. Instead, Akriti delivers my tray to my room without speaking. I don't get warm milk tonight, either.

The Universe or God or Fate or whatever has started the ball rolling. I am the ball, and the speed downhill is about to increase.

21.

A Slice of Israel

EVERYTHING HAPPENS FOR A reason. I am where I need to be, when I need to be there.

If I hadn't had the heated exchange with Pradeep last night, I wouldn't have felt the need to escape this morning. Leaving before breakfast, I race to the only place I feel secure: the coffee shop.

I've worked hard to avoid reading news from back home while I'm here. My friends and my husband know not to tell me anything. Long before I left the US, I had decided to be fully here in Nepal. Keeping up with news from the US would make me feel as if I have one foot in each country. Whenever I go to the coffee shop, I sit far away from the massive flat screen television if they are playing a global news channel.

Today, however, the television catches my attention with yet another hurricane in the US. Fixated on the moving images, I begin absent-mindedly setting my satchel and notebooks down.

All at once I turn my head to see a massive bear of a man looking at me from across the table, and I flush. "I'm sorry!" I laugh. "I'm blocking your view!"

He smiles and says it's all right. We are immediate friends.

His name is Saami, he travels here frequently on business from his home country of Bangladesh. Saami doesn't have a high opinion of NGOs here. This is becoming a common conversation for me, and I tell him the folks at CGN really are the good guys. He's shaking his head.

We drop easily into deep conversation. When he mentions that he went to Shabbat last week, I must look envious. He tells me the story of how he met the rabbi of Chabad House many years ago, and how he was invited to break bread with the group. He had trouble once, when one of the dinner participants pointed to him and said he shouldn't be allowed there. The rabbi made it very clear that Saami was their brother, not their enemy, and that he would always be welcomed when he's in Nepal.

Saami is Muslim. Since halal meat is almost impossible to find in Nepal, Saami rarely eats meat while he's here. On Shabbat, he prefers to eat kosher at the Chabad House.

"I would love to go to Shabbat," I breathe in envy. "I crave some kind of sanity around here."

He smiles. "You can't. You're not allowed to know where Chabad House is, and you don't get invited. You have to either go to the embassy for clearance, or visit with someone who is approved."

My heart skips a beat.

He smiles. "So, if you go with me for dinner tonight, you can then go any other time while you're here because I would introduce you."

I'm elated.

We agree that we'll meet here at the coffee shop at 8:00 p.m. It's a date.

I'm going to Chabad House tonight. I'm so excited, I'm floating.

⌒

I haven't been out much after dark. At the elder care home, they lock the gate at the entrance to the stairwell early every evening, so it doesn't make sense for me to be out late. Plus, women have been attacked here, Westerners and Nepalis alike. It's not common, but it happens, and this is why Saami has volunteered to walk me back to the elder care home after dinner.

As I'm headed to the coffee shop, I notice there's a nightlife feel in the streets. I emerge from the alley into Thamel, and the scene is mesmerizing. Streams of lights pour down buildings and logos are lit up everywhere. Everything is sparkling, music is playing, and the streets are alive and lit up with rotating lights to lure people into restaurants. Procol Harum blasts from the Irish pub's open windows.

Saami is enjoying a coffee when I approach, and asks if I want tea. I whisper that the coffee shop has closed for the night, and he chuckles in response, says it doesn't matter. He knows the owner, so the employees can't leave until *he* leaves, and if they try to kick him out, it won't go well for them. It's no wonder they look a little bitter.

"Anyway, I go to dinner later, to give everyone their own time," he adds without pretension.

It's nice to sit out on the upstairs patio and listen to the nightlife below us. Thamel cuts off traffic through this part of town to keep everything quiet for the tourists at night. I hear people talking and laughing. I hear business being transacted, happy shouts here and there. I could enjoy this kind of nightlife.

෨

Chabad House is hidden. This section of the neighborhood is dark.

Saami and the security guard greet each other with broad smiles, clasping hands. The guard turns, opens a gate behind him, and Saami's pace slows as we head down the walkway beyond, between two buildings. The air feels different, somehow, and the atmosphere is calm, lightened.

We emerge into another world, into an Eden of sorts. Gentle lighting, a grassy area, walkways, a dormitory to our left. To our right, tables are set up outside with umbrellas and young people sitting around, speaking Hebrew, engaged in conversation. A kitchen, a community gathering room past the seating area. Signs in Hebrew. Books. Couches. Children and families. No one is shouting. All is calm. A slice of Israel has been relocated here. In the midst of the madness that is Kathmandu, here is sanity.

Saami and the rabbi greet each other as old friends. I am introduced to this beautiful man, who speaks with a heavy accent and who nods as Saami says I am a good friend. Saami says I am here for three months doing work with elders, adds that he would like me to be welcome here in his absence.

The rabbi engulfs my hand in his. "Welcome," he says. "Shalom," I reply. The word slips from me. I hope it doesn't seem pretentious.

It is a commune in every sense of the word. There is community, solidarity, self-sufficiency, and safety in numbers. But why have a security guard at the gate? Who are they in danger from here? The answer is simple: Jews are a minority. "My God is better than your God" is a mindset that knows no borders. Religious persecution exists wherever religion can be found.

Saami and I sit off by ourselves, away from the young people, relaxing on cushioned benches, eating from a low table. Our conversation, as before, winds around multiple topics. I tell him about taking my refuge vows as a Buddhist, my childhood growing up Christian. We talk about religion, the New Testament, the history of Christianity, the Qur'an. We talk about the history of "my God is better than your God." He tells me that when he prays five times a day, he prays for all the children of Abraham, and talks about being disappointed that all three religions see the others as the enemy. I tell Saami what Anna, the ex-pat from Cuba, said to me: "God came to us several times, and gave us several different ways to get to Him, and instead we use this to kill each other."

We start to talk about my work and the troubles I'm having, and Saami divulges his history with the NGOs in Nepal. He managed a project where he assessed and investigated NGOs for the Ministry of Women, Children, and Social Welfare. His work closed thirty-eight NGOs, and had fines levied against a dozen more. He has no patience or respect for them.

Saami asks what I want from CGN. I tell him I want them to let me choose where to live and let me do my own work. Since their hostel is not finished, I can stay with friends, and CGN can pay my friends the daily rate that they would normally pay a host family. It seems apparent that they don't have a real elder care program, if the so-called elder care home where I'm staying is all they had for me. If I could get a refund on the program fee that CGN charges volunteers, I'd be thrilled. I doubt that will happen, though.

Saami announces we will get this taken care of. He makes a phone call, talks for some time to a man he knows, then hands the phone to me. I begin explaining my situation. I tell this man the conditions where I'm living. I say that it is not an elder care home at all. He tells me he will take care of it.

After hanging up, I ask Saami who I just spoke to on the phone. It was Saami's former boss at the Ministry of Women, Children, and Social Welfare.

"What?" I exclaim. "I just told the Ministry all that?" Saami looks surprised that I didn't realize what was going on.

My heart stops. I've just reported the elder care home to the government. From what I understand, Pradeep and Garima have never registered this elder care home with the Ministry. Based on Saami's previous work with them, I now know this could result in the home being fined or shut down, and heavy fines levied against both Pradeep and Garima as well.

The world has tilted.

᠀

As promised, Saami walks me home from Chabad House. We walk at an easy pace, neither of us in a hurry to rush me back to the temple grounds. There's still much to talk about.

Just a few feet from the gate to the temple grounds and the elder care home, Saami gets a pained look on his face. I tell him I don't want him walking me into the courtyard, and that I don't want any of my friends in this place. He looks down at me, concern in his eyes.

"Didi," he says, calling me his sister in Nepali, "even if it weren't against my religion to enter this place, I wouldn't do it anyhow. I can feel it from here. There is *so* much darkness here. We *have* to get you out of here. And we have to do it soon. *You cannot stay here.*"

His intensity catches me off guard. I tell him I know it's bad. Saami says he will send me a verse from the Qur'an to pray. He says that Muslims are given specific prayers to recite during Dashain, to dispel the negative energy and black magic Hindus don't realize they're invoking through their rituals and animal sacrifices. He will email one to me tonight. We agree to meet back at the coffee shop at 8:00 a.m. tomorrow.

As I crawl under my mosquito netting, I consider the possibility that I may be forced to leave tomorrow, or I may not. Either way, I can't take the risk of needing to pack at the last minute.

The packing that took me weeks to handle before I left the US takes me just about an hour to do now. I am crazed but precise. I know where everything is going, where everything belongs. When that task is complete, I crawl beneath my mosquito netting again and email my husband to tell him what's happened. He responds almost immediately. "Stay safe, babe. Let me know what happens."

I text Toon from Netherlands. The morning after Howard's dinner party, I had told Toon and Howard how bad things are here. Toon is still awake and sends a response. "Follow your heart," he says. "It will guide you."

Saami has sent me the verse from the Qu'ran. I reply, thanking him, calling him "brother."

Considered one of the greatest and most powerful verses in the Qu'ran, the quote he sent both recognizes and exalts the one highest power, regardless of name. Calling upon this highest power, those who repeat this verse believe it will dispel evil and demons: Satan cannot dwell any place where this verse is recited.

At first, I am whispering as I read aloud, repeating the verse over and over. Soon, though, my voice gets stronger, more confident, and I begin to rock back and forth as I read.

Surah Al-Baqarah 2:255

God! There is no god except He, the Living, the Everlasting. Neither slumber overtakes Him, nor sleep. To Him belongs everything in the heavens and everything on Earth. Who is he that can intercede with Him except with His permission? He knows what is before them, and what is behind them; and they cannot grasp any of His knowledge, except as He wills. His throne extends over the heavens and the Earth, and their preservation does not burden Him. He is the Most High, the Great.

22.

Meeting the Authorities

I'M READY TO LEAVE when Akriti arrives at 7:30 a.m., bringing my tea. She's almost an hour early today. She doesn't seem to notice anything different or frown that all my things are packed up. Everyone here has been subdued since I had the heated discussion with Pradeep.

I down the tea and pack the biscuits in my day pack where I keep food for the homeless. Then I'm back at the coffee shop by 8:00 a.m. Saami arrives a short time later, and his phone rings right away. It's Dhan, the man from the Ministry with whom I spoke last night. Yes, Saami says, she's right here. Yes, he says, she'll come right down. He hangs up and tells me that Dhan is parked downstairs and wants to meet me.

Dhan is a small man on a small motorcycle, but he is of a high caste and holds one of the highest positions at the Ministry. He asks me if I know how to get to the elder care home from here. I tell him yes, I walk this route many times a week. He says, "Take me there."

My mouth is open. I look to Saami, and the alarm must show on my face. Saami says it's okay, he'll watch my things while I'm gone, so I climb on the back of Dhan's motorcycle, and we head out.

I am numb when he pulls into the courtyard, and feel as if I've left my body. Dhan walks with his helmet on. He peers through the gate into the shrine room and asks to see my room. We ascend the stairs, passing the kitchen on the way up, and I unlock my door.

Dhan looks dismayed as we slip off our sandals. "This is your room?" he asks, just to confirm. I tell him yes. I take him to my toilet closet and his brow furrows. When I flush the toilet to show him that it only drains sewage from the bottom and is now spraying water from the pipe leading from the tank to the bowl, he shakes his head—he's seen enough of my room.

Daya and Mahti are poised in my doorway. As we put our sandals back on, Dhan glances down the hallway, looking up at the empty lightbulb sockets, and walks a bit before pushing open a door to peer into the next room.

Daya catches my attention, gestures with her chin towards Dhan: *Who is he?* She has a look of borderline disgust on her face, one that I've been seeing for a long time with anything related to me. I shrug without shrugging. My face says, "I don't know." Even though I do know who he is, I have no clue how to handle this situation.

We make our way back to the stairwell. Daya and Mahti stand aside to let us pass. Dhan asks about the floor above. I tell him it's empty. We go up anyway so he can at least see for himself the conditions of those rooms as well. When we come back down, Daya and Mahti have gone. I'm sure Daya is on her phone, reporting to Pradeep. I'm sure she and Akriti and perhaps even Hajuraama are huddled in conference. In suspicion.

I tell him I will show him the old people's room. His face says it all as we walk down the second-floor balcony. He can smell it already. I press the door open, and Dhan has a physical reaction to the stench, drawing back in alarm. He shakes his head. "I have seen enough," he says. Hajurbaa is sleeping on his side on one bed and doesn't know we're there.

Dhan takes pictures with his flip phone as he walks, takes a call on his smartphone jammed against his ear inside the helmet which is still on his head. He takes a photo of a sign high on the wall near the door to my room, and a picture of a handwritten sign posted outside the shrine room, then a photo of the banner hanging on the shrine room gate.

Akriti has joined Daya and Mahti, now, and all three stand to the side in the courtyard with us. They do not question the authority he possesses. Akriti looks to me for answers. My face is clear, dispassionate, lacking in information and emotion. I am frozen, not so much in fear, but in the unknown of it all.

He asks for a chair, and Akriti jumps to get him one from the stack. He gestures for them all to sit, so Daya grabs a few more. I hear him ask who is in charge of the money. I know enough Nepali by now, and all of a sudden I realize what's happening. Daya has already called Pradeep and told him this man is here. I imagine she said I brought him to the home. Pradeep can't come down, she tells Dhan. She calls Garima, the second in command.

Dhan looks at me, waves me off. "You may go," he says, being very polite. "You do not need to remain for this."

I turn and speed out of the courtyard without looking back. I'm running up the road, weaving around shoppers, walkers, rickshaws. Panting, I call Saami and tell him I'm heading back. He tells me to take my time. I tell him I'm running and I'm freaking out as I yell into the phone, *"Saami, he's going to audit them!"*

Saami is chuckling. "Of course he is, didi. What did you think would happen?"

All I can say is, "Oh my God," over and over.

He tells me to slow down, that it's all going to be all right.

Still, I'm panicking. I've just exposed Pradeep and Garima to the government. While they deserve everything that's coming to them, I am aware that I'm a volunteer with a Nepali NGO, and everything I do reflects on CGN. Now, I may have just caused trouble for Aabi, CGN's founder and president, and the rest of the staff.

As soon as I sink into the deep leather chair along the windows back at the coffee shop, I order a bottle of water. I'm still in a state of shock. When the waiter brings the bottle to our table, I grab it from his hands, crack it open, and drink right from the bottle, the non-Nepali way. Saami is still chuckling a bit. He asks what happened, and I give him the quick rundown: Dhan saw the basics, and he saw the old people's room, and that would be enough for anyone to say this is not right.

Saami says, "You know you can't go back there tonight."

I'm nodding. I have to go to the services shop to see Dil. I have to move to his hotel. Many things are falling into place in my head and in my life here. All the pieces are slipping, one by one, into each neatly-fitting slot. I tell Saami I'll be okay, that I'll get help in moving. Dil is a brother.

When I tell Saami that I'm worried about the backlash, he asks if I'm concerned that they'll come after me or try to find me. I tell him yes, that I don't know what to expect.

"They will not bother you," he says, shaking his head. "Partly because you're American, but also because you came with Dhan. They don't want this trouble for themselves. But yes, they are vicious."

Saami tells me I need to call Manesh and tell him I'm moving out today, and I'm dialing the phone as he's talking. When Manesh answers, I say that I've had enough at the elder care home, that I've completed my commitment to him, and I'm moving into my friend's hotel this afternoon. He says he understands. He's not at all upset. My brother Manesh has two speeds: calm and calmer. "We are still meeting on Tuesday?" he asks.

"Yes," I say. "Manglabaar. Teen bajye." Tuesday. At 3:00 p.m.

"At the office?"

"Yes," I say, calming a bit more. "At CGN's office."

୭

Dil is surprised to see me. The two young men in his services shop look up when I enter.

I sink onto the bench along the windows facing his desk, exhausted. I tell Dil I'm not in a hurry, but he senses otherwise and gestures towards the stool in front of him. One of the two young men who have been talking with him takes his leave, nodding at me as he goes, and I lower myself onto the stool.

Words spill out of me. I tell Dil that things have become very bad at the elder care home, and that I have to move into his hotel today. He is nodding. I ask if he knows of a good taxi driver that he trusts, someone who can help me move my things. He says he does, but that he can help me move instead, that it would be no problem. I tell him I don't want him to close his shop, and that I'm willing to take a taxi, but Dil is standing, taking his keys. No, he says, we will go now. We will get you out now.

Dil looks to the young man still sitting nearby at an unused desk, who has heard and understood every word. The young man is already standing up in anticipation of something. Dil says a few words to him and he nods, replies, nods to me and leaves.

"Please," Dil says as he comes from behind his desk, holding his arm towards the door.

And that's that. He locks up behind us, we walk to the t-shirt shop across the way to tell them he's stepping away, walk to the shop two doors down where he talks to his friend there, and then we're off.

"I do not want them to know where I am going," I say as we walk.

"Then we do not tell them." He is very clear. He seems to know what these people are like. In fact, everyone around me seems to know. I'm the only one who's just getting it.

We walk down a side street, and as Dil greets another shop owner, I can further see how people appeared on my path on this journey for a reason. I just have to trust that everything works itself out.

"I have told them that I'm going to my next assignment," I tell him as we approach the temple grounds. "That is all. I do not know what they will do, but I do not think they will like this."

Dil makes a decision. "I tell them I am your friend, and I help move you to your next assignment in Thamel."

This sounds perfect. I'm bracing myself. For what, I don't know.

We are calm as we walk into the courtyard, climb the stairs, and slip off our sandals before we enter my room. He is moving along with me as if he's been here before. I point to the bags, packed and ready to go, and tell him, "All this." He is taking a hold of the red duffel when Daya and Mahti arrive in my doorway.

It begins.

Daya is yelling, Dil is replying, and Mahti is shouting—I don't know if Mahti is angry with me, or if she's just upset that I'm leaving. Dil and I are grabbing things and moving towards the door, but Mahti and Daya aren't stepping aside. Dil just stays calm and keeps telling them that he is my friend and that he is taking me to my next assignment. They back up to let us through, to let us put our sandals back on, but Daya doesn't give us a lot of room. At one point, she blocks me to force eye contact between us. "Do you call Pradeep?" she shouts in clear English. What am I supposed to say to this? "I don't report to Pradeep" or "He's not the boss of me"? Which one of those would work?

I focus on remaining silent. On remaining non-reactive. I focus on getting the hell out of there.

Akriti is at the bottom of the stairs, hands behind her back, brows furrowed. Daya is on the phone behind us. Mahti is shouting from behind Daya, and I still can't decipher where she's at emotionally. I want to give Mahti a fierce hug; I will miss her above everyone else. My heart breaks for everything she's going through, and for her deteriorating relationship with Daya. But I don't hug her. I don't say goodbye.

Dil and I walk out through the gate, and I follow his directions. "Across here," he says, "Up this way," and "Over here." We walk, and my bags don't feel heavy. In fact, I can't feel anything.

We pass beneath an arched sign which marks a temple area, and start our short walk down an alley with shops set on either side. The noise from traffic quiets. At the end of the alley is Ganesh Temple, and to the left I'm surprised to see a courtyard. Shops and apartment buildings surround the temple and an open dirt area, making the temple part of the shops in a very natural way. Three doors down, up onto a tall step and into the tiny lobby at Dil and Puja's hotel.

Through the open door behind us, in place of traffic, I hear laughter, neighbors visiting, children playing. In place of horns honking, I hear someone strumming a guitar somewhere.

Dil explains to Puja, in Nepali, my situation. Puja is his business partner and girlfriend. She is the one he says he will marry one day, but Puja doesn't mind that they are still unwed. Together they own the services shop which Dil runs, plus this hotel, and a second hotel in the vacation hotspot of Pokhara. They also run a nonprofit which takes food, clothing, blankets, and mosquito nets to the poorest regions of Nepal. They are a middle class power couple, dedicated to honesty, integrity, and lifting up others.

Puja nods as Dil explains my story, smiles at me in sympathy. He has to go back to work, but I'm in good hands, he tells me. As Puja grabs a key from behind the counter, she tells me that she'll get me settled in my room and we can take care of the details later. Together, we pack-mule my things up to the fourth floor.

As she swings open the door to my room, I almost weep at the sight before me: A spacious room, painted soft yellow, white comforters atop twin beds, a nightstand between them. A bathroom with a real toilet, a sink, and a shower (a shower!) and a sliding door. Off to my right, through a doorway trimmed in dark wood, is small kitchen area with a deep sink and a tall faucet. Plenty of counter space. A large table and chairs. Screens in the windows and real drapes.

Puja tells me dinner will be served around 6:30 p.m. and asks if that is okay or do I want to eat earlier? I tell her it's fine. Just fine.

As soon as she leaves, I set to unpacking. I feel relieved, calm, elated. I'm sorting, setting up things in the kitchen area, and feeling how surreal my world has become.

I message my husband, and he's still awake, so I call. We are both tearful and relieved and know the worst is behind me.

I message Saami, who's on his way to Bangladesh for a few weeks. I tell him I'm settled at my friend's hotel. He replies that he is happy for me. He tells me about the delays in his flights. We text as two old friends who have a few minutes to catch up.

In the midst of all this, I race to the toilet four or five times as my body releases the tension that has built up during the last month at the elder care home. I have never been more grateful for a toilet that flushes. I take my first shower in a month, complete with hot water, and I can't even wrap my head around how good it feels. At the elder care home, I was hunching over in the toilet closet, perching on the toilet seat lid that wasn't attached, trying not to let it slide off from beneath me, and was washing myself down with the cold water from the bidet sprayer.

At long last, though, it all catches up to me. I curl up under the covers, close my eyes for just a few minutes.

I wake up at 7:30 p.m. I slept eight hours. I don't know if I've missed dinner, but I'm too groggy to drag myself upstairs and find out. Outside in the courtyard, lights stream down on Ganesh Temple, and flicker and flash in a second-floor room in the building behind it. Young people are playing popular music. It's a clean-cut dance party. My cousin in Steamboat Springs refers to it as the "dharma disco" when he sees my video on social media. I watch the scene, noshing on CocoCrunchies and an apple for dinner, washing them down with water. I smile at my cousin's nickname for the young people's gathering. The term "dharma" means many things, including divine law, or a teaching centered on a universal, moral law. It's used quite often in Hinduism as well as my own practice of Buddhism.

Having bolted from the elder care home, I swear to myself never to set foot in there again. While I believe that the situation will improve now that they have been reported to the Ministry, I am mistaken. I won't realize how wrong I am until one year from now, when I return to Nepal and break my promise to myself.

But right now, none of that is known. Right now, I believe I will never return to that dark hell. There is only *now*, only here.

And *now*, here, I lie on my bed in this bubble of compassion and love for all humanity, check messages and emails, then fall asleep again to the sounds of the neighborhood.

III. The Oasis

"This is worship: To serve mankind
and to minister to the needs of the people.
Service is prayer.
A physician ministering to the sick, gently, tenderly,
free from prejudice and believing
in the solidarity of the human race,
he is giving praise."

~ 'Abdu'l-Bahá

"Whoever is kind to the poor, lends to the Lord,
and He will reward them for what they have done."

~ Proverbs, 19:17

23.

Forcing Others to Stop

DIL AND PUJA'S HOTEL is almost a shock to my system after my month at the first elder care home. The hotel seems to overflow with kindness, compassion, and joy, and it feels as if every guest I meet here embodies these qualities, just as Dil and Puja do. Most of the hotel's patrons have come to Nepal on multiple occasions, choosing to stay here each time because Dil and Puja become family overnight. Others stay here because they've planned a trek through Dil and his services shop; Dil has arranged the trek, guides, flights, and all the details one would never be able to coordinate on one's own should he or she be traveling to Nepal for the first time.

Within hours of my arrival, I am back to feeling as if I'm home again.

๛

Stepping out of the hotel lobby, I squint in the sunshine, pause to look around. This morning I am heading to a meeting at the Chhatrapati Free Clinic. I've dragged eleven patient transfer belts along with me to Nepal, and today I am going to introduce the president of the board and the medical director to these thick, woven belts. In the West, we use them to support unstable people as they sit down or stand up, and to help stabilize them as they walk or move.

The kids playing in the dirt area yell and wave at me, and I smile and wave back. Near the market in the alley, a young boy of about five is kicking around a small pumpkin squash with an older boy. The youngest one and I share laughs and smiles whenever we see each other. He likes me for some reason, and I like him for all the reasons in the world, especially his laugh.

I spy a five-rupee note on the ground, pick it up, spin around without thinking.

A beggar sits on a stoop selling trinkets in one corner of the area. His eyes are on the five-rupee note, now in my hand. I imagine they have been on the money since someone dropped it. I consider this: Someone dropped it, no one picked it up. Not a single shopper in the market, nor the faithful coming to the temple. Not even the poorest man on the street. No one picked it up because it was not rightfully theirs. This is their way, and perhaps the way it has always been. I walk to the beggar, and he holds out his hands, right hand on top of left, as if receiving a gift. He takes the money from me, closes his eyes, folds his hands over the note and holds them to his forehead in gratitude.

If I'd left any earlier, what might have happened? Five rupees isn't a lot of money, but to a beggar it's a start. No one else was going to pick it up. No one else was going to give it to the beggar.

As I weave through traffic and shoppers, though, I begin to feel less than pleased with myself. Why didn't I give him more money from my satchel, or some water and biscuits from my backpack? I keep my pack loaded now for this very reason, so why didn't I give him some? Why did I settle for just the five rupees? On the way back, I tell myself, I will take him by the hand, as a brother, and buy him a meal. I make a promise to myself.

At the chowk—the five-way intersection—near Chhatrapati, I spy an ancient man, stooped with age, with a bad leg and a cane, trying to cross one of the roads. I step out and stop traffic, daring people to hit me, then reach my hand back to the old man. He shakes his head. *No, go on without me,* but I insist again. *Come along,* with one swift downward motion of my hand. He gazes at me partly in disbelief, partly in gratitude, as I creep along with him. At one point he gestures again for me to go on without him. I shake my head and force another car to stop while we inch along. As we arrive on the other side, he nods again and again in gratitude, and I nod again and again in respect, before we head our separate ways.

Right away, I hear a man say, "Madam." I ignore it. I don't know what to make of hearing the word and can't imagine it's meant for me.

But this man persists and says, "Madam," just a tad bit louder. I turn to see Pradeep's friend, the one who served as a translator the night I had the heated discussion with Pradeep.

I ask how he is. He says he is well. He says he misses my presence at the elder care home. I nod and tell him thank you, and that I have much work to do. I tell him I will be in Pharping several weeks at an elder care home there. He is nodding, still trying to take it all in, gazing at me with warm eyes and a gentle face. Then we excuse ourselves and go our separate ways.

Dating its history back to 1951, during Nepal's earliest struggles for democracy, the Chhatrapati Free Clinic is the largest free clinic and hospital in Kathmandu. Its motto is, "We believe that medical care is a basic human right, that no individual should suffer or die just because he or she is too poor to pay for it." Their outreach programs serve the needy across the city, and they have been trained by the United Nations Development Programme on search-and-rescue tactics as well as disaster management. After the earthquakes of 2015, they provided free resources for tens of thousands of Nepalis throughout the valley.

Feeling as if I'm in a dream, I sit with both the president of the board and the medical director, who are overjoyed with the transfer belt I show them. They call me a "godsend," and declare the belts "gifts." I tell them I brought plenty to pass out. We schedule time for me to train emergency room staff, nurses, and physiotherapists on how to use a transfer belt in various situations. They ask if I would go to Kalikasthan to train EMTs there. How can I say no?

As I leave the clinic, still in a daze from everything that has begun to happen, I pass a woman leaning against a small temple. She's chatting with a toothless, old, homeless woman, sitting on the ground. I stop short and slip my backpack from my shoulders. The old woman looks up at me, dumbfounded, as I hand her a bottle of water and package of biscuits. The woman talking to her chuckles. "Say, 'Namaste,' Aama," she says, trying to prompt the old woman to respond to my actions. She doesn't. She just stares. I smile and remove the plastic safety slip from the lid.

After sitting with the homeless man in black, I made the decision to just plant little seeds of humanity during the day, to just show a little kindness to the elders who need it. The God in me, the Light in me, sees the Light in them. That is the meaning of "namaste." That attitude is the root of kindness. Maybe, *just maybe*, I can inspire others to do the same.

Several locals have stopped to watch, and there is no animosity, no spitting. One man smiles and says, "Welcome to Nepal," as I begin to walk past. I stop, smile in return, and say, "Thank you, but I live here." A broad smile cracks his face.

Squeezing through the small crowd of shoppers in the alleyway market on my way back to the hotel, I spy the same little boy out playing with the same pumpkin squash. He sees me as he's preparing to kick it to his new partner, laughs and points to me again, and I laugh and point back at him which delights both of us even more.

The beggar is gone. Disappointed in myself, I realize I am too much in observer mode, too much a tourist still. This morning I was focused on my own agenda, and neglected to stop and take just a few minutes to serve this man. Just as with the old beggar in Thamel and the young shopkeeper, my inaction, or tiny actions, are not who I want to be. I can do better.

24.

Moving Forward

MANESH PAUSES AT THE top of the stairs, outside Aabi's office, CGN's president and founder. "I am taking you to Africa!" he announces with great humor as he swings open the door with a flourish.

A wave of heat nearly knocks me backward, and I laugh at his joke. I have never been shy about my big laugh, and back at the elder care home, Garima told me my laughter is needed in Nepal. She said it is a good thing. Now, Sunjiya and Geetu look down the hallway at my outburst, stopping their conversation with CGN's bookkeeper.

There is no spot to sit on the black leather couches that would not burn bare skin. Aabi's drapes haven't been installed, and the windows are open with wall fans blowing steaming air around. We find a couple of seats but will move halfway through the conversation to avoid sitting in the sun, which moves across the sky at remarkable speed.

We start our meeting, as per Nepal custom, with small talk. When it's time for business, though, we both get right to the point. Manesh tells me that after they heard of the problems at the elder care home, they removed this program from their website. I'm pleased but confused. "So, do you even *have* an elder care program?" I ask.

He explains that in the past they had two elder care homes for the program. One home can't house volunteers any more, and CGN has yet to find a suitable host family nearby. The second home never housed the volunteers, so CGN used a local host family. That host family is unacceptable now. He doesn't say why. When I submitted my application, they found themselves *with* a volunteer, but *without* an elder care home. I decline to ask why they didn't just tell me to choose another program. *They wanted the money*, I tell myself. To give CGN credit, though, they did believe they could find a place before I landed in Nepal. Manesh had spoken with Pradeep one year before, and when he followed up with Pradeep again, upon my arrival, it seemed like it could be a good fit. CGN now knows, however, that they can't use that place.

His next question stuns me a bit. "How did the Ministry come to the facility?"

My heart skips a beat, and I stammer out an answer. "I told a friend about the conditions at the elder care home, and he had me talk to someone he knew. I didn't really understand who I was talking to. Suddenly, everything happened."

Manesh nods, smiles, then moves on.

He asks how they can make it right. I start to tell him that I'm staying at my friend's hotel, and before I finish the thought, he offers to reimburse me the same daily cost as they would reimburse a host family. He then asks, "What else?"

"Let me help you redesign your elder care program," I say. "I have been in touch with other elder care homes and have introduced myself." I tell him I've found one home in Pharping that can use my help, and Manesh is pleased. He will call to arrange for a visit for both of us. "Also," he reminds me, "Aabi will have other work for you." Ah, yes, Aabi had asked for my help with various projects when I first arrived. They'll get what they can out of me, but that's all right. This is what I signed up for—not just to do elder care, but to help CGN as well because of my master's degree in international business.

࿊

During Dashain and our thirteen-hour temple tour, I had watched out the window as we careened down the road away from Dakshinkali. When I first saw the banner, I craned my neck backward to ensure I'd read it correctly and could remember its location as we flew past: Senior Citizen Nursing Care Home Pharping.

I made a mental note.

As the end of Dashain approached, I knew I would need to find another elder care home. I honestly didn't have an immense amount of faith in CGN, regardless of what I told others. Sitting at the coffee shop in upscale Thamel, typing away on my little smart phone, I found three elder care homes. Writing to each in English, I gave them a quick review of who I was, why I was in Nepal, and how long I'd be here. I finished each email with one simple question: "Do you need my help?"

The only response came from Pharping. Shaha, the young man whose NGO runs the elder care home there, was delighted to hear from me. Yes, please, they could use my help.

ॐ

CGN's driver, Akkal, handles the roads like a pro, and Manesh naps in the front seat the day we make our trip to Pharping. My first trip out here, during Dashain, was a heart-stopping ride in a bus at the very edge of an unstable dirt road with nothing below but trees, rocks, and wrecked buses. Today, Akkal pauses where needed, dodges reckless drivers, and refuses to take chances. It's a completely different experience. We park on the main street near the water gardens below an elaborate Hindu temple and a Buddhist monastery, then walk back down the road to climb the stairs to the elder care home.

Shaha greets us with a warm smile. We chat over tea and biscuits, and his warmth never fades. Shaha says the elders could benefit from some new energy and a fresh face, and as he gives us a tour, I use my experience from the first elder care home to assess this place. How many elders live here? Nine, he says. Six women and three men. Will there really be work for the volunteer? Yes, he says. They could benefit from a little massage, some help walking, and lots of company. He adds that one woman hasn't bathed in several months. If I could get her to bathe, he says, it would be wonderful. I smile. Oh, I can do that, I tell him.

We gaze into the wash facility. One side has a shower wand, hot and cold running water, and a semi-automatic washing machine. The other side has a traditional squat toilet, which is a ceramic basin that fits in the ground. It's a fancy pit toilet, really, and I've used them frequently here. Manesh looks at me. He asks if I'm certain it will be okay, and I tell him it isn't a flush toilet, so it can't clog, and he laughs with me.

The room that would be mine is overwhelming in both size and amenities. Blankets, low tables, chairs, windows with screens and safety grates, a peaked ceiling. It's huge even by my own Western standards. The door has a lock, and the room opens onto a balcony that gazes out across the road and into the forest beyond.

After the tour of the grounds, we head back to the sitting area outside the kitchen, where Akkal has been visiting with the caregivers and the elders. Maya, one of the caregivers, brings out Nepali donuts and more tea. The food here seems abundant, in vast contrast to the first elder care home where I stayed. Thanks to Lions International, there is also a water filtration system on the grounds, so the elder care home never runs out of clean drinking water. The entire situation feels good. It feels right. When Manesh asks what I think, I reply that I'd like to stay here, and Shaha is delighted. We tell Shaha that we will discuss it all, and that Manesh will call him with details.

Once back at CGN's office, Manesh and I agree to a two-week stay. Akkal needs to return to Pharping after two weeks to pick up volunteers from a monastery up the street, so it makes sense for me to return with them. One week from today, Akkal will drive me back to Pharping to begin my stay.

૨

Leaving the coffee shop later that afternoon, I recognize the homeless man in black, sitting in a new doorway today. I touch his shoulder before sitting down with him, and he is elated to see me. I hand him the rest of my water from the coffee shop. I didn't drink from this bottle, so it's easy to share. He says he was afraid I had left for my home country.

As he did the other times we visited, he asks me again how I knew he was there, if I am married, and if I have children.

He asks where I'm staying and I gesture around the corner. He apologizes again, as he does each time we meet, for complaining when we last spoke. I assure him that I never noticed it.

This man lives in a constant state of now, with the knowledge that something has happened before this, but without the burden of having to remember it all.

He is happy today, and that makes me happy. Perhaps he will have good memories from our few visits. Perhaps he will appreciate being treated as a fellow human, and being treated as worthy of someone's time.

Perhaps he will remember it all as a dream.

25.

The Silent Young Man

TONIGHT IS ONE OF my last nights at the hotel. I venture to the roof for dinner, the bright, eating area stark against the void of the night. In homes all around us, families are gathering and cooking outside, all of us pockets of light in the darkness hovering above Kathmandu.

I arrive to find a young man in a light blue t-shirt and shorts sitting at the table outside the kitchen window. I can't discern his age. His back is straight, his hands folded in his lap, but his head is hanging so far forward that his chin is resting heavily on his chest, beneath a weight the world has forced upon him. I'd no idea the neck could extend and fold the way his is extended and folded. As I look at him, it strikes me that his body has reflected this shame for many years, that his soul may be impossible to reach.

A young woman sits to the side. Her long hair is pulled up into a ponytail. She wears glasses, a short-sleeved, peach-colored top and jeans, and is wrapped in a printed blue shawl. She is talking with the man standing to the side of the young man whose head hangs down.

This man is fortyish, wearing a khaki t-shirt and blue shorts. He smiles. He is jovial. And generous.

I've brought my camera with me tonight and capture a moment where the young woman and the man are smiling at each other over the young man seated between them. The man's hand is on this young man's back. The scene is well-lit, the immediate background framed in plants and flowers and pots; in the distance, the darkness of the night is dotted with far-away lights.

As I swap out lenses, I ask Puja about the young man. Her quick smile fades. She says the man found him on the street. She and Dil have agreed to let him keep the young man here. No one knows his story. He won't speak.

When the young girl leaves, I venture over to talk with the man. He's from Malaysia and is a frequent visitor to Nepal, always staying with Dil and Puja. This afternoon he found this young man standing on the side of the road in front of a hospital, pants around his ankles, having soiled himself multiple times. The young man was cold. Shivering. The man from Malaysia says he has no idea how long the young man had stood out there. He fights back tears. "Who would do this? Who could walk past another human being like that?" I shake my head, feeling his agony, sharing his emotional pain. "I could not leave him," he says.

No one seems to know anything about the young man, not even the hospital where he was found. This man from Malaysia doesn't know who else to talk to. His biggest concern is that he's only staying in Nepal a couple of days on this trip and will be leaving soon. He says Dil and Puja have agreed to keep the young man at the hotel if this man from Malaysia can't find another place before he leaves. He has offered to pay Dil and Puja for their kindness. "I have to go back and make arrangements so that I can bring him home with me," the man says.

I hate to talk about this young man in front of him, as if he isn't there, but I end up doing just that.

Does he speak? No, he's never really uttered a word. He has whispered some words in English.

Is he ill? No one knows.

Can he control his bowels? It doesn't seem as if he can. He hasn't had an accident at night, but during the day it seems like a different story.

We talk some more. No one knows the young man's name. He is mostly unresponsive to questions and comments. The man from Malaysia has explained to him that he's safe now.

I excuse myself as Puja brings a bowl of food for the young man, places it in front of him, hands another bowl to the man from Malaysia. She rubs the young man's back a little bit, speaks to him in gentle Nepali and in English, telling him he is safe and that his dinner is here.

After a while, as I sit and eat my own dinner across from Puja, I glance up at the young man to see his hands move up, creeping in to grasp the bowl and bring it to his mouth. He spoons the rice and curried cauliflower into his mouth without looking up.

The next night, the man from Malaysia tells me he has found a care home that will take the young man. He tells me about the woman who runs the place, says he's done his homework, researched her, inquired at the Ministry of Women, Children, and Social Welfare. He gives me all the information and tells me if I am looking for volunteer opportunities, she could use my help. Right now, though, he says he worries that the young man will think he's being abandoned. The man says he needs a few weeks to get everything in order so that he can come back to take the young man home with him.

Halfway through dinner, halfway through his bowl of food, the young man whispers something and the man leans in to hear, then helps him from the chair and guides him downstairs to their room. They leave behind a puddle on the floor beneath the chair.

IV. Serving the Elders

"Recognize the Lord's Light (Spirit) within all,
and do not consider social class or status;
there are no classes or castes in the world hereafter."

~ Guru Granth Sahib Ji

"Whoever gives the poor money is blessed sixfold;
whoever does it with a kind word is blessed sevenfold."

~ Talmud, Bava Batra

26.

Finding My Own Footsteps

TRAVELERS COME TO NEPAL seeking answers, just as anyone turning to religion or philosophy or a spiritual path also seeks answers. We look outside ourselves instead of inside ourselves. Humans tend to hope that something bigger than we are will tell us who and what we are supposed to be.

Siddhartha Gautama—the Buddha—was not creating something new; instead, he was showing people what he had uncovered within himself, what is within all of us. He was showing us that we create our own misery and suffering, and that we have within us the power to rise above all that we see and all that we create within our minds. He proved to us that the answers lie within *ourselves*, not within religious dogma or superficial spirituality.

When his first great student wished to accomplish what Gautama had, Padmasambhava did not follow in Gautama's footsteps, or go to find the famed fig tree beneath which Gautama became enlightened. Instead, Padmasambhava came to the mountains to meditate in the cave now called Asura Cave. It was his intention to find his own footsteps. As the legend goes, upon his reaching enlightenment, he walked through the mountain and came out of it through a second, nearby cave entrance.

Both of these caves are located in what is now known as Pharping. Just as Christian and Jewish pilgrims flock to Jerusalem to feel closer to Jesus or to their Jewish history, so, too, do followers of the Buddhist path flock to Pharping. They hope to become enlightened just by walking the path that Padmasambhava walked and meditating in the cave where he meditated.

The teachings of the Buddha and of Padmasambhava, it seems, are lost on these pilgrims.

⇜

The days flew past at Dil and Puja's hotel, time picking up speed with each moment and each meal. Here at the Pharping elder care home, time seems to fly even faster. Akkal drove me, and took my bags to my room without asking. He visited with Maya, the caregiver working today, as she served us tea and biscuits. After staying long enough to be gracious to my new hosts, he departed, and I was left on my own, smiling from ear to ear.

I have found where I belong. This is my pack, and I am family, welcomed into their world as if I always belonged here. Two of the three male residents become my Dhais—my older brothers; the third man, the oldest of all the residents, becomes my Baa—my father. The six female residents become my Aamas—my mothers. Since it becomes obvious that I struggle with their names, I quickly give each resident my own private nickname.

Here, my name is "Alena," with a long first "a." What's in a name? Nothing. It's just a label.

Pushpa lives on-site, and manages the elder care home. She is in charge of the three caregivers who come and go, and she is like a sister to me. She's about my height and very lean, with a small belly. I believe she's around my age. Pushpa speaks English around me, but not around Shaha, and tells me that she's self-conscious about her English skills.

She takes her tea and the paper up onto the hill in the mornings, sits on a low bench with her back to the sun, and reads the newspaper. Whichever caregivers are on duty that day—Reeta, Beena, or Maya—usually join her. During the day she sits in the seating area and reads, visits, or watches television, keeps an eye on everyone and all the goings-on.

Earlier today, my second full day here, Pushpa had me lie face-down across her lap on the couch in the seating area outside the kitchen. Then she pounded the hell out of my aching, twisted back. Up and down, side to side. She didn't even ask. She just knew, as a big sister would, that I needed her help.

When she was done pounding me out, she put me in the side-lying position, and this is where I have stayed for a while, finishing an email. I am

140

going up to the market to buy eggs, but need to stretch first. Just my walk yesterday morning up through the hills has thrown my twisted spine into fits. I'd feel better if I'd stretch, but I haven't been good about it.

☙

The elder care home is situated on a massive property that includes the Sheshnarayan Temple and its various water gardens. There is also a Buddhist monastery built next to the cave, known as Yangleshö, where Padmasambhava emerged after attaining enlightenment.

Shaha runs the NGO responsible for the elder care home. He's about thirty years old, is about my height with a slight build, and has a conservative, short haircut framing his round face. He wears Western-style clothing, a baseball cap, and always has the smile of someone who feels quite at peace and pleased with his world.

As with many Nepalis trying to eke out a living here, Shaha does a little bit of this, a little bit of that. He runs the elder care home, runs a messy stationery and printing store in town, teaches yoga, and is a broker/dealer of undetermined goods.

When his 5:30 a.m. yoga class is finished in the large building on the property, Shaha and his class members gather in the seating area while two of the women from the class make tea and serve it to everyone. Shaha sits on the couch, and his friends gather around him. They talk a bit, and he smiles as a wise one might smile at the goings-on of his students.

The yoga class fees are supposed to help support the elder care home. Shaha, however, doesn't collect fees from his friends, and his only students are his friends.

Beena is a retired nurse and one of the caregivers here. She is very short, and is perhaps in her forties. She has a sweet, round face, bad teeth, and bad skin. She is good-natured and gentle, very smart but meek, and she is rotund but not obese. Even though my little sister insists that she does not like to have her photo taken, she still laughs as I click away.

One day I will run into Beena on my morning walk. She will tell me I inspired her to go out at 5:00 a.m. to take a walk herself. She climbs up the hill in town with her painful bad knees, but always greets me with as much cheer as she can muster. I will earn Beena's love and respect tomorrow morning, when I stand up for her while we're in town. This is the morning my Chicago really comes out.

27.

The Chicago in Me

DASHAIN IS OVER AND it's Tihar now, the Festival of Lights. Tiny lights are strung along the upstairs balcony, and small oil lamps have been placed around the grounds at the elder care home.

Today the local elders and honors-level high school students are being celebrated at a big event in the heart of town. Shaha told me about the event yesterday and invited me, with great pride, to attend. He said Pushpa and Beena would take me. This morning, however, Pushpa and Beena don't want to go and I don't want to go if they aren't going—but after two of our elders arrive at the festivities and we aren't there yet, the call comes: Shaha wants to know where we are, and so we go.

It's a slow walk with Beena's bad knees, and we take our time hiking up the dirt road, past the carnival filled with young people, set up on the soccer field. We navigate around the steady traffic of cars, motorcycles, and scooters, and past the police checkpoint at the edge of the market. Today they are stopping and searching all red SUVs. Papers are being examined, bags opened. Yesterday, it was all Land Rover-style SUVs, with expedition packs and bags piled on top and tourists stuffed inside. Tomorrow it might be local buses or white cars, or scooters and motorcycles.

The stop-and-search checkpoints are difficult for me to grasp as a westerner, but it's just a normal occurrence for the locals. I haven't yet met anyone who can answer my most general questions, so I don't ask why the police have these checkpoints here in Pharping. I can only assume it may be a deterrent against future violence from the Maoists, who started the civil war, and who've never given up fighting towards a now-vague goal.

Today's gathering is a big event, and we find seats under a massive tent. I am aware of being the only Caucasian here. Most of the audience is either under age twenty-five, or over seventy years old. Many of the young people are dressed in the traditional attire of the Newari tribe, in black and white pinstripe outfits. All of them have red paint on each cheek, either two slashes, or Newari symbols. Later they will march around the square in a parade, and then return to the stage to perform traditional Newari dances.

Newars are the original inhabitants of the Kathmandu Valley, and the people at this event are the descendants of that history. Modern Nepali civilization was built by the Newari people, and this country's traditions have been handed down by the Newars.

Newars terraced the land and farmed the valley and traded with those from other lands. It is the Newars whose art and architecture and culture survive to this day. Historical Newars likely were Buddhist, and they have never stopped frowning at the practice of animal sacrifice. Most of the festivals that the Nepali people celebrate, and that attract tourists, are traditional Newar festivals.

On this day during Tihar, Newars across the valley will march and sing and celebrate. Two years from now, I will sit in Kathmandu Durbar Square as tens of thousands of Newars crowd the streets, hour after hour, in a raucous celebration of their heritage. I will be in awe as each tribe's tall flag pole spins high above the crowds.

As we watch the ceremony, I notice Beena become agitated. A short while later she scoots her chair forward. In a few minutes, she does it again. At this point, she can't go any farther. We're really crammed in, and her knees are now almost touching the back of the chair in front of her. I ask Pushpa if we can leave, and she says to give it ten more minutes. We've been here a half hour, and it is just plain loud with male and female speakers yelling into microphones with the volume turned all the way up. I am feeling the stress of the noise and of being packed in like cattle. I pray for a breeze even though it isn't hot under the massive tent.

Then Beena asks Pushpa if we can leave. That's when I look down at the back of Beena's chair and see what's been going on: A large young man, in traditional Newari dress, is stretched out in his chair behind her. His right foot has been hitting one of the rear legs of Beena's chair as he lounges and visits with his friends. In an effort to get away from this constant knocking, Beena has continued to scoot forward, and somehow his foot has been chasing her this entire time.

I turn and shout, "Oy!" over the din, but the man doesn't hear me. When I grab his leg, he doesn't notice that, either. So, I shout louder and grab his arm, and one of his friends gets his attention as well. When he looks at me, I point to his foot and shout, "Stop kicking her chair!" He puts his hand to his ear, pulls his feet back, leans forward and asks, "Sorry, ma'am?"

Now I shout in a voice loud enough to be heard over the microphone on the stage. "Stop kicking her chair! You're being rude!" I never knew I could be this loud.

"Yes, ma'am!" He sits straight up.

"Knock it off, *now*!"

"Yes, ma'am!"

"Don't mess with my sister, or you'll regret it!"

"Yes, ma'am!"

There's no question that I'm angry, and he gets it. He nods. His friends are laughing that he's just gotten a verbal butt-kicking by a white woman old enough to be his mother.

When I turn around, I see several women around us, smiling and chuckling, nodding in approval. I look at Beena, ask if she's okay. Her lips are pursed as she fights back both her horror and glee at what I've done. Her entire body is shaking as she fights to hold in her laughter, and she grabs my left hand and pulls it into her lap, squeezes it in gratitude. I encourage her to slide her chair back, so she can have a few inches of room. I want her to re-establish her territory. When she scoots back a bit, I tell her to scoot back even more, which she does, and gets comfortable once again.

I've been here only a few days, but apparently I will fight the biggest, baddest-looking eighteen-year-old to defend my little sister.

We can't leave right away. Not after that scene. I wait about ten more minutes, during which time the young man is on his very best behavior, then look at Pushpa, her chin resting in her hand. Okay, that's it. "We go," I say, and she tilts her head in agreement.

We weave our way through rows of scattered red outdoor chairs, with Pushpa greeting people she knows along the way. The three of us glance at each other as we move, co-conspirators skipping away from our obligations, hoping that Shaha or his friends won't see us leaving.

~o

Beena makes tea, and the elders gather in the seating area to be served. Pushpa and I are laughing about our outing in town when we are greeted by a young father and his family coming up the front stairs from the road. They are following the new Nepali custom, created by young parents, of taking food or gifts to the elder care homes on their child's birthday. They want to teach their children to respect their elders, something which other adult children across this country seem to have forgotten. The mother sits with their pre-teen son and younger daughter, holding a large bag with blankets in it.

The father guides his youngest daughter, perhaps just four years old, and they collect a blanket from the bag, then present it to one of the elders. The father takes his little girl from elder to elder, holding her hands from behind her. I snap photos on an angle, capturing the gratitude in each old person's face, their hands held together before them, "Namaste," to this young soul. The girl, wide-eyed, standing before this ancient person, father behind her. I love these photos.

~o

At 7:30 p.m., I relax on my bed and realize the road is quiet, save for a motorcycle now and again.

Beena asked me earlier if I was bored. I said no. I'm not. There's very little, if anything, for me to do right now. I don't care. It's nice to be here.

It's also nice to realize that my definition of work is not the only definition. In the West, elder care includes washing their clothes and bathing them, but this is not what the elders here want or need. They want my company, my stories, my photos. They want to interact with me and share their world with me, even if we don't speak the same language. This is elder care—and by its definition, this is my work here.

I'm also learning to feed my soul by following my heart more. I can sit in the Buddhist shrine room at the monastery during services, close my eyes, and breathe in each moment of chanting, of blaring horns, beating drums, and crashing cymbals. I drop into the nowness of it all and feel my soul fill to overflowing.

The television is blaring in the sitting area outside the kitchen. Dwarf Dhai must still be watching. Grumpy Aama and Black Aama are chatting down in their room. They'll be up late.

28.

Snores

OF THE NINE RESIDENTS here, I find myself drawn to three women in particular. It has been easy to find nicknames for them: Grumpy Aama always looks unhappy about something; Black Aama has a very distinctive face; and Folded Aama's legs are permanently folded up against her body.

These three women share a room beneath mine. This is a simple building made according to traditional Nepali construction, with a loose, powdery mortar thrown onto disintegrating bricks or concrete blocks, and then smoothed over to hold everything together. Once dried, the rippled, bulging product is painted with non-latex, chemical-free paint. This building is four years old and has chunks of mortar falling off in places, cracks in other spots, all remnants of the 2015 earthquakes on top of normal aging out here.

Also, here they use untreated wood, and ants, pigeons, and mold have made themselves at home along the eaves and the peak of the rotting roof. Flooring for the second level consists of unfinished wood planks with no subflooring. Over these planks is a very thin layer of carpet. Taken all together, the smallest noise—from the pigeons in the peak above my room to someone coughing in the room below—can be heard as if they are in the room with me.

During the day, Grumpy Aama and Black Aama talk a lot in their room, and nap. There's also the occasional argument—at least it sounds like arguing. Outside the room, though, they don't speak. Black Aama socializes with another resident whom I've nicknamed Goiter Aama, but Grumpy Aama socializes with no one, and Folded Aama stays by herself. My three favorite Aamas speak Newari, and I am assuming I'll have trouble communicating with them. I'm wrong, of course.

All night long, Grumpy Aama's and Black Aama's various snores compete with the packs of arguing dogs outside to see who can be the loudest. The dogs are drowned out. The Aamas' snores are akin to a Three Stooges symphony: A sigh, a groan, a higher sigh, a multi-toned groan.

Black Aama stands at about five feet tall. She is nearing eighty years old, from what I can tell. When not arguing or yelling in her room, Black Aama is very soft-spoken and gentle. She lets me massage her lower legs and knees sometimes but never lets my hands anywhere near her feet or slippers. It would be too humbling, too low, for me to touch her feet.

When Grumpy Aama comes out of their room, she will sit either on the low cement wall lining the walkway outside the lower dorm rooms, or in her self-assigned chair inside the seating area, but only until the food is served. Once she has her plate, she'll waddle back to their room to eat.

When she's in her chair and waiting for food or watching television, she always sits sideways, facing the kitchen. Grumpy Aama never changes the station or the volume. I can't say I blame her, since the channel and volume buttons all seem to just turn the volume up somehow. If she's the only one left watching and has lost interest, instead of turning the television off, she just wanders off, which annoys Dwarf Dhai no end. I think she knows this and just does it to irritate him.

Folded Aama is in her seventies and has very short gray-and-white hair. She is lean, and has a long face with sad eyes. Both legs are permanently bent against her chest. Her left leg is so tight, she can't move it, but she has some movement in her right leg, and uses it to help her crawl up the low steps and up the hill to hang up her laundry. She hobbles around on the ground, inch by inch, moving her things with her.

She comes out of her room, climbing up and down from her bed, several times a day, for tea, snacks, meals, and sometimes to just hang out and get some sun. The first finger on her right hand is deformed. It's folded forward and off to the side at the first joint, her fingernail pointing down towards her palm.

Despite her disability, she washes herself almost every morning—far more often than any of the other residents here. She washes her clothes daily and washes her dishes after every meal, doing all this at the outside tap in very cold water.

Folded Aama arrived at another elder care home more than ten years ago. Pushpa arrived at that home a few years later, and then they moved here to Pharping four years ago. Folded Aama has never told anyone about her life, about her history, or how her legs ended up stuck in this position. She cries when asked. Shaha tells me that he has had therapists come to try to work with her but was told her injuries are permanent. There is no way to stretch the tendons or straighten her legs or give her any semblance of a normal life.

Folded Aama eats alone at the half-wall outside the Dhais' room, with the caregivers taking food and tea to her.

She mumbles whenever she speaks to someone. Folded Aama has learned that I will help her, and sometimes asks me for little favors throughout the day. Whenever she sees me, she talks to me. I can't make out anything she says, but I understand her gestures. She just has things to tell me. I listen and nod and try to be understanding.

॰

Maya is making popcorn tonight. It's being cooked over the adobe stove in the corner of the kitchen. Nepalis don't prepare popcorn the way Westerners do. We sit together outside, huddled under blankets, and pass the burnt, almost-popped kernels around as we watch the tiny television on the desk near the kitchen. It never occurs to me to see if I can successfully pop the kernels myself and then show them how to get the same fluffy white balls. This is how they eat popcorn, and I accept it.

Maya is a few inches taller than Beena, and a healthy plump as well. She's older than the other caregivers, perhaps as old as Pushpa and me. She has long, henna-colored hair and good skin, and she is always pleasant but not too cheerful. Maya is patient with Goiter Aama as she relates her many woes, and listens to all the residents but is not taken in by their ploys and complaints. Her clothes are just a little more expensive than those of the other caregivers.

On the evening Dwarf Dhai's lightly fried, curry-seasoned flatbread disagrees with my sensitive gut, Maya will lecture me in Nepali and nurse my intestines back to normalcy. She walks home every evening that she works at the home, waving goodnight to us as she leaves if we're still out after she's closed up the kitchen.

Reeta is the third part-time caregiver here. She is slightly shorter than me and perhaps in her thirties. She cooks and cleans and washes clothes for the residents, squatting at the outdoor tap and scrubbing. One day Reeta asks me something in Nepali, which I take to mean she wants to cut my hair. I panic. I tell myself it's all part of the adventure. All I have is my little fold-up scissors, which aren't quite scissors at all. I go to my room to get them along with a sheet and my hair clips. When I return, I understand she wants me to cut her hair. First, it's to her shoulders. I say no, I'll just trim it. Then, as I'm clipping her hair up, she says again up to her shoulders. I say no again. Then she compromises to halfway up her upper arm.

Women don't wear their hair short in Nepal. Long, shiny, flowing black hair is a point of pride for them here, even if they wear it up in twists or back in a ponytail. I worry that Reeta would regret the decision to cut her hair short, and I don't want to be associated with that regret.

I take a small lock of her hair, and the carnage begins. Her hair is slippery, and the scissors aren't cutting. It's more like hacking. After the first lock is cut, I let go, and her hair bounces up almost to her shoulders. It's crooked. I have to straighten it. I panic. I am sick to my stomach. I should have started with a trim to see how the scissors worked.

In the end, she's upset, I'm upset, and I tell her to hack my hair to make it up to her. But Cheerful Aama sees it and gives her the thumbs up, as does Pushpa. They like it. It makes her look younger and, when it's not pulled back, frames her face well. For days I'm sick about what I did, even though she reassures me it's fine, that she likes it. I understand her angst, though, and can't seem to get over my mistake.

29.

Together a Family

WHEN MANESH AND I first visited Pharping, Shaha told me that the woman I call Black Aama has refused a bath for the past three months, and that he's concerned. Manesh didn't seem alarmed, so I explained that bathing is a critical role of the caregiver. It allows us to inspect the resident for signs of abuse and skin breakdown, as well as rashes or untreated wounds.

This morning I'm racing around the grounds trying to photograph an elusive eagle after my long, pre-dawn walk. Two retired nurses arrive, along with two young and very sweet EMTs. One of the EMTs tries to convince Goiter Aama to see the doctor; Goiter Aama wants none of it.

Of the two nurses who arrive, one exudes confidence and leadership. She is decisive. This is Padma. She is in charge of the nurses' organization that helped to establish the elder care home.

Today I tell Shaha that Black Aama refused her bath when I offered it yesterday. Padma hears, and as the two of them march off to talk to Black Aama, I stay behind. When Padma notices I'm not with them, she turns and gestures to me to come along.

After a brief conversation, Padma explains that Aama didn't want a bath because she has some eczema on the back of her neck, and shows me by taking Black Aama's collar down a bit. Padma says she'll bring some cream tomorrow for her to use for the next four days, and tells me to rub it into her skin every night. She has confidence in me, somehow, without even knowing me.

I ask Padma and Shaha to tell Black Aama that I bathe elders for a living, and that the room will be warm for her shower, in case this is something that worried her. They translate into Newari, and Aama seems pleased to hear the news. I tell her I'll bathe her tomorrow morning when the sun is hottest.

When it comes time for a group photo, we are all together a family. We sit, stand, rearrange ourselves. Pushpa sits next to me. We nudge each other. I sit next to Black Aama and in front of Troublemaker Aama, who pokes me from behind. The nurses want photos of themselves seated next to me, and Pushpa and I try several times to get Kali, the dog who lives on the grounds, to pose with us.

I have been here nine days. I don't want to leave.

ॐ

In the room next to my favorite three Aamas are Goiter Aama and Cheerful Aama. Whenever Reeta or Beena spend the night, they sleep in the spare bed in this room.

Goiter Aama is about my height and lean with a little belly. She has two teeth left that I can see. It is hard to look at her at first because of her massive goiter, but you have to look through that and see the beautiful person beneath, in spite of how whiny she is.

She keeps her long gray-and-black hair in a bun at the back of her neck and has kind eyes. Even with her many woes, she likes to smile. Goiter Aama is never rude to anyone and never raises her voice.

Cheerful Aama could have popped right off the cover of a Far East version of The Saturday Evening Post. With good teeth and a quick, warm smile, she is plump and wears dresses, sometimes not getting out of her pink flower-print night dress all day.

I never see her cranky, even though her toes are crossed from bunions, her right knee doesn't straighten all the way, and her left knee doesn't bend much. Because of all this, she is slow and careful when she walks.

During the day, Cheerful Aama hobbles about unassisted, but by evening, the cane comes out. The first time I offered to rub her aching feet, calves, and knees, she resisted. Even when I insisted, she had trouble letting me touch her feet. She looked around for a braided mat for me to sit on so that I wouldn't be sitting on the ground. Within minutes of having my hands on her legs and feet, I could see the tension leave her body. She sat back, smiling, becoming chattier by the minute. After I was done, she expressed her enormous gratitude, pressing her palms together in front of her and telling the others about my good deed.

When I offered to rub her feet a second time, she didn't argue and grabbed the braided mat right away. She wasn't going to pass up the opportunity to feel better. The third time I rubbed her feet, though, she didn't seem to be as appreciative. She chatted with others while I worked on her and didn't chat with me. When I was finished, she didn't express as much gratitude as she had on other occasions. Now she just gestures to me whenever she wants me to rub her feet, and I oblige when my schedule allows. I want to do this favor for her, but it has started to seem that she expects it of me as if I'm a servant, and she no longer acts grateful when I'm done. I just remind myself that I am here to serve, and I keep doing this for her.

Troublemaker Aama earned her nickname early on. When I was taking pictures of the facility, she kept trying to get me to include Folded Aama in the photo, who was bathing, nearly naked, at the outside tap. Troublemaker Aama is just over five feet tall with thinning, dyed-black hair cut to her chin. She wears good clothes—a mixture of modern Nepali clothing and Western. Her teeth are good, and she's proud that she is Nepali, not Newari like some of the others at the home. The irony, however, is that the entire town is Newari.

The man I call my Baa ("father") is married to Troublemaker Aama. He is just over five feet tall, has very short gray hair, and is bald around the crown of his head. He almost always wears a topi, the traditional men's pointed cap. Baa is slender, has most of his teeth at eighty-seven years old, and is very hard of hearing. We all have to yell when talking to him. He walks bent-kneed and is bow-legged, though whether from genetics or from life experiences, it's hard to tell.

Baa is always happy. In the mornings, if it's warm enough, he'll have his tea, then go up the hill to sit in the sun. One day, as I'm wandering with my camera, he calls, "Alena! Eagle!" I spin and look up to where he's pointing and see a little bird flying. When I look back at him, shaking my head in amusement, he's laughing.

30.

Black Aama's Bath Day

Today is Black Aama's bath day. She is not pleased.

I go to the room with the shower and set out all my tools of the trade on the semi-automatic washing machine, including the lavender and goat's milk soap. The washing machine is basically an agitator with a separate spinner. I have to use the shower wand to pour water into the agitator when I want to wash or rinse my clothes. When that's complete, I take my clothes out of the agitator and put them in the spinner. The entire process is a bit of an ordeal, and for anyone handling the high volume of wash from a home such as this one, it would be too time-consuming. The caregivers use a large basin and the outdoor tap on wash days instead of this machine. Considering the difference between hand-scrubbing fabric and the motion of this agitator, I don't blame the caregivers for doing the wash by hand. I'm pretty sure the clothes and bedding come out cleaner that way.

Grumpy Aama seems as if she's making an effort to smile as I enter their room. I smile back. I ask Black Aama if she's ready—

No, she doesn't want a bath. Black Aama is adamant, but I am far more skilled at convincing reluctant elders to bathe than she is at convincing the caregiver that she won't give in.

We have a short discussion, her speaking in Newari and me responding in English. I fold my arms across my chest and give her a stern look. Black Aama looks away, gestures. She's fine, she is saying. I raise an eyebrow and change the look to disapproving. I wait. She relents, collects her bath things, and drags her feet behind me all the way back to the shower room. It's early, and we are expecting a visit from a children's school in a few hours. I'd like to get this done.

157

Black Aama is the quintessential cranky old woman being forced to do something against her will. She gets out her hard bar soap in the broken plastic soap container, her rough scrubbing fabric, and her almost-empty bottle of shampoo, muttering to herself the entire time. Every item gets set down with a bang on top of the semi-automatic washing machine. There's not much room left on the washer for her clean clothes, so she gestures and mutters and wants my towels off the washer. I set them in my bucket and put them outside the door.

It's a cozy room, with just enough space for the two of us and the red plastic chair I've brought for her to sit in. This should be interesting.

Her knit cap comes off, and she unravels her long hair. She gestures for me to turn on the hot water. When she undresses her top half, three layers of clothing come off, including a traditional heavy, short jacket, a heavy silk undershirt, and a tank top. As she unfolds her skirt from the front of her waist, out comes a small pouch. She holds it up to me, explaining what it is in Newari. As if performing a magic trick, she unrolls the next fold of her skirt, and out comes a tiny flip phone. She holds it up. "Mero babu," she says, pointing to the phone. "Qatar." As it turns out, no one knows where her son is, not if he's still in Qatar or if he's still even alive.

Next, after stripping down to just a thin skirt from beneath the other skirt and two shawls wrapped around her waist, she reaches over to check the water temperature. "Tahto," she mutters. Too hot. I nudge the tap back a bit.

Muttering some more, she dumps her dirty clothes in a heap onto the washing machine. I want to put them outside the door, since there's just no room on the washer anymore, but Black Aama will have none of that. I'm to leave everything piled up on top of itself.

Finally, she's down to just her thin, pink lunghi—the fabric that women use for modesty when bathing in public. It is a long stretch of fabric that's stitched together to create a tube. The tube slides over their heads, and then they gather, fold, and tuck the fabric just like a sari. It's long enough that women can wear it up to their armpits but short enough to wear around their waist—as Goiter Aama and Black Aama do during their baths.

Black Aama checks the water temperature again: "Tihso."

Seriously? I barely nudged the tap. How can it be too cold? I check the water myself and notice no difference, but she wants me to nudge it back up, so I do.

I've been making myself useful while waiting for Black Aama to undress; I've lathered my dark blue bandanna with the luxurious soap. As she takes a seat, checking the water temperature again, she waves off my rag. She shows me her hard bar of ancient soap, starts to rub it into her scrub fabric. I hold the bandanna close enough to her nose to get her attention, explaining that I've already soaped up a rag.

It works. She gets a whiff of the scent, and her face lights up. Her soap bar goes back on the washer with a bang, and she grabs my bar, begins to soap up her scrub fabric. I am starting on her back as she starts on her face. She reaches for the wand, checks the water temperature again, and it's perfect.

Black Aama has gone from grumpy to chatty and happy. She scrubs and scrubs some more. She gives me one of her scrub fabrics to do her back, and has me scrub it three times.

At one point, I have her lean forward so I can wash the folds around her waist. Holding the skin folds open, I see the sores. They are long and bright pink. I need to wash and dry the folds as best I can without aggravating the skin, then report this to Padma, the nurse.

When I start to scrub her lower legs, Black Aama doesn't object, but when I reach for her feet, she is appalled. She pulls her feet in and holds one finger up in the air, admonishing me. I am not allowed to touch her feet. I don't argue with her.

We take so long in the bath that Pushpa yanks open the door at one point to yell at Black Aama. I gasp and say, "Tihso!"

"Tihso, tihso!" she hollers back, mocking my concern about the cold outside, emphasizing the fact that she doesn't care. Her tone is clear. We are taking far too long and using too much water, especially after Black Aama didn't even want the bath to begin with.

Having said her peace, Pushpa slams shut the thin aluminum door. For a long moment, the only sound is the water pouring from the wand behind me.

Black Aama looks at me, holds up her hand and puts her index finger and thumb together, then opens and closes them ever so slightly, saying, "Nit, nit, nit," each time—the equivalent, essentially, of "Bitch, bitch, bitch." The tiny finger gestures are dismissive of Pushpa's actions and her complaints, and I am chuckling. Aama's comedic timing is spot-on, and she is chuckling as well, smiling at me. She finally nudges me and we get on with finishing up the final rinse.

It is at this point that I realize I don't want to leave after two weeks. I don't care what it takes to get me back to the city. I want to stay for *three* weeks.

ॐ

Every elder here has a story. Many years ago, Black Aama's son decided to marry his wife's sister. In Nepal, men can marry more than one woman without divorcing the first wife, or even the second wife. After the wedding, the son and second wife left the country and were never heard from again. With nowhere else to go, Black Aama continued to live with the first wife, who stopped taking care of her. Alone and neglected, Black Aama was discovered by a social worker and was brought to Shaha for lifelong care.

Now Black Aama is clean and happy, and she's combing out her long hair in the sunlit courtyard when dozens of children, from eight to fourteen years old, begin to come in. They are all dressed in near-matching outfits of red, blue, green or yellow polo shirts with their school logo. The teachers are serving as chaperones, and with them all are the school administrators, Suraj and Devina.

I am surprised and delighted to see Padma the nurse with them. At my request, Shaha starts to translate about the sores I found on Black Aama, but Padma understands enough English and heads towards Black Aama's room before he's finished speaking. Shaha and I tag along.

Black Aama unfolds and unties her lower garments so Padma can inspect the problem, then Padma turns to me with instructions. Black Aama will need ointment rubbed into the sores once daily, in addition to the ointment for the eczema on the back of her neck. The challenge is how to get the ointment for her sores to Pharping soon. I tell her I have packets of triple antibiotic ointment upstairs, and Padma is delighted. Yes, she says, go get some. The sores don't need an antibiotic ointment, but it's all we have, and it will do for now.

Padma next gives Black Aama instructions on how to wear her clothes from now on. The fabric from her skirts is causing this, so she's to wrap the shawls around her waist before donning her skirts, and not tie everything as tightly as she has been.

Now Padma embraces me, clasps my hands, touches my face. I have endeared myself to her not only for getting Black Aama bathed, but for finding and reporting the sores. I try to remind her that this is simply my job as a nurse's aide, but that doesn't matter. All that matters is what I've done here and now, and for this, she is forever grateful. It's not just Padma's loyalty that I've won, either: Padma is Suraj's mother, and the future mother-in-law to Devina, and my dedication to these elders leaves no doubt in any of them that I am family.

The children have been set about their tasks in sweeping and cleaning. In reality, they are stirring up more dust and dirt as they try to sweep, and they make a mess in the downstairs bathroom. I will be in there later with gloves and a pail, washing urine off the commode toilet and the floor, and washing dirt off the sink.

On the couch in the seating area, Suraj, the school's chief executive calls out to the kids that if they want to skip their evening class because of how long this trip will run, they need to discuss it with their teacher. Seeing as how he's in charge, I laugh and ask him if he's ever heard the American phrase, "passing the buck." He hasn't. I explain that it happens when someone doesn't want to make a difficult decision, so they decide someone else should do it instead. Suraj laughs and says he does that all the time, so he must be good at it.

While the chaperones pass dishes to the children so they can assist in serving the elders, I join Suraj and his colleague, Devina, in the seating area. As usual, I wait until all the elders are served before I take any food. Suraj explains that he can't eat anything here and didn't bring his food. Devina shakes her head, smiling, and begins to unpack the food she brought. She pulls out his patties, his fruit, and his greens. He smiles at me, says she takes good care of him. He sees that I pass on the meat when Maya brings out my plate and asks if I'm vegetarian. I tell him yes: no meat, no alcohol, no gluten. His eyes brighten, and he tells me his diet: no meat, no dairy, no gluten, nothing fried. Devina chimes in, and the conversation turns to how our diet as humans has evolved further than our digestive systems have. We talk about illness and diet, cancer and cures.

The kids have long since left with the chaperones, and Padma is off visiting with Pushpa and the elders. Suraj, Devina, and I are lost in our own world. As we talk, I realize I know Devina. I know Suraj. I know Padma. It goes beyond an immediate connection or friendship. We have been here before, been through personal challenges together, loved each other as family, and fought for each other, in eras past. I don't have all the answers, and I hope I never think I do. But I know this, here and now: Suraj and Devina and I will never lose each other. Not here, not now, not ever.

31.

The Brothers

Dᴡᴀʀꜰ Dʜᴀɪ sᴛᴀɴᴅs ᴀʙᴏᴜᴛ four feet tall, looks to be in his late seventies, and is quite hard of hearing. He seems to be mentally challenged along with having a speech impediment. He is rotund at the hips, and when he speaks, he reminds me of the Tasmanian Devil. He is bow-legged and has a stiff walking style, waddling his weight side to side.

Dwarf Dhai loves to make flatbread. Several days a week, he owns the kitchen for a few hours with his laser-like focus on his work. His arms and hands are a blur as he mixes the dough, separates it into balls, rolls them out on an upside-down stainless-steel plate, and fries them in the pan on the countertop burners. He uses the little adobe stove in the corner of the kitchen to heat water, and to keep his flatbread warm after it's made.

Smoke billows from the open edges of the kitchen roof whenever he cooks. He tends the fire, tends to his baking, and has no time for conversation—unless I am just about to leave for town, in which case he grabs a fresh, hot flatbread for me. One afternoon I head into the kitchen just for fun. Walking into the wall of smoke, I cough and wave my hand in front of my face, then squint and feign blindness, stepping slowly into the room and reaching for things that may be in my way. Dwarf Dhai swats me on my tush and gives me an "Oh, you silly girl" look.

Dwarf Dhai has lost most of his teeth and has a heart of gold. We speak in different languages but universal gestures. He looks down from the seating area and yells at the traffic below, motioning to them, far away and through the trees. I tell him they can't hear him. He complains anyway and yells at them.

One time I stand to see what he is complaining about, and see a large van turning around on the narrow road below, which is a precarious and traffic-blocking move. Another vehicle, an SUV, is backing all the way down the road. The two nearly collide. The SUV then also turns around, backs up, and parks. Dwarf Dhai seems to complain that they are going to the Hindu temple here on the grounds where the elder care home is situated. He says this is why they're parking.

I tell him that's not what the driver of the SUV is doing. He says it is. I gesture no, then pantomime unzipping my fly and peeing like a man. I point and tell him that's what the guy is doing. This results in roars of laughter from everyone. Dwarf Dhai slaps my arm and bends over in his chair, laughing hard.

Even though he seems to adore me, whenever I lift a finger to help Folded Aama in any way, Dwarf Dhai has something to say about it. I can't understand a word he's saying, but he yells at me, and I yell back. I yell about Krishna and God being in all of us, and about no one being greater than another. He gestures at me and I keep on, before he finally dismisses me.

Slender Dhai is about my height, thin, and stooped just a bit. He has a full head of dyed-black hair, which he has just had buzz cut. Slender Dhai appears to have mild dementia. He has the perpetual look of a man who knows he has worries but has given up on them. He is soft-spoken and mumbles more than speaks. I have never heard him raise his voice or make any gesture in anger or frustration. He has very dark skin and bad teeth. He is in his mid-to-late seventies, from what I can surmise.

Every day, he takes the forty-five-minute walk to Dakshinkali Temple to worship. This is the temple I visited with all the other women during Dashain. Slender Dhai can be gone for hours each day. He takes his time, walks to and from the temple, and visits with many members of the community.

Slender Dhai has family, and often spends the night with them, but they don't feel they can care for him properly. As with life in the West, it becomes a challenge for adult children to take care of their parents when dementia sets in, and Slender Dhai's children have chosen to bring him to this elder care home, where he can get the daily care he needs.

32.

Chhath Puja

ONE AFTERNOON I NOTICE some unusual activity on the grounds of the temple. When the vertical light bars go up and the tents are raised and the massive speaker is perched on its stand, I finally make a comment.

Standing in the seating area outside the kitchen, I lean over the railing a bit and look out towards the temple water gardens. Then I stand upright again, sip my tea, and see Pushpa, who is seated on one of the couches, look out and follow my gaze. "What is this?" I ask. She seems weary in advance of the celebration.

Beena glances over her shoulder at the commotion, then back down at the cup of tea she hugs in her hands, shakes her head with a wry smile.

"They go all night," Pushpa says in clear English, resting her chin in her hand.

Dwarf Dhai gestures towards the night club atmosphere on the temple grounds and turns away, annoyed.

Pushpa senses my disbelief and says, "All. Night." She looks at me, chin still resting in her hand.

Perhaps it's because night closes in, but somehow the volume seems to rise as the darkness descends. Night travels onward, and the volume somehow travels upward even more.

All night it is, then.

అ

This elder care home was constructed on ancient temple lands, and the Hindu temple here on these grounds is the Sheshnarayan Temple, one of the four Narayana temples in Nepal. They were constructed in the fifth century, after the valley had been conquered by the Licchavi clan. Some experts believe the Licchavis built these temples across the valley according to the four cardinal directions, so that all the people of their kingdom could have the opportunity to more easily worship on important dates.

Too tired for my usual brisk, hilly walk at 5:00 a.m., I stagger downstairs with my camera bag. My plan is to walk around the grounds and look for interesting photos. Dwarf Dhai sees me coming, rushes out of the kitchen to stop me. No, no—I'm going the wrong way. I should go to the temple. I should go get food from them. I start to protest. I'm still in my black leggings, crappy t-shirt, and inside-out hoodie. I'm not dressed for company. He is insistent, and so I go. Out the back road, around the monastery, and towards the party.

At the bottom of the stairs near the water gardens, I step my way over to the next staircase. Looking up, I see a crowd gathering far above me. They are collecting on the very steep staircase that leads to the Hindu temple, and to the cave where Padmasambhava emerged after becoming enlightened.

I am called over to join the group. Young men, young women, a few in their forties, children as young as two—there must be thirty people, most of whom are calling to me, gesturing to join them so I can be in their group photo. They want me to be a part of their world for this moment. I decline their invitation, but I do take a few photos of them having their group picture taken. A beaming young girl turns from taking her own photo of the group to smile at me, still inviting me to join. I'm struck by her beauty.

If I had been angry or irritated by any of last night's noise as I huddled under my blankets, I wouldn't have been able to stay angry once arriving here. These people are welcoming and gracious, and want to share their world with me, even without knowing who I am as a person.

From there, it seems to descend into chaos. I take more than one hundred photos. People are everywhere. Old and young, and all ages in between. The young kids and young adults are still dancing under the massive tent and aren't going to be satisfied until I join them. I dance. They cheer. Young men work the laptop that drives the music that's fed into the commercial-sized speaker high on its stand.

Everyone wants their photos taken—families want portraits taken, the teens dancing want to be captured in action, friends want to document their love for each other. I keep snapping away on my camera, falling in love with these people who love me unconditionally. None of these folks will ever see these photos, but that doesn't matter to them. All that matters is that I am capturing this moment in time, and that it will be saved, somewhere, forever.

A young woman tells me this is Chhath Puja. "Today we thank the Sun for all he gives us during the year. We celebrate two days." She then asks if I've gotten tea yet. No, I haven't, and this isn't acceptable to her. She turns to someone, and within seconds I have a small, hot cup of tea. Next, she asks if I've eaten. When I shake my head no, this also isn't acceptable. It takes just a few seconds again, and I have a small bag of bananas and peanuts.

Near the koi pond, three men sit, engaged in political discourse. One leans in towards another. He wears a beanie, brown slacks, and a black thermal top with red a stripe up each side of the top. The third man in the group sits up, gazes straight into my lens. I snap my camera. Of the five photos I take of this group, this one best captures the moment.

I frame a shot of an old woman leaning against the centuries-old post from the shrine along the back of the gardens; a policeman appears off to her side, hands in pockets, staring me down. Policemen have been appearing almost every time I point my camera.

Next, I frame a shot of a woman with a steep streak of orange up her forehead and into her hair, sitting in a blue outdoor chair and wearing a red, draping kurta. She's talking to a young woman standing next to her, wearing a pink sweatshirt and blue jeans. Before I can snap the shot, an officer appears behind them, standing on the steps to the ancient shrine, feet wide, bag of free food in hand, staring me down. He's soon joined by another. I take the photo anyway.

Is this an attempt to intimidate me for some reason? Why are they working so hard to make their presence known and ruin my photos? Tourists can be tiresome, I know—I live in a tourist destination in the US—but tourists here in Nepal bring precious resources and money into the country. Why harass me? I decide to focus on ignoring them.

Arriving now is a very old man in a beige knit tunic with a hoodie framing his face. Over the tunic he wears a bright yellow rain jacket, and a long gray insulated vest over that. He walks with a walking stick and is stooped at the waist, bent half over. When he sees me hold up the camera, he forces himself to straighten up. This man I notice more than anyone else; our paths were meant to cross today, and in a few weeks, I will understand why the Universe or God or Fate put us in this place at this exact moment.

Framing the shot and snapping away, I see Cheerful Aama with her cane in the background. She has come all the way from the elder care home. Oh, my God. This woman's level of arthritis and pain would sap the joy out of anyone's life in the West. But no, she has walked all this way, down all those steps.

I shout at her and rush to her side. She is smiling, as always. Gritting it out through the pain. I help her over to the small shrine under the tent. She places a few flowers that she's picked and dips her head, blesses herself. We circumambulate the tiny structure three times. She wants her picture taken, and so I stand back, focus, snap a few photos as she leans on her cane.

All around us, everything is vanishing into cars, getting packed into bags, and perched on scooters. The koi pond, water gardens, and grounds are littered with garbage. Someone will come back later today and tomorrow to pack most of it up. The koi, though, are dying one by one, in water polluted with tea and garbage. They will die, and people will put new ones in their place.

Cheerful Aama and I have finished our photo session at the small shrine. I hold out my elbow, and she grasps it. We walk back out from under the tent and across the wide walkway separating the water gardens. Now, we are headed towards the steep staircase that leads to the Hindu temple and Yanglesho, the cave where Padmasambhava purportedly emerged after becoming enlightened.

Catching my breath as I realize what's to come, I check myself. It is not my place to tell her not to climb this staircase. There's no place to stop if she gets tired. She knows this; she lives here. It's not the first time she's climbed up, and it won't be the last. I've seen other elderly people do it.

We are gently passed as we climb the structure. No one rushes us. A few give me warm smiles as they turn to watch the Westerner help the old one.

When we reach the top, Cheerful Aama sighs, leans against the wall, and rests for a moment, spent. We laugh together, and she nods, taps me on the arm. Good job, she says. We made it.

She made it. I was just along for the ride.

I stay with her as she moves from shrine to shrine, touching fingers to forehead and heart. At one point she asks me to place some flowers up a few steps at the tiny gate to a tiny shrine. As I'm coming back down the steps, she holds out her hand as if to help me. I stop and give her a horrified look. "Nnnnnooooo," I say, and she laughs. A few others who are watching us laugh with her.

We are done up here. Now down another series of short flights of stairs. This place is a maze of stairs, walkways, shrines, and temples, Hindu and Buddhist, old and older. Step by step, with me now one stair below Cheerful Aama, we head down to the landing area in front of the staircase leading up to the Buddhist shrine room. This staircase is heart-stoppingly steep, even for me.

Cheerful Aama pauses, looks up. I sputter, "You are *not* going up there, Aama! There is *no way* you are going up there." A young monk standing nearby overhears, and tells Cheerful Aama, in Nepali, that the shrine room is closed. As she pleads her case to the monk, I take the flowers from her hand and ask the monk to please place them in the temple. The monk agrees, Cheerful Aama relents, and we continue walking across the front of the monastery.

Next, she wants to climb the stairs off to the side of the monastery to circumambulate the small Buddhist shrine up there. So up we go, one step at a time again. We circle the shrine seven times, a man in tan slacks and a white shirt passing us doing his circuits, his prayer wheel spinning. Cheerful Aama places her flowers, and we both pay our respects.

Back down now, I pick up her cane at the bottom. "Are we done now?" I ask. The words are English, but the tone is universal. She nods and laughs.

Cane in one hand, she takes my arm, and we walk all the way down the back road and down the hill, where she collapses onto her straight-backed wooden chair next to the couch in the seating area. I collapse on the couch beside her. We are laughing. I download my photos to my phone and scroll through them with her. Maya brings us tea and biscuits, and Cheerful Aama tells her about our morning. I promise to rub her feet, and I will, without complaint, later this morning.

Pushpa comes down to visit. Dwarf Dhai collects my bag of bananas and nuts to share, and Black Aama wants me to come sit with her and show her the photos as well.

Life is good.

33.

Having a Chat

BLACK AAMA IS SUPPOSED to have cream applied to the eczema on the back of her neck every night. Beena was going to do it instead of me, but she isn't here every evening. I have my glove on my right hand as I knock on the open door. All three Aamas are on their beds, Grumpy Aama sitting cross-legged on hers. Black Aama ushers me in, pats her bed next to her. I tell her I need to put her cream on. The three chat as Black Aama pulls the box with the cream in it from under clothes and bags. I ask her how her neck is. She gestures that it itches.

Their room has no carpet, only a fake wood floor. It's very sparse compared to the other rooms, and there is no separate bathroom with a sink and toilet as there are in the other rooms. Mine also has no bathroom.

None of these women own much. There are no shelves, no cabinets. Just the three beds—the wooden platforms that we all use—and some things piled on windowsills and in bags on the floor.

Before I can put the cream on, though, we are to have a chat. Black Aama points up to the ceiling, and in her gentle, soft-spoken way, she mimics me walking. "Boom, boom, boom," she says. I laugh, and Grumpy Aama laughs with me. Folded Aama smiles. Black Aama chatters on, points to the cracked outer mortar on the wall and to a place where a piece has fallen off. Now I am doubled over. I yell that my walking is *not* that noisy. We are all chattering now. I say that at 5:00 a.m., when I come down the stairs, I am quiet. That is not the problem, says Black Aama. I am loud the rest of the day.

I remind them that I can hear everything, too. I point to Black Aama and Grumpy Aama and make loud snoring noises. This delights Folded Aama and

Grumpy Aama, and Black Aama denies that she snores. She points to Folded Aama. I don't let her get away with it. I point to her bed and to Grumpy Aama's bed, point to my ear then up to the ceiling: No, no, no. I hear it from *this* side of the room, I say.

Black Aama insists that she doesn't snore, making soft mewing noises as she pretends to sleep. Grumpy Aama laughs and disagrees. Folded Aama laughs from where she hugs her knees on her bed. We are having a grand time.

Finally, I agree to walk like a "musee," even though we don't have mice here. I stand and mime an exaggerated bent-knee, vaudeville-style tip-toe across the room and back. They all laugh some more.

Now it's time for them to get to know me. After being here almost two weeks, we are just now getting the chance to sit together. Black Aama is the designated questioner, but Grumpy Aama joins in as well. I am questioned in broken Nepali and Newari and English, and my answers are as choppy as their questions.

Do I have a home in America? I tell her no, that I live in rooms, like this. It's the best way to describe an apartment right now.

Husband? Yes.

Children? No.

Oh, oh, sad. Black Aama clucks her tongue. Grumpy Aama shakes her head, also sad.

Really, no children? No, no children. A dog.

They laugh. I tell them her name is Daisy. Nepalis love that name.

How long am I in Nepal? Three months.

Do I like Pharping? Yes, very much. Very, very much.

Do I like it here in the elder care home? Yes. Very, very, very much.

Will I miss them when I'm gone? Yes. Very, very, very much.

Will I come back? Yes, next year.

About that, I've already made up my mind.

Satisfied with my answers, Black Aama hands me the ointment tube, and I puncture the seal with the pointy end of the cap. The medicine has not been used, even though Beena was under instructions to apply it nightly. Grumpy

Aama and Black Aama chat as Black Aama loosens her top, pulling it down in back. She reaches back to hold her hair out of the way.

I dab cream on the affected area, then begin rubbing, ensuring that it is well absorbed into the skin. Black Aama shifts, holds her hair from her left side with her right hand and points with her left hand: Itch! I scratch just below her neck, on the back of her left shoulder. The itch moves. She struggles to rearrange hands and hair and points again. I reach my hand down her shirt and keep scratching. We all laugh as the itch moves and fades. I go back to rubbing in the cream.

When I'm done, Black Aama wants to see my gloved hand. She holds it in both of hers, my palm up. She blows on my fingers as if to cool them from all the friction from rubbing. I can't help but laugh. She blows a few times more before I pull the glove off, looping the thumb of my left hand under the wrist and pulling up so that the glove turns inside out.

I check if she's good. She nods, saying, *"Thik cha."* She's good.

It is time to say good night, so I stand up and bow, and we all say, "Namaste."

I turn to the door, reach backward with each foot to slide into my shoes.

Black Aama says, "Okay!"

I say, "Okay!"

She says, "Good night!"

I say, "Good night!"

We all giggle.

By sheer force of will, I walk lightly back to my room, and again during the night as I creep down to the bathroom three or four times. I never once pound the floor again.

Somehow, the Amaas never snore again.

They do, however, have a heated exchange a day or so later at—yes, I can't believe it as I check my phone—2:45 a.m. I growl out loud, but not *too* loudly, that they can't expect me to walk quietly all the time if they're going to argue at 2:45 in the morning.

Suddenly, quiet.

34.

The Money

SHAHA AND HIS BUSINESS partner have made a seat for me on a stack of boxes of paper. The stationery store is messy, cluttered, overwhelmed, and layered with dust and grime. As Shaha and I talk about how I can help him get a grant for a new roof, and perhaps even a new dorm building, he says that, above all else, the wash facility must be replaced soon. He says it was damaged in the earthquakes and could collapse any day. He has the estimate, the plans, everything.

He opens one drawer and pulls out two pieces of paper, stapled in the top left corner. The first page is the detailed estimate, the second page is the technical drawing. I glance at the total in Nepali rupees. My heart stops for a long moment. I grab my phone and convert the estimate into American dollars. I stare at the amount.

Shaha is talking, and I'm not hearing him. I'm hearing another voice: *The money was never yours.*

Before I left the US, friends, coworkers, and family members all donated money to help support me with the expenses of this trip. They understood that I would be without an income for three months, and also understood the financial cost of such a journey.

The estimate for the new wash facility is within four US dollars of those donations.

Shaha says that he knows nothing about fundraising or grants. He is uncomfortable asking for money.

I hear the voice again: *The money was never yours.*

Over the coming days, the voice will nag at me, keep me awake at night, and follow me through the dark hills on my early-morning walks. I cannot escape it.

I call my husband around 4:30 a.m., Nepal time, on a Wednesday. Not that it matters, but I recall it was Wednesday because I felt time slipping away from me in Pharping.

As I explain to him that I'm considering donating all the money I collected to the elder care home for their wash facility, and as I have a brief nervous breakdown about being financially destitute by the time I'm done with this trip, he waits to make sure I've taken a breath.

He then asks, "Do you want my opinion, or do you just need to vent?"

I sigh. "I want your opinion."

"Okay. For starters, you know as well as I do that there are cost overruns on every construction job. So, you are donating just the cost of this quote, not the cost of the construction project as a whole."

As we continue to talk about this crazy idea I have, my blood pressure drops back to normal. There is a Western Union office here in town at the same shop where I buy my mobile data, and I'm pretty sure I know where the one is in Thamel, near Dil's shop. I can get the money here or there. Or somewhere. So I don't have to make a decision right now. Right now, it's time for my walk. Time to hike up and around the hills, trying to memorize as much as I can before my time here runs out.

I put my phone away and head out into the familiar, pre-dawn darkness.

35.

Long-Lasting

My walk this morning fed my soul, as usual. Out through the valley, up and around and down hills, winding past ancient homes scattered along the road, and past other gatherings of houses. I walked as far as I'll ever walk in the mornings. There's a point where the hair on the back of my neck stands on end, a point where my gut tells me to turn around.

There is no walking a bit further, no checking out what's up ahead a few feet. I've tried to just explore some more, but my brain, my mind, my body—some force somewhere in my DNA—stops me. I walk no more than sixty-five minutes out, turn around every time at the same small woodpile by the side of the road, and come back.

This is home. The reddish-brown ribbons of dirt stairs, cut into the green of the terraced land and rolling hills, stairs created perhaps hundreds of years ago, by hand, by the people who lived and died in this valley. The cows low as dawn approaches. Roosters crow their dominance over their territory. Entire flocks of birds burst into spontaneous, joyous song. People in simple homes wake up and begin to stir, their lodgings filled with life, not with the excesses of the West.

Every moment, it seems, brings a new memory to cherish. Yesterday, as I headed back from the market with a bag of fresh apples, I stopped to buy a roll of CocoCrunchies at the little sundry shop up the road. When I turned to leave, I saw a duck coming up from the nearby school yard. Her right leg was stuck in the handle of a plastic bag. She waddled and complained, dragging the bag. Waddle, quack, drag, waddle quack quack, drag drag.

I tried to sneak up from behind the duck, half-heartedly reaching down towards her, but the woman at the shop called out, "Ai! Ai!" I stopped and stood back. The duck picked her way around rocks, dirt, and trash, complaining all the while, and headed to the shop. She hopped up the low step and headed straight into the back. To mamma. The woman behind the counter bent down, disappeared from sight.

Seconds later the duck emerged from behind the counter, stood in the doorway, fluffed herself up, and shook herself off. Smiling, the woman held the bag up for me to see.

☙

My departure date from this elder care home has been changed to November 8; I told Aabi, CGN's president and founder, that I want to stay one additional week. He agreed. Akkal will pick me up at no extra charge.

Walking off these grounds will be one of the hardest things I'll do during my time in Nepal. I know it already. Even Pushpa told me this morning, after I'd teased Baa as we all sunned ourselves on the hill, "Alena, you leave here... long-lasting."

36.

Ekadasi

AFTER A QUIET NIGHT, the noise is building in the streets below. Vendors who camped out the night before have started to set up; the shops below the elder care home are open and serving tea and fried sweets. Other sellers and beggars staked out their spots on the temple grounds last night, I imagine.

I stretch my body in bed, trying to extend my hands as far as possible in one direction, pulling my legs in the other direction. It is pitch dark out.

A real photographer would be out there.

I throw back layers of blankets, nearly leap from the bed and grab some clothes.

Today is Ekadasi. One legend says that this is the day Lord Vishnu wakes from his slumber to preside over religious celebrations across the universe; another legend says that this is the day Varuna, the god of water, rises from the bodies of water to live among the people. He chooses to do this since, at this time of year, the water is becoming too cold live in, even for a god.

Many Hindus fast on this day and worship at one of the four Narayana temples across Kathmandu. Others do not eat salt or meat products on this day. Their diet will consist mostly of peanuts and fruit.

And here, at the elder care home, they will also eat Dwarf Dhai's flatbread.

At 5:30 a.m., as I come around the upper level of the courtyard, smoke billows already from the roof of the kitchen. Dwarf Dhai sees me through the window, asks where I'm going. I hold up my camera, and he salutes me. I salute back.

Down the dark front stairs inch by dark inch, and the scene before me is surreal. I begin to snap pictures, glance at my camera from time to time, adjust settings. It doesn't matter what I'm shooting, I just start capturing it all, even though there's too much in every frame.

Vendors are set up on the side of the road, their peanuts, fruits, and vegetables laid out on tarps. Pots are cooking over fires; small tables stand here and there. The shop below the elder care home has its fill of customers buying small plastic cups of hot milk tea and fried sweets fresh from the oil. The Nepal police force are warming themselves with both. I try to capture it all, my camera clicking away.

A cousin of mine once told me that this is how we photographers process the world around us: We must view it through a lens, review it, study it, stay separate from it. Perhaps this is why I'm driven to document everything, or perhaps it's because I fear I'll lose precious moments from this trip as time takes me further from these days, weeks, and months—and so I need to capture every moment possible.

There is also the reality that Nepal is changing quickly. The old ways will be gone one day, lost to a history few may care about. How many more years will vendors be able to set up on the side of the road like this? Which practices will die, and which will survive, as Nepal evolves? What will tourists and visitors witness in five years, ten years?

I make my way up the street, and the sky starts to lighten a bit. Past the temple, up the hill, searching for my next photo, and the next, and the next. Soon it is daylight.

I move back to the water gardens and see a young girl in a red hoodie, lingering. She wanders, hands deep in her pockets, hood up. I train my camera on her and wait. I wait for that moment when she turns to look off in another direction.

A policeman walks over, steps up onto the ledge behind her and turns his back to me. Then his colleague joins him and they both turn towards me, point somewhere in the distance. I capture it all. It's not that they want their photo taken; it's that they want me to know they're there, watching.

I don't know why they're photobombing me, and I don't care. I decide to beat them at their own game. Most of the police are standing on the ledge on the other side of the koi pond, so I walk to the street and stand right in front of them. I start to snap away at passersby, taking photos I don't care about. When they least suspect it, I turn my camera on the police and capture the moment as they tell me not to take their photo. I remove my camera, smile an apology, and try not to laugh.

Although still unsubstantiated, rumors abound that both the UK and the US provided extensive paramilitary training to the police force during the civil war, to give the authorities a fighting chance against the Maoists. The female officer on the ledge fascinates me. She has earned her way onto the force, going through the same, rigorous training as her male colleagues. Nothing was watered down for her. No doubt she could take down any of the men around her.

Before they realize what's happening, I take two steps forward, touch my forehead and reach for her left boot. She exclaims and pulls her foot back, laughing in surprise and discomfort.

I look up at her and say, "Female police…respect. Namaste," and do a one-handed bow, my other hand still gripping my camera.

It is a sincere gesture on my part, and they can feel it.

Now it's time to head back to the other side of the koi pond and patiently wait for photo opportunities to arise. Within moments an officer comes to stand near me, off to the side. His smile is warm as he greets me with, "Good morning! Namaste." I smile and reply, "Namaste," in return. Hands in his pockets, he watches the people moving around, and stands guard for me.

The photobombing has stopped.

There is much, still, to sort through all around me, and I know the area will be packed with people soon. I keep aiming my camera, looking for *the* photo. People are standing in line around the edges of the walkway over the water and up the stairs, waiting to get up to the temple. The steps coming down the other side are crowded with beggars and vendors.

As I expected, within a few minutes the crowd has ballooned. I feel like a real photographer. I feel like my father's daughter. During the Korean War, he served as an Army photographer, and wrote home saying he never felt more comfortable than when he held a camera in his hands. And *I* am feeling comfortable with this camera in *my* hands, as I snap, review, adjust settings, zoom in, zoom out, completely enjoying the morning.

37.

Tea for Folded Aama

TODAY I AM DETERMINED to crack a coconut myself. I am working off frustration as I lean over the compost pile, stripping the fibers from the outside of the shell. I want to pound something, and cracking a coconut is just what I need.

I arrived back from my walk as the yoga class was just ending. As usual, Shaha's group of friends made tea. I emerged from the kitchen, where one of the young women had handed me a steaming cup, and joined them in the seating area. That's when I glanced over to see that Folded Aama, sitting just a few feet away on the cold, hard cement, had none.

When I asked if there was tea for her, they looked at each other and said there wasn't any left. I said if I'd known there wouldn't be any tea left, I would have given Aama my tea. I told them that where I come from, the elders are served *first*, and—more importantly—not left out. My mother would have never let me hear the end of it if I'd not served an elder first.

No one thought about her. Not even Shaha with his big statements about lifting up others and serving the community. Even after my unhesitant verbal reprimand, not one of them went back to the kitchen to prepare a cup for her. When they were gone, I added some hot water to the pot, boiled it a bit, and served her some tea. It was weak, but it was better than nothing. And she received it with gratitude. It was a hot beverage for a crippled woman sitting on the cold ground.

There are no special considerations for someone like Folded Aama. She can't get into a chair, and no one will give her a thick cushion to sit on so she's not perched on the cold cement all the time. No one thinks of sharing with her. As much as I love this country, there is a general lack of compassion for others in this culture, and that breaks my heart.

As I was serving the weak tea to Folded Aama, Dwarf Dhai, standing nearby, gestured to me to stop. I snapped. I yelled, "*Stop it! Apparently, I am not like you people!*" He threw up his hands at me and continued to berate me. I continued to yell back. Disgusted, he stormed off to the kitchen.

I have no idea why he is always enraged whenever I help Folded Aama, and the truth is that I don't care why he reacts this way. I don't care what he thinks. I only know that his attitude doesn't mesh with my values as a human being.

So, I am not pleased when Dwarf Dhai appears beside me at the counter in the kitchen and insists on helping me with the coconut. I want to work out my frustrations and some of those revolve around him. Still, I give in when I realize I am not quite doing it properly.

He grabs a heavy, pointed knife and, talking the whole time, pokes at the three indentations at the top of the coconut, trying to pick out the soft shell. He doesn't have any luck. While he goes in search of a better tool, I try my hand at it but give up because I like my hands and fingers intact.

After scouring the drawers in the desk outside the pantry, he finds an old screw. First he scrubs it, pours some boiled water on the tip, rinses it again. Then he starts prying.

Little by little, the spots give way. I grab a cup, and he pours the coconut water into it for me, smiles when I down it in one gulp, not even bothering to strain out the bits and pieces of shell.

Next, he takes the long, rolling-pin-style stone, which is the equivalent of our pestle in the West but used also as a rolling pin, and just starts smashing the coconut on the cement floor. There's a targeted, gentler approach that I saw on a video, and I convince him to let me try tapping firmly on its circumference. We squat down together in the kitchen, while I chase the coconut around the dirty gray cement floor, both of us laughing.

We give up at the same time. I hand him the pestle as he is reaching for the coconut, and we resort to the tried-and-true method: Pound it until it cracks. Then keep pounding.

I grab the heavy knife he was using, and together we crack and peel and pound and scrape, dropping larger and smaller pieces of flesh onto my metal plate. He waves off my offers to try some. He doesn't like coconut. He just likes cracking them.

When we're finished, I take the plate and offer some to the elders as I walk around the grounds. It turns out most of them don't like coconut either, but Grumpy Aama takes some. Then some more. Then a few pieces more. Later this afternoon, she will retrieve them from the folds in her skirts, one by one by one, handing them back to me, sheepish.

When I return to the kitchen, Dwarf Dhai has washed the screw we used on the end of the coconut and gets my attention. He shows me where he's going to store it in the top left drawer of the desk. We have something we do together, and he likes that.

The next day, however, he's on a rampage again, and although I think I know why, I still ask Reeta and Pushpa what he is upset about this time. They tell me it's because I took Folded Aama's wash up the hill and hung it out on the cement wall for her this morning. Really? This time I can't get upset about it. This time I just think it's getting ridiculous.

Striking a defiant pose with my right hand on my hip, I yell back at him, gesturing with my left hand. He yells again, dismisses me, and turns to walk away. I mimic him as he walks, complete with sticking my tush out. When he turns around, I straighten up and innocently point to something inside the pantry. He shakes his head, dismisses me again, and I turn to see Pushpa and Reeta wiping tears of laughter from the corners of their eyes.

Later, when he is making flatbread, Reeta and Pushpa send me into the kitchen. I'm hesitant but finally go in, muttering to myself. I hear them chuckling as I enter and greet him—and am promptly sent out of the kitchen.

They send me back in. I sigh, but like any dutiful child, I obey, going back into the battle zone. This time he figures the only way to get rid of me is to give me a fresh, hot-off-the-griddle flatbread. Today he's grilling them in curried sunflower oil, and the flavor is out of this world. I head back in to tell him how good it is, and he tries to get rid of me by giving me a second one. I see Grumpy Aama sitting in her chair, so I ask her if she wants half. Yes, she does. I offer the other half to Black Aama, who doesn't want it, so I head straight to Folded Aama, who is grateful for it. When Grumpy Aama sees that, she scowls at me and then scowls down at her flatbread, but eats it anyway.

అ

After dinner, we are all back to normal. Now Dwarf Dhai is sitting in his usual spot in front of the television, watching the children's singing contest show. Beena sits in the chair against the half-wall, watching every moment. I brush my teeth behind them. I am cheering for one particular young girl, but one of the young boys really comes out swinging tonight. A commercial comes on for special shampoo. A woman is flinging her long, dark, shiny hair around in ultra-slow motion. She runs her fingers through it, looks at the camera. Her mouth is just a bit open in a toothy, pleasant, sexy smile. I tap Dwarf Dhai on the shoulder with my left hand, still brushing my teeth with my right hand. I gesture to him, to the television, to his nearly bald head, mime washing his hair, point to the television again. He gives me that look, shakes his head, smacks my leg. He resumes watching television. Beena chuckles. I keep brushing.

Nepalis are free with their emotions, and quick to forget their anger with each other. I am becoming more Nepali every day.

అ

The next morning, I have lost track of time while out walking. These hilly walks and long sessions of stretching in my room have loosened and strengthened my hip, and it's wonderful to move without discomfort. Shaha's yoga class is done already, and tea has been served.

I reach over the half-wall of the seating area and put my things on the table. One woman offers me tea. I say yes. Now that I'm no longer moving briskly up and down hills, the cold is registering with me. I check with Folded Aama; she has been served tea, to my relief. She thanks me, gripping her cup, holding it for me to see.

Pushpa pats the couch next to her, telling me to sit, and Shaha tells me it's 6:40 a.m. He asks how long I've been walking. I've been out two hours, which surprises them. I grip my own steaming metal cup between both hands and sip, enjoying these early moments of my day, and these last moments with my family.

࿋

Dinner is finished, and the Aamas are tucked into their room below mine. Black Aama is on a roll, throwing out comments. Grumpy Aama is on her own bed, wheezing with laughter, probably rolling around with joy. Folded Aama laughs and adds her own comments. Black Aama laughs at her own jokes, and queries Folded Aama, who responds. Black Aama throws a comeback and has the room in stiches again.

She does a high-pitched impersonation and gets chuckles, gets serious for a moment.

I stare up at my ceiling. Tomorrow I will pack up my things, and Akkal will take me back to CGN's building, to their not-yet-completed hostel. I feel as if I will be leaving a part of me behind, as if this elder care home and I belong together always.

Tomorrow morning, a part of me will be torn away from me when I leave.

38.

Time to Go

SHAHA TAKES THE NEWS very well. We sit in his shop, and I explain about the donations. "This is not my money," I tell him. "This was money donated by other people to me." He is nodding in understanding.

"Then we start on the new building very soon," he says, smiling at the thought of building his new wash facility. Since it's available at any Western Union in Nepal, I can pick it up in Thamel and bring it to him. This is the right thing to do. The money was never mine.

These are my last few minutes in Pharping for a little while, so I choose to take a leisurely walk back to the elder care home, savoring every moment. On the back road that runs behind the elder care home, young monks are kicking their ratty, ancient soccer ball around. One has stripped off his robe and is wearing black sports shorts and a yellow shirt. A few stand by the fence. Several pause to greet me.

We are all teary-eyed. Reeta hugs me. Pushpa and I bow, touch cheeks. She is quiet. Cheerful Aama stands, starts crying. I hug her and get weepy, tell her not to cry. Slender Dhai rushes out to give me a blessing, pressing a large red dot of tika paint onto my forehead. As he prays for my safe travels, he reaches back into the small paper pouch he received at Dakshinkali this morning, pulls out marigold petals, then tucks them into my hair on top of my head for good luck. I am fighting back tears of gratitude as we say our goodbyes.

Goiter Aama and Black Aama are crying. Goiter Aama can't even speak she's so emotional. Black Aama cries, "Mero babu, mero babu." My baby, my baby. We hug. She places her hand on my head, gives me a blessing.

As Akkal and I head up the hill to CGN's SUV, Baa calls to me from the chair with the makeshift cushions outside the yoga building. I go to see him. He bows, and I touch my forehead to his hands. He is choked up, keeps nodding. Akkal and I continue up the hill, with me turning and waving as I walk. Pushpa, Reeta, and the others wave back. I stop to say goodbye to Folded Aama, can't understand what she says in return, but nod and say, "Namaste," over and over. Pushpa, Reeta, Cheerful Aama, and I keep waving until I am in the SUV. It hurts to leave, but it's time to go.

V. No Peace for Nepal

"For you were called to freedom, brothers.
Only do not use your freedom
as an opportunity for the flesh,
but through love serve one another.
For the whole law is fulfilled in one word:
'You shall love your neighbor as yourself.'"

~ Galatians 5:13-14

"Spend in charity and do not keep count
for then Allah will also keep count
in giving you what you need."

~ Sahih al-Bukhari

"Every act of kindness is charity."

~ Prophet Muhammed

39.

The Stranger

As Akkal winds through the streets of Naya Bazar, I can't help but smile. I know these stores, I know every twist and turn on these roads. We arrive at CGN's offices, and something feels different. I feel different.

When other volunteers come to CGN's building to hang out and get on Wi-Fi, they go upstairs to sit on the uncomfortable couches outside the offices, or sit in the stairwell. During my first month here, when I needed to escape the so-called elder care home, I would sometimes come to CGN's offices. Being too old to fit in with the young volunteers, and not knowing the employees at all, I'd refill my water bottle at the cooler in the corner of the kitchen, and visit a little with the two women who cook for us. Then I'd wander off through the neighborhood.

Now these two women, Rekha and Muna, greet me as an old friend as I enter the front door. Squealing with joy, Muna rushes back into the kitchen to be sure they have tea for me, and Rekha hooks her arm through mine, walking with me as a sister.

Muna is Akkal's wife, and their eleven-year-old daughter is Monika. The three of them are moving into one of the downstairs rooms, where they'll live. Muna will clean and cook for the volunteers who'll stay here, and Akkal will continue to be CGN's driver and help with cleaning and maintenance.

This first floor is busy today. Muna's sister and brother-in-law are helping with the move-in, and CGN employees are visiting the kitchen to look for tea since it hasn't been taken upstairs to the offices yet. Adding to this activity are the workers everywhere, who are busy completing construction both inside and outside. Saws, hammers, and drills create a cacophony of sound, and everyone is talking and yelling. It makes me smile.

Rekha serves me tea, and we talk about her kids and her husband's new job at the airport. As she becomes preoccupied with other duties, I venture upstairs to the third floor, where the offices are, having a good look around at everything that's changed since I was last here three weeks ago.

Geetu, the volunteer coordinator, looks at photos with me, listens to my stories from the first elder care home and from Pharping. She says Akkal told them all the women cried when I left Pharping, and I say yes, I cried a little, too.

Sitting at a spare desk in the office, I begin to write up my report on the loaner laptop that Geetu finds for me. Manesh arrives and also says he heard that the women cried when I left Pharping. This seems to please everyone.

It is a calm, comfortable afternoon for me. Hot air blows in through the open windows. Outside, off in the distance, the black kites call to each other as they search for food along the polluted river. These large black-and-brown striped birds will become my favorite photography subject in the next few weeks. Now, though, I sip my tea and type away, as employees chat and laugh all around me.

Who is this person inhabiting my body? Who is this confident woman who came back from Pharping? Just three weeks ago, I was uncomfortable here. I didn't know anyone well. I didn't know the language well. I didn't feel I fit in. Now here I am, in the offices, acting as if I belong here.

So what changed in three weeks? Somehow, some way, there is a new entity inhabiting my skin and bones. A stranger is moving my body, creating this smile that isn't fading, driving a new confidence. I am not me. Or I am finally me. I can't tell.

☙

Akkal is doting on me, making sure everything is perfect. Am I okay with the sheets for curtains in my room? Do I have what I need? I ask him about the hot water system on the second floor, and we figure it out together. In Nepal, they use on-demand systems for hot water, even at the sinks. It's an efficient and inexpensive way to manage water. When I discover that the Wi-Fi has been turned off, Akkal says that tomorrow he will ask Aabi to leave it on overnight. Anything I need, anything I want, Akkal wants to accommodate me.

It's not nearly dinnertime yet, but I wander to the kitchen anyway. Everything smells so good. Akkal asks if I am hungry, and I reply, "Aliali," meaning, "Just a little." Monika, Muna, and Muna's sister are all pleased with my casual Nepali. Akkal says it's good that I am hungry, tells me he will call me when dinner's ready. I drift back to my room, change into my long sleeved, gray t-shirt, black leggings, and gray zip hoodie—my sleepwear these days. Voices drift up from the stairwell. Water runs. Pots are moved, stirred. The pressure cooker pops and hisses. A plane flies overhead. I soak it all in.

I haven't lain down on my bed. If I do, my eyes will close and won't reopen all night. I rested my head on the laptop earlier, when I was alone in the office, and dozed off.

At long last, dinner is ready. Muna places a blue plastic outdoor chair in front of the cardboard-covered crate under the kitchen window. Muna's sister puts a dish piled with tarkari and bhat in front of me, and then Muna brings me a small bowl of dal. I hear the women say, in Nepali, that I should have a proper table. I don't want to eavesdrop, but I don't want them to worry. I say, "Thik chha," and they are delighted that I'm fine. In fact, I'd much rather be sitting on the floor, eating the old-fashioned way.

They hover, holding their breath in anticipation. After my first bites, I announce, "Mitho sah." Faces light up, sighs of relief. I continue to eat as we chat. Do I need more rice? No, no. It is a little too much rice for me as it is. Don't finish if it is too much, they say. I tell them they can make the food spicy for me. I tell them I had achaar at lunch, which is an extremely hot and peppery, pickled vegetable dish. Now they're surprised and happy. Now they know they can cook normally for me. More dal? No, thank you, this is enough. More bhat? No, Monika says, it is too much for her already. I eat while they watch.

Finally, on a full stomach, and having been refused my attempt to take my dishes to the sink, I say good night to everyone and make my way back upstairs.

As I brush my teeth, I wander down the hall, flicking off lights in rooms. Earlier today Manesh told me they'd hired someone before Dashain in September, which is almost two months ago at this point, to come in and put up drapes. The drapery rod hooks were hung, and they haven't seen the guy since. Manesh laughed as he told me this story. Same with the windows, he said. The last two were only just recently installed. Welcome to Nepal. I now understand why nothing gets done around here: It's because nothing gets done.

Teeth brushed, I stand at my window, take a long look outside at the peaceful, quiet neighborhood. My month of fresh hell at the first elder care home is far behind me, far away from my reality. Staring out the window at the tall homes down the street, I listen to the sounds of my new world, absorbing life on this side of the city.

I think back through my journey here. One week in orientation, cut short because of my delay in arriving, followed by the four weeks of fresh hell. After that, ten days at Dil and Puja's hotel, and then three weeks in Pharping. Time has flown by, and I have just three weeks remaining now.

Pharping felt wonderful and comfortable to me, and if it were possible, I'd have stayed there for two more weeks. The dust was too much, though. My lungs couldn't handle more of it. As painful as it was to leave, I needed to go.

Aabi will be back in the office tomorrow, and we'll talk about the work he has for me. I suspect it has to do with designing new materials for their elder care program, but I'm sure there'll be more. When I met with him during my orientation, he alluded to needing my business skills.

Collapsing into bed, drawing the comforter over me, I am giddy. I am also naïve. No one has told me about the expected violence that will accompany the upcoming elections. They wouldn't tell a foreigner like me about their fears. It isn't the Nepali way to burden a guest with their private nightmares.

So, for now, I am relaxed, happy, and at peace.

Punjabi music plays somewhere outside. Children run around, playing in the dark. A motorcycle passes. Mothers call their children in. I fall asleep to the sounds of barking dogs and music.

~

November mornings are cold in Nepal. We haven't yet hit the coldest time of the year, mid-December to mid-January, but when the hot water system stops working and you're stuck rinsing in cold water with a head full of soapy hair— well, it might as well be the coldest time of year.

Shivering in my skimpy towel, I try to determine what happened. The power is on downstairs, from what I can tell as I stand at the top of the steps. The power is on in my room as well. No power in the bathroom, hallway, or other rooms up here, though.

Teeth chattering from the cold, I stand on the stairs and say a meek, "Namaste." Akkal responds right away from the first floor. How did I sleep? Very well, but I have no power. Where? Most of the upstairs. He comes up, looks around, grabs a piece of cardboard, then reaches up and flicks a breaker in the small box high on the wall next to my door. I have power again. Joy!

No joy. He is downstairs as I fiddle with the hot water system. It still isn't working. I have no hot water.

Forget it. After rinsing my hair in cold water, and dressing as fast as I can while shivering uncontrollably, I stop in the kitchen for a quick tea with my new family before my morning of errands. Akkal promises to look into the situation with the hot water.

~

At the end of the street, men play an early morning game of badminton in a dirt lot scattered with garbage. They pause to say good morning and wave. I wave back and greet them in return. Across the road and a soft left here.

Wending my way through Naya Bazar, I pass the shop where Rekha helped me to buy a kurta. And here's the shop where I saw a woman weaving silk scarves for twelve hundred rupees each—a bargain price. I pass the spot where I saw the large brown bull who flinched when I went to rub his head, but who fell in love with me after discovering true kindness. And here is the restaurant where I stopped for an ice-cold orange Fanta on a hot day, and where I left my blue bandanna behind by accident. I feel like I've lived here all my life.

When I arrive at the busy street which runs along the edge of Naya Bazar, I find a father trying to cross the road with his very young son. A younger man has arrived at about the same time I have, and, without uttering a word, the younger man and I step out ahead of the father together, negotiating the speed of cars and motorcycles, estimating intervals. We each hold out our right hands at motorcyclists as we step into the path of the little white car we both know will just miss us. A few steps farther, we order a bus on our left to slow down, and all four of us make it safely across.

Dil is pleased to see me. He orders tea from across the street, and we spend time catching up. I tell him I am going to donate money to have the wash station rebuilt at the elder care home in Pharping, and that I've sent money to myself here in Nepal. It's available at any Western Union office. Dil and Puja run a small NGO of their own, and use the donations to take food and necessities to the poorest regions in Nepal. In the spring, they take mosquito nets, and in the winter, they take blankets and warm clothes. Dil and I decide to transfer my money to his NGO's account for temporary keeping. Then when I'm ready to go back to Pharping, Dil will give me a check made out to Shaha's NGO. This gives Dil a sense of relief because even though he knows I trust Shaha, he likes ensuring the money goes directly into an NGO instead of someone's hands.

Walking back to the hostel, I'm smiling. This is the right thing to do. All the donations people gave me for my trip were really for this single purpose. The proof is in the numbers: The total donations came to within just four US dollars of the construction estimate, and the Western Union fee itself was four US dollars. You just can't argue with those numbers.

Young volunteers are in CGN's building today. They sit on the uncomfortable couches in the front room outside the office upstairs, busying themselves on social media. I take my seat in the comfy chair at the spare desk in the office, typing away on my loaner laptop, sipping tea.

Aabi comes up and greets the volunteers, then comes into the office and sees me. "Ah," he says, "How are you?" I smile. I tell him I'm well, that Pharping was wonderful. "And you're staying here, now, I hear?" Yes, I say, and use an American phrase: "It's good to work out the bugs before—"

He panics. "We have bugs?!"

I laugh, no Aabi, not actual bugs. *Issues*. It is an American phrase. I tell him about the hot water system on the second floor. He says he thinks it draws too much power for their circuits. He promises to look into it, but I wish he'd just let Akkal handle it.

"You are writing your report?" Aabi asks, and I tell him, yes, it's almost done. I tell him I will give him a copy of the guidelines I've created on how to determine whether an elder care home is a good partner or not, and he smiles at the news. "Good," he says. "This is good."

Next up, he wants me to put together a presentation about doing elder care at the home in Pharping. "It tells volunteers about this assignment," he says.

Last, he mentions that he will need rules for the hostel. "Other hostels, I see they have rules for those who stay there. Can you do this also?" Of course, I tell him. I'll do some research and put something together for him.

Aabi smiles. "You are easy," he says, and I take that as a compliment.

40.

Death by Meditation

CAMERA IN HAND, BAG slung across my back, I stand at a corner as traffic flies past. So many choices. So many different directions to explore. I want to capture as much as I can in these last days.

Life here in Nepal changes quickly. Just ten or fifteen years ago, motorcycles and scooters didn't clog the roads. The vendor who pushes his bike through the streets, with a massive basket on the front end loaded with fruits or vegetables, is a fading reality. One day electric rickshaws will replace those pulled by bicycles. Today's young women eschew traditional attire in favor of fashionably torn jeans and crop tops, exposing skin in a way that, a few years ago, would have seemed improper. Westernization is creeping in from all sides.

My father was stationed in Germany when he served as an Army photographer during the Korean War. I have dozens of his photos from that time. Dozens of moments in time in Stuttgart, Strasbourg, Baden-Baden, and other cities. All snapshots of a life that vanished.

As I roam, I notice an obscure archway at a corner. Since these generally lead to some kind of religious spot, my curiosity is piqued. Beyond the archway, I find a very long set of broad stairs deep in a forest, conjuring an image of masses of people moving to and from the cement building far beyond. Or maybe it's a wall. The entire scene is quite uninviting, and part of me thinks it's that way for a reason. As I finally approach the top of the stairs, I notice a door cut in the cement wall and decide to walk through.

Inside is another building to my left, on a foundation about three feet above the area in which I'm standing. I can't make heads or tails out of what

I'm seeing. It's a cement structure with a wooden roof and fancy eaves, similar to some of the oldest construction styles here. Ahead of me, the broad cement terrace continues; to my right, a cement half-wall overlooks a forest and an overgrown garden, with a steep set of steps cut into the wall leading down into the forest. Old rugs hang over the half-wall. A younger woman comes up the steep stairs, eyes me with suspicion, and disappears into a small room I hadn't noticed back towards the outer wall. I hadn't even noticed the posters hanging on this outer wall as I walked past them. Everything here seems utterly out of place and disjointed when taken all together.

Peering over the low wall, all I see is forest. It feels as if this whole place is hiding by design, and yet the steps leading up to it suggest it's a gathering place for large crowds.

Caving in to curiosity, I turn around and go up the few short stairs and in through a doorway to this tall building with the wooden eaves. As I step back in time, I step also into the territory of a large and vicious, black guard dog.

I jump as he lunges, snarling and barking, his chain just long enough to let me walk forward and into the small square courtyard set lower than the entryway in which I'm standing.

It's a very strange scene to me. In the middle of the courtyard is a statue of Buddha on a pedestal. To the left is an open area with photos lining the back wall and a steep old wooden staircase leading up to the second floor. A donation box sits near the staircase. An old woman in ragged clothes sits on the cement stoop off the courtyard, smoking. A squat younger man in a tattered knit top and ratty old knit pants sits next to her. Above them are traditional windows with ornate wooden shutters.

While the design and feel of this place is similar to the inner courtyards at other palaces and religious residences, there is something different about this place. Here, the wood *appears* to be hundreds of years old, but it isn't cracked or weather-worn. It seems as if it's been protected—sealed or varnished somehow. It's also dead quiet in a creepy sort of way. Only the old woman and the young man are here.

My guess is photos aren't allowed, and I don't even try to test that guess. I step down into the courtyard and begin my circumambulation around the statue, finding there are two smaller busts I don't recognize. The old woman is motioning to me with gestures I can't quite understand. The young man says "Shoes," and I get it. I walk back up to the entryway, where the dog considers lunging at me but stops with one subtle movement of the old woman's hand. Now in my stockinged feet, I finish my route, look around as I walk, and feel as if I'm missing something significant. I've still seen no one else, heard no noise. No birds, nothing above, nothing outside. It seems as if this place is in a vacuum.

Smiling and nodding at the woman, I walk into the open area under the residence, next to the stairs, and look over the photos on the wall. It is a long line of portraits of various sizes, appearing to date back more than one hundred years. I look for a clue among the names and titles but can't figure it out. Are they swamis? Are these two people Jainists? They have a statue of Buddha, but that doesn't necessarily mean they're Buddhist by our Western definition. Soon, the young man approaches, smiles, and gestures that it would be okay for me to go upstairs.

I make my way up the steps. They are steeper than they appear and quite narrow; only the front halves of my feet fit on each stair. And much to my dismay, each step is slanted downward, the polished wood making my trip up a precarious one. I have no idea how I'll be able to come back down, since there is no railing to hold on to.

At the top of the staircase, I enter a residence with a traditional low ceiling and windows slanting outward. A delicate carved railing prevents people from falling into the stairwell from above.

Lining the walls here are more portraits framed by garlands. Still more paper flower garlands are draped from the ceiling and over fixtures. Just up to the right of the stairs is what appears to be a large coffin. At least, that's what it looks like. It's hard to tell since it's draped with multiple fabrics and even more paper flowers. In front of the coffin is a gold railing with a carpeted stoop in front of it—something like a kneeling altar. I wander along the wall behind the coffin, looking at the portraits.

When the young man comes up the stairs, he motions for me to come around to the front, and tells me I'm on the wrong side. Then he kneels in front of the coffin. I join him on the floor, and set my things off to the side.

The young man begins to talk. His right eye looks one way while the left eye gazes at me. He speaks in a low, gentle voice in broken English. Every ounce of his being radiates peace of mind, compassion, and love. He tells me that's his guru in the coffin, and that his guru died three years ago, here in this room. He comes here to talk to him.

I try to make out the rest of the room. An old blanket is folded over the back of a straight-backed, ancient wooden chair. Next to the chair is a small table. Also along that wall is a small chest of drawers, and a door leading somewhere. On the wooden floor is the usual, very thin layer of carpet, this one a faded red color, and on top of that, where we are in front of the altar and coffin, are area rugs. Layered on top of the area rugs are the pastel sheets on which we're now seated, the young man with his legs folded underneath him, and me sitting cross-legged.

All these photos on the walls upstairs and downstairs are their gurus, he says. He tells me he has been without a guru for these past three years, and that when a new guru is needed, a new one will arise. I ask him if he worries about what will happen if no new guru comes. He says no, he does not worry. I ask him how many others live here; he says just the old woman and himself. I ask him who will carry on this work if no guru comes; he says he doesn't know and that it's not his concern. He says they come to do meditation here with the dead guru, that he comes every day to talk to his dead guru and to listen for his answers. He tells me he can hear the guru speak to him, and that it would be good for me to meditate here, too. I smile and remain noncommittal on the subject.

The young man gave up everything he owned to come live here. He says others could not understand how he could give up all his belongings. He says he works every day to reach samadhi. This is all he lives for: to attain the ultimate union with all that is, and to transcend his body. I ask him if he is in contact with his family; he says he has no family any more. I ask if he is Hindu; he seems horrified. The answer is no. I don't know if there is any particular spiritual belief system at work here or not.

He tells me another teacher and two students reached samadhi here on these grounds. He says the teacher and the two students decided that they would meditate until they reached samadhi and that the teacher's last words were, "The next time you see us we will appear dead but we are not dead; we have reached samadhi." He is in love with this word, or perhaps just the concept.

I have at least a dozen questions flying through my head, but most seem impolite, and I can't figure out where to start with the other questions. It doesn't matter. He wants to show me where the teacher and these students achieved samadhi. We head back down the stairs, him in his bare feet navigating the steps with ease. I move with caution, coming down on an angle, my feet not fully able to land on each step. It would be easy enough to just take my socks off, but this doesn't occur to me. My brain isn't working properly, and I seem to be disconnected from my body.

The young man is heading off across the courtyard. We walk through that small wing of the building and emerge into another world. A long marble walkway rises above the forest floor, and my first thought is, *"Where the hell did this come from?"* When I was out on the terrace earlier, I walked to the half-wall above us and looked out and down, and none of this was here. Sure enough, this walkway and these low shrines are tucked into the forest, hidden. I try to pick my way carefully along the marble walkway, since it is loaded with bird feces and small chunks of dirt, but there's no hope. I cringe when I consider that these dirty socks are going back into my shoes when this is all done.

We inch around an ancient tree marked with tika paint in the middle of the walkway. Ahead of us is a small shrine made of marble, and at the end of the walkway, another shrine built of brick and mortar, painted the red and yellow of Hindu buildings. There are two small ironwork doors on the front, painted gold. A cement spire, painted red and gold, rises above this into the forest. The young man swings open the golden doors, and tells me with pride that this is where the teacher and two students attained samadhi.

I peer into the building. It can't be more than five feet in each direction inside, and probably four feet high. He encourages me to go in and meditate. I shake my head no, tell him I'm okay. He points to the three stone slabs on the cement floor. He tells me that's where the teacher and the two students were found. He reassures me that it's okay to go in. He says, "They are not buried here. They are buried below."

That doesn't help me any. He is smiling, waiting for me to enter.

Standing here, in this other-worldly place, on a marble walkway rising from the forest floor, staring into a tiny shrine where, if I'm interpreting everything correctly, three people *meditated themselves to death*, I struggle to tell him I don't want to go in.

Let's not even consider the horror-movie possibility of him shutting and locking the doors behind me, then walking calmly back down the marble walkway away from me as I scream to be let out.

A slight shudder shakes my bones. I tell him I would like to keep looking around. It's a gentler way of saying that I don't want to go in. He is so proud of this spot and so proud of his fellow practitioners—I still haven't worked out quite when this happened—and I find it kind of him to want to share these holy places with me. But me going in there? It just isn't going to happen.

We navigate the narrow ledge around this shrine, and make our way back past the marble shrine and to the tree. A small clay slab at the bottom has the imprint of feet in it; they are the feet of one of their previous gurus who prayed here at this tree.

This is a sacred spot for him. He is emotional and proud of this tree, these shrines, this history. The people who have gone before him are those on whom he's built his life, his belief system, and on whom he pins his hopes for the future of his soul.

We walk around the tree, with me admiring it as I pass by (I have to give any life credit for surviving one hundred years in this harsh climate), and head back into the courtyard.

At this point, the young man's entire personality seems to shift. He asks me if I would like to see where they have their classes ("classes"?). He tells me they have a very important guru (I thought the dead guy upstairs was his guru?) who has "one million followers" and that I "can find him on YouTube."

What the hell. I'm feeling adventurous.

With the dog ignoring me at this point, I head over to my shoes and look at the bottom of one sock, preparing to brush it off: it's spotless. Sliding it into my shoe, I look at the bottom of the other sock: also spotless. I follow the young man out of the courtyard and along the terrace towards the front of the building, then past the smaller structure attached to the side of the building. Like magic, a walkway appears between this smaller structure and the outer wall. My head is screaming, *"And where did this come from?"*

We emerge into a massive, modern field house. All along the walls are posters and banners, and I can't make out what they say. I start to walk in, but he ushers me instead into a small area draped off from the rest of the field house. We step through sheer fabric hanging from above and into a shrine room, complete with a low table and cushions on the floor. There is a large carved, wooden chair with elaborate pillows, a colorful tapestry, and a footrest with wooden shoes on it. The young man's face is glowing now. This is where he comes to meditate, he tells me. This is where he feels closest to his guru. (I won't deny how confused I am at this point.) He instructs me to sit on the floor facing the chair and footrest, and, with a flourish, he removes the tapestry from the chair.

The sight beneath causes me to jump and move off to the side. This seems to hurt his feelings. He explains that it's just a photo of his guru.

A life-sized photo of a forty-ish man is positioned on the chair. This man's hair is pulled tightly behind his head, and a full beard reaches down from his chin towards his white tunic. It's apparent he's alive in this photo, but his face is devoid of expression. Vacant eyes stare out of a flaccid face. Even though I've moved off to the side, it feels as if he's still staring right at me.

I think of all the photos I've seen of various teachers and lamas—Paramahamsa Yogananda, Sri Nisargadatta Maharaj, just to name two—and I can see wrinkles around their eyes. Calm, compassionate, peaceful faces. I think about the images of Bishop Desmond Tutu and the Dalai Lama laughing and playing with each other.

But this man has nothing. No emotion. Nothing.

Now I'm really starting to feel uneasy.

The young man sits on the floor next to me. His face is different from when we were in the residence at the start of our visit. Now he is beaming with admiration. He is talking a little louder, a little faster. He tells me this is a great guru, and mentions again all of his followers. He says that "we do for our yoga" here. This guru, he says in awe, reached samadhi twice this year. "Really?" I ask.

Yes, he tells me. He reached there once in April and again in August. It is true because his guru says it happened.

Now there's even more pressure for me to stay and meditate. Yet again, he tells me that this is a good place to meditate. He tells me I can stay as long as I want, and says he can sit here for hours. This is his third attempt to get me to stay. He's not proving to be a good recruiter.

I've come to the decision that it's time for me to go, so I'm a little more direct in my response to this latest approach to winning me over. "I don't meditate in front of shrines or statues or photos," I tell him. "I don't believe in doing this because to me it feels as if we are worshipping that person or statue or shrine. I meditate on my own without anything in front of me."

He reassures me that it's just a photo and that his guru is a very holy man. This is a holy place to meditate, he says.

Changing the subject, I look out through the gauzy fabric separating this space from the rest of the field house. "You have classes here?" I ask. He says no. There are no classes here. The posters along the walls of the field house, from what I can make out, indicate otherwise. And he also asked if I wanted to see where they hold classes. We may be getting lost in translation somewhere.

Taking the opportunity to glance at the clock on the wall, I stand up, telling him I have to leave and thanking him for his time. As I start to head out into the open area of the field house to wander around a bit, he stops me. He tells me not to go that way. He says it is not good. I am ushered out the way we came, barely setting foot in the field house upon leaving the sanctity of the shrine room.

Although I am saying my goodbyes, he is not done with me. He tells me to look up his guru on YouTube, wants to be sure I remember the name. He is delivering his sales pitch even as I head towards the door in the outside wall, but it's apparent he won't follow me into the stairwell that leads to the outside world.

At the bottom of the stairs, I again pass beneath a skyscraper of a dead tree, laden with black kites yelling at each other and stretching their striped wings. I stop to admire them before passing beneath the archway and out to the street corner. It feels good to step back into the flow of life. Something lifts from me—a dead feeling. A feeling of being suspended in another universe for a while.

I take a deep breath, feel myself smiling.

When I get back to CGN's building, I slip my shoes off outside the door and grab my slippers from the shoe cabinet in the hallway. Socks off, slippers on. It's past 3:00 p.m.

Muna calls to me in Nepali from the kitchen doorway: Do I want tea?

"Dhanyabad, bahini!" I call out, thanking her in Nepali, and calling her "little sister."

In the kitchen, I sit with Muna while she makes tea for us. I am with my family, and it is good. All that just happened at the religious site feels far away, as if it were a dream, and I keep the experience to myself. Even though anyone here at CGN—either Manesh or Geetu or Sumira—might be able to shed some light on what kind of religious or spiritual tradition that young man practiced,

I never ask them. I just want to let the experience exist as it happened, without explanation. I don't enjoy having to find answers for everything.

Muna hands me a steaming cup and smiles. "Love you, didi," she says.

I smile in return, happier than I ever imagined I could be in life.

"Love you, bahini," I reply.

41.

History Repeats Itself

THE STORY OF KATHMANDU is a tale of unity, division, civil strife, conquest, and unity again. Originally named Kantipur, Kathmandu was a small, thriving, independent city in the valley. During the Malla Dynasty, which lasted from the twelfth to the eighteenth century, Kantipur and the surrounding areas experienced a time that can be compared to the Italian Renaissance. Unfortunately, Yakshya Malla left his kingdom divided among his three sons after his death in the fifteenth century. This resulted in civil strife between the newly formed three kingdoms of Kantipur, Patan, and Bhaktapur. The ensuing wars weakened each kingdom and the surrounding independent principalities. As a result, the area was ripe for invasion during the eighteenth century.

For better or for worse, the victorious invading ruler, Prithvi Narayan Shah, united the valley, and is credited with forming what is considered modern Nepal. The Shah Dynasty lasted just two hundred and thirty-eight years, and ended in May 2008, when King Gyanendra vacated the palace two years after the civil war ended. His departure formalized Nepal's transition to a democratic republic. With the end of the monarchy, the palaces of Nepal's three ancient kingdoms, and their vast, expansive, and walled grounds, were finally opened to the public. Around each palace is an area known as a Durbar Square.

These squares are filled with temples and markets where craftsmen sell their wares on tables in grand, cement and stone courtyard plazas. More shops are tucked away in nooks and crannies, creating an ancient and complex maze of restaurants, sweet shops, clothing shops, and souvenir stores.

Devina has already taken me to visit Kathmandu Durbar Square, and today she and Suraj will take me to visit Patan Durbar Square. We have kept in touch since that day in Pharping when they brought school children to visit the elders.

Patan Durbar Square is much less packed than Kathmandu Durbar Square, and filled more with tourist groups huddled around guides. Suraj tells me stories about his childhood near here, and both he and Devina talk about how, early in the morning, if you stand still and quiet, you can hear the voices and activity of those who lived here hundreds of years before. All three of us smile as we stand in a courtyard, in front of an ancient shop made of wood, with moss and grass growing from its roof. We are surrounded by activity, but we stand still and quiet, smiling and happy.

From there we descend into a massive plaza. Suraj motions in front of him. "Do you see this plaza?" he asks. It's wide and vast, and stretches out far in front of us with a few temples at the far end covered in scaffolding and tarps. "You could not see the end from here," Suraj says. "Here was a row of temples, five or six temples, and you could not see past one from here. All gone with the earthquake. They were all destroyed." He sweeps his arm out, seeming to wipe away history the way the earthquakes did twenty-nine months ago.

Behind us, a small group of tourists stand close together on a cement platform raised about four feet above the ground by a brick and mortar base, evidence of another temple that vanished from history on April 25, 2015, on the day the earth shook and life here changed forever. The tourists tower over an Asian woman who gestures around the plaza and motions to the palace on our right. They hang on her every word as she tells them the story of this place, the story of that day, in what sounds like Dutch.

All at once, as Suraj's words echo in my mind, I register the horror that happened in this land just over two years ago. I've been here a couple of weeks shy of three months. I've seen the remnants of that day. I've noticed the buildings and homes being propped up by long planks of wood, and homes crumbled to the ground, still waiting for final demolition and removal. I've heard the stories from Shaha, Suraj, Devina, and others. I've seen the cracks in walls, witnessed the building-sized gaps in a row of shops, evidence of something lost forever.

None of that, however, registered with me before. Now, standing here in this plaza, my skin prickles, and I feel cold. The earthquake struck at 11:56 a.m., local time. How many people were in this plaza? Hundreds? Friends meeting during lunch, shoppers visiting with shop owners, children running around, tourists listening to their guide. People sitting on the temples and enjoying the sunshine. Worshippers praying for their loved ones and for themselves. Men arguing politics as they sat drinking tea. I can hear the sounds of laughter, of children playing, of people shouting to get someone's attention.

How did it feel to be thrown off your feet all at once? To have the initial question in your mind, *"What the hell is happening?"* before you realize the earth is tossing you around as if you were insignificant? Are you too stunned to scream at first, before the screaming starts? Do you run, and if so, where would you go? Reaching to help someone as they are crushed under rock and stone that had stood tall for hundreds of years. Getting separated from your children, your loved ones. Watching your world fall apart in minutes that must have felt like weeks.

Earlier this week, Devina had shown me a video taken after the earthquake. She and Suraj had driven out to the farthest sections of Kathmandu, their car loaded with food, water, and sweets. Suraj had videotaped Devina as she distributed their goods to patient, grateful, and traumatized people. One woman, speechless with grief, touches Devina's head, blessing her, puts her own palms together in front of her, bowing and thanking her. A second woman leans in and tells Devina this speechless mother watched, helpless, as her two children were crushed in the earthquake. She hadn't spoken a word since.

I think of the elders around the city and consider all they have seen, all they have lived through. The monarchy was all they'd ever known, a system that had survived for an eternity. Earthquakes repeatedly shattered their world throughout the twentieth century. Still, they endured. Their children grew up, moved on without them, oftentimes leaving the country for greener pastures. Then everything collapsed all at once: civil war, followed swiftly by the end of their monarchy and life as they knew it, with another devastating earthquake to top it all off.

Back in Pharping, Shaha told me that after the first earthquake struck, he rushed to the elder care home to check on the elders. They refused to leave their rooms. As aftershocks rattled everyone's bones, Shaha, his friends, and the caregivers all tried to convince the elders that it was unsafe inside their rooms. "We tell them it is not safe," Shaha said. "We tell them they can die if they do not leave their rooms." He told me this story while we were at his mother's house for the feast of Brother's Day during Tihar, the Festival of Lights. We stood on the roof, looking out at the land as he vanished into his memory of that day.

"They tell us they do not care. The old people say if they die in their home, that is where they are to die." He shook his head, looked at me, still speechless in recalling their words.

ॐ

Even as we are family, finding each other again after being separated for a lifetime, Suraj and Devina are, first and foremost, Nepali. Family aside, I am still a guest in their home country, and because of the Nepali concern about alarming their guests, Suraj and Devina don't want to warn me about the upcoming elections. Devina mentions that they have a school picnic planned soon, but also says that it may be cancelled. She doesn't say why, and I don't bother to ask.

As much as I want to be a local, I am still very much an outsider. I am a tourist.

When I notice the small parade of noisy people marching through the streets along the edge of Thamel while I'm out running errands one day, I register that it must be related to politics, but I don't give it much thought.

At the center of this small parade is a pickup truck with a loudspeaker attached to the roof, crawling through the streets to block traffic and attract as much attention as possible. A man is yelling through an electric bullhorn attached to the loudspeaker, and the effects are just what this group wants: an ear-shattering distraction for everyone within earshot. Walking alongside the truck are about a dozen young people and middle-aged adults, banging drums and waving Communist flags—the flag used by the Maoist Party. More people are packed into the back of the pickup truck. I don't understand enough Nepali to fully comprehend what the man with the bullhorn is saying, and I can't imagine it has anything to do with violence. Although I don't trust these Maoists, I can't let my brain go there. I just want everything to be okay here, to finally be peaceful.

In the end, I'm oblivious to reality.

42.

Forever Grateful

ON THE DAY I am to present the check for the new wash facility in Pharping, Suraj drives, and Padma sits in the passenger's seat. The car bucks from side to side, and Suraj eases his way around traffic, rocks, and holes, muttering to himself in Nepali from time to time. Padma announces she could come to Pharping every day if she had a driver like this. Suraj translates for me, and both Padma and I laugh. He is not amused.

During dinner at Padma's house last week, I told her and Suraj that I am going to donate the money to rebuild the wash facility at the elder care home. This delighted Padma. She wanted to be sure I got the credit for the work, though, telling me that we should have a banner for the side of the building with my nonprofit's name on it. Nonprofit? I looked from Padma to Suraj and back again. I told them I didn't have a nonprofit.

Padma waved me off. Then I should have a banner with just my name on it, she proclaimed. I needed to get the credit for the wash facility, however it was to be done. After a short discussion, I convinced her that I didn't need the credit, that my ego wasn't tied to this donation.

Today, as we near the elder care home, Suraj tells me his mother wants to go to Dakshinkali first, to do a puja—a service—for an ailing friend. I tell them I won't go in with them, that I'm uncomfortable there with all the animal sacrifice. Padma understands and shakes her head, telling me in Nepali that it won't be like that today. Suraj translates and says his mother wouldn't come on those days, either. The Newari people don't believe in animal sacrifice.

Suraj adds, "You know the days they do the sacrifice?" I tell him yes, Tuesdays and Saturdays.

He says, "Today is not Tuesday or Saturday. I promise no sacrifices today." Then he glances at me in the rearview mirror. "I promise," he says again.

Of course, they are right, and today is a good day to visit Dakshinkali. It is a good day to watch the most devout as they worship. This religion is their truth, and it is who they are. This is who Padma is: a mother who's come to pray to Kali for her friend's health. These are the pilgrims who are here because this religion, this belief, is not just in their hearts and minds and bones. It is part of their soul. Only a small percentage of people who come here actually practice animal sacrifice.

It is good for me to remember that solemn and peaceful Slender Dhai walks all this way, every day, from the elder care home. And it is good for me to reflect on my own journey with what humans call God, and to bookend my visit to Nepal with a new memory of this beautiful temple.

ॐ

Maya calls to Pushpa, who comes to the balcony, then down the stairs. She calls Shaha to tell him we've arrived.

Cheerful Aama, Black Aama, and Maya call out as I pick my way down the back hill. My smile is so wide I'm afraid it will crack my face. Cries of "Oh!" and Black Aama weeping, "My baby, my baby!" fill the air as we clasp hands and hold our foreheads to each other. Cheerful Aama stands and hobbles to meet me.

Goiter Aama is sitting on the stoop and greets me. She is always pleased to see Padma. Shaha arrives within minutes and smiles as he sees me.

The group is together, sitting around the courtyard. Grumpy Aama is out with Goiter Aama, and Folded Aama is off to the side. Troublemaker Aama has come downstairs, and Cheerful Aama sits in her usual spot near the kitchen. Something feels different.

I notice the new man right away, and exclaim, "I know you!" He nods, not understanding. Flipping through the downloaded photos from Chhath Puja on my phone, I soon find the one I took of him. He is the old man in the gray hoodie who pressed hard against his walking stick to stand upright when I took his photo. I hold up the phone for him to see himself, and he smiles, nods, points to the phone, points to me. Is he staying here now? All the resident rooms are full on the first floor, so I can't imagine where he'd sleep.

When I mention to Shaha that the elders are in very good spirits today, and all seem to be wearing new clothes, he tells me the elder care home hosted a puja over the weekend. A family paid money to rent the yoga building and the upper seating area in order to hold a special service for a loved one. It is this puja, Shaha tells me, that has put all the elders into such a good mood. They have some money in their pockets now from the other night. It has made a difference in their attitudes.

Indeed, it has: Grumpy Aama is smiling, and willing to sit between Black Aama and Goiter Aama, as we pose for photos while I present the check. I ask Suraj to please explain to everyone what is happening so they understand what the fuss is about. I hear murmurs and see heads nod and smiles spread across faces. Slender Dhai clasps his hands before him and bows to me. Cheerful Aama is grateful.

After the photos, I take Shaha aside and ask about the new man. "Yes, he is here now," he says, and begins to tell me the story. This man has four grown children in the area. They all told him they can no longer afford to feed him. He came here for help, and Shaha told him he has no room for him, but if he comes in the morning and stays, he can have tea and food and can rest when he needs to. Then Shaha discovered the man was being turned away from his children's homes at night because they claimed they suddenly didn't have room for him. Shaha realized he could let the man sleep in the yoga building at night, and approached the children with a liability waiver so their father could live in the home. The children, though, won't sign the waiver. So they won't feed or house their father, but won't let Shaha take the responsibility of doing it, either.

After Shaha found out this man's family had given away or thrown away all their father's belongings, he made the decision to keep him here full time. If it weren't for Shaha and his friends, this man would have nowhere to lay his head at night, and would have nothing more than the clothes on his back. Now the community has come together to give him some more clothes, and to help him settle into his new home.

The man, whom I nickname Peaceful Dhai, is quiet. He barely speaks and just nods and is forever grateful. When he was first turned out of his son's home, he decided, "I will walk, and where I drop, I will die." Fortunately, he found his way to Shaha's elder care home.

As Shaha tells me this story, I see his smile falter and a sadness in his eyes. The very idea of turning out one's own parent is beyond his grasp. I understand the depth of his compassion, the drive to do something, the need to help elders in these situations.

࿔

This departure feels almost worse than the last. More tears, more blessings from Cheerful Aama, from Goiter Aama, from Black Aama.

Suraj makes his way back down the disaster of a road, telling me that he thinks the day went very well. He laughs a little as he says that Shaha thinks I am going to donate the money for a new dormitory roof and new kitchen next year.

"I will *what*?!" I exclaim from the back seat. "I'm not made of money!"

He is laughing. "He says you will help collect donations for him."

Ah, yes. A grant. I need to find a way to help Shaha find a grant, as I'd promised.

As the car rocks side to side with the road, my thoughts turn to Shaha, to his deep compassion, and to the growing problem of homeless and abandoned elders around the world. I think about how I managed to raise a bit of money for this trip. A little voice nags at me: *"You did this once. You could do this again."* I consider how Padma had assumed I was already running a nonprofit. She has undying faith in me, it seems.

That's where I'm headed, I realize. I could help more elders in more countries. I could do this. I could form my own nonprofit.

This...*this* I could do.

43.

Simmering

SEVENTY-EIGHT DAYS AGO, I stepped out of Tribhuvan International Airport in Kathmandu, into the blinding sun, and into the dust and heat that is Nepal. The trip had taken me from the airport in Seattle to Epsom, England, through New Delhi in India, and on to Kathmandu.

Because I hadn't applied for a transit visa to collect my bags in New Delhi, I'd been forced to remain in Epsom while I waited out the required five-day period between my application date and travel date.

While stuck there, I had earned my keep with my friends Dee and Jon. They manage a field where they board horses, and I'd helped out by scooping manure and painting a shed. It was hot when I left. Now it's the end of November, and I can't figure out where the time went.

Today is Thursday. I have just five days left here in Nepal. Soon I'll be headed back to Epsom after a stop in New Delhi again. *Back to Epsom?* Was I ever really there? It seems like a dream. For close to three months, now, I've questioned what's real and what isn't. I'm no longer certain that I know.

I'm standing in my room in Naya Bazar, staring out the window as the neighborhood wakes up. It's cold. I can hear the vegetable and fruit vendors calling out as they wheel their produce-laden flat carts through the streets. "Cau-*lee*! Ah-*loo*!" Children are playing somewhere up the block. The usual dogs are having their morning arguments. Someone revs up a motorcycle.

My work for Aabi is complete. I've finished the PowerPoint presentation on elder care at the home in Pharping; the new assessment protocols for determining whether or not an elder care home is a good fit for CGN are done; and I've finished the hostel rules and completed the list of items to address before he opens the hostel to volunteers. Top on the list of items: Please fix the hot water on-demand system in the shower. It rarely works. Next up: There are only six outlets in each of the larger rooms, and all the outlets are near the door. With Aabi expecting to cram ten volunteers into each room, how will they charge their electronic devices? Has he even considered the load on these circuits? The list of items goes on, including adding cabinets that lock so people have a place to store their personal items.

Earlier this week, Monika tried to explain to me that I should not go out on Friday, which is now tomorrow. She had said it would not be good for me to be outside. Mistaken in my belief that this was some kind of holiday because of the upcoming elections, I had asked her what they were celebrating. She replied, "No, no celebrating. Fires in the streets, burning. Police outside, and roadblocks."

Tomorrow is also the day that Devina's school is supposed to hold their picnic—the picnic that may be cancelled. I'm still not sure what's happening, and it hasn't occurred to me to just ask someone. I have one foot in tourist mode, in blissful ignorance. The other foot is in Nepali mode, knowing in the back of my mind that something has been simmering beneath the surface of daily life here for the past couple of weeks.

It's time for me to consider the implications of what may come, and to think about the violence the Maoists are planning. It's time for me to realize I'm more than a tourist here.

"Didi!" Muna calls from the bottom of the stairs.

"Hajur?" I call back, using the common catch-all word to ask, "Yes?"

"Tea!" comes the reply.

"Okay!" I say as I turn from the window.

It's time to begin my Thursday. Life as a Nepali, continues.

ॐ

After a day of taking photos, going to visit with Dil at his shop and Puja at the hotel, and browsing the area, it's grown dark. It's not yet dinner time, and the neighborhood children aren't out playing as usual. It's so quiet outside that it catches my attention.

When I wander downstairs, I find the front doors to the building locked from the outside. Really? Muna, Akkal, and Monika are all gone, without having told me where they were headed or when they'd be returning. I press on the eight-foot-tall, carved wooden doors, and they give way a little. I continue to wrestle with them until the latch outside wriggles itself free. I walk to the driveway gate, and one gentle press tells me it's locked on the outside.

This isn't the first time Muna, Akkal, and Monika have done this to me. The last time they locked a day laborer in here with me by accident. Tonight, though, I know I've been locked in for my safety. Ten years of civil war, ten years of bodies in the streets and people disappearing, would make anyone want to protect their loved ones left inside the home. Tonight, I am that loved one.

At long last, I hear a scooter pulling up outside and the sound of a key in the lock. Monika swings the gate open and laughs at the sight of me standing in the middle of the driveway, arms folded across my chest, leaning on one hip and tapping my other foot, pretending to be angry.

Akkal navigates the scooter through the entrance and onto the driveway, and both he and Muna also laugh at me.

"You locked me in again!" I yell as he shuts off the engine.

"Sorry, didi! We do not think we will be gone long."

Monika is excited to tell me about her first "scootie" ride and loops her arm through mine, guiding me down the hallway to the kitchen. Muna is shivering from the cold, so I wrap her purple and black shawl a little tighter around her shoulders as she begins to make tea. Then I tell Monika to go get her mother's slippers for her, which she does without hesitation.

Muna smiles at me as she switches out her sandals for her slippers, saying, "Love you, didi!" Her smile seems forced, though, and I can tell she's tense.

As we sit in the kitchen as a family, enjoying the tea, Akkal explains that Muna is worried about being able to get passport photos tomorrow. He says they expect the shops to be closed because the Maoists have called for a general strike. I've never seen Akkal without a smile on his face, but now it disappears. "The Maoists don't want peace," he says.

Muna understands enough of what he's said in English and turns away, upset. Akkal has the look of a father concerned for his family's safety. Monika continues sipping her tea; this is her parents' history, not her own. Born just after the civil war, she isn't flippant about the potential violence, she just hasn't experienced it for herself. It's different to have lived through something versus having only heard about it in a story.

࿏

From 1996 to 2006, civil war raged in Nepal. A staggering eighteen thousand people either died, were abducted, taken into custody, or taken hostage. Another three thousand people—men, women, and children—went missing. The Maoists refer to this horror as "The People's Movement."

The Nepalis have not been the same since. Continued political disagreements left the government unstable, so much so that a constitution wasn't signed until just two years ago, in September 2015. By then, the earthquakes had torn apart much of the country. The Nepalis couldn't catch a break.

Nepal is now a federal democratic republic, and at the highest levels of power, politicians continue to play games. Nepal's first elected prime minister was the same man who instigated the civil war against his own people. He resigned in protest before his term was completed, because the elected president at that time rehired an official whom the prime minister had recently fired. That same prime minister was recently *re-elected*, only to step down six months later after serving half his term. Apparently, his political party had agreed to split the term of office between the leaders of his party and a second party. It's enough to confuse any global political observer, and more than enough to frustrate any Nepali citizen. This is a country relatively new to democracy, and it seems this democracy exists only on paper.

In two days, on Saturday, November 26, Nepal will hold the first phase of its national and state-level general elections. The second phase of the elections will take place on December 7. The Maoists have called for the general strike to happen tomorrow, Friday. Their expectation is that shops will remain closed, that shop owners do not need to earn a living tomorrow, and that people will not need to buy food or sundries or anything else. It is unclear what the Maoists hope to attain by calling for and expecting this strike.

44.

The General Strike

TODAY IS FRIDAY, THE day of the strike. Very early this morning, around 4:30 a.m., a small group of young adults marched through the streets, blowing horns, pounding snare drums, and banging cymbals. When the same thing happened during my first month at the elder care home run by Pradeep, Daya said it was related to politics. When it happened during my stay in Pharping, Pushpa said, "The Maoists," and shook her head.

By 7:30 a.m., Monika finds out school is open and rushes to get ready. Ten minutes later, I'm out with my camera. Some shops are opening. The streets are quieter than normal. A few motorcycles pass, a scooter here and there. Children are being walked to school. A bull searches for something to eat, while a year-old puppy chews on a dry weed nearby.

I turn down an unfamiliar street, then another. I reach the river. At one corner, three men are squatting next to a tiny pile of burning garbage. They hold their hands out over the small fire, trying to get some warmth. Blue-gray smoke fogs the space between them. I cross the dusty bridge and keep going, snapping photos as I wander. The atmosphere is subdued, not quite tense, and I'm trying to capture this feeling. We are all waiting to exhale. A chicken races across the road up ahead of me, accustomed to trying to beat traffic that doesn't exist today. Dogs challenge each other in a vicious battle. Who owns this section of street?

A genial-looking, round-faced man appears next to me. "Good morning, ma'am." He is just shorter than me, and in his thirties. He wears jeans and a blue down parka.

"Good morning," I reply.

"And how are you?" he asks.

"I'm well, thank you."

"And where are you from?"

The conversation goes on as we saunter along. He is a trekking guide, and has talked to many people from around the world. How do I find Nepal? He is delighted when I reply in Nepali. We converse a bit, simple phrases that I can handle. This is how they generate business: Get to know a tourist, introduce your services, exchange information, sell them on a trek. Many of these guides, however, don't take "no thank you" for an answer the first, second, or third time. Their behavior can be obnoxious towards a woman traveling alone. Today, though, I don't mind. There's nothing he can sell me today.

We stop at a corner and I get serious, lower my voice. "What do you think about this strike?"

"Ah, ma'am," his voice also low, "we do not know what to make. The political party, one party, says strike. The government says no, we do not do this. The government says we will beat you if you strike. So, we do not know."

"Many people I talk to are concerned," I say. He takes a light hold of my elbow, leads me out of the street onto an empty section of sidewalk. "It does not seem many will strike," I add.

"The one political party does not like the government," he replies. "They do not want peace. They have bombs. Do you understand? They make bombs."

A slightly older man, dressed in a shirt and sweater vest, has stopped behind the trekking guide. I make a motion; the guide stops talking. The man in the sweater vest lingers; the guide remains silent. After a bit, the man in the sweater vest leaves, and I give the guide a subtle nod.

"Tomorrow is the election," the guide continues, his voice still quiet. "They do not want this. They bomb before. Election is not good for them."

"In my country," I say, "we have democracy. It is not perfect, but it is good. We have choices."

The trekking guide says democracy is not the same here. He talks about how nothing gets done in the government. If you want something done, you pay money over the table, but nothing *gets* done unless you pay money *under* the table. He says, "The government wants more and more, and the people have no more to give."

I say it seems that people have no choice. He tells me they don't. The government threatens violence if people strike; the political party threatens violence if people *don't* strike.

He checks his watch; it seems there is a start time to the strike. He says again the election is tomorrow. The results will be announced Sunday. *Do you understand this?* he asks. Results on Sunday. Today is not the most dangerous day, he says.

A young chick breaks from his siblings and runs across the street towards us, hops up on the sidewalk next to me, and pecks. The guide laughs. The chick then makes the precarious zigzag back to its siblings, a motorcyclist screeching his brakes to avoid it. The man in the sweater vest has returned, lingering once again behind the trekking guide. I gesture and we cease our conversation yet again. Who knows who this man in the sweater vest is? He may be a Maoist, or he may know people who are. In this environment, who knows what would happen if the guide was caught talking to me about these issues?

At last, the man in the sweater vest sees me staring hard at him over the trekking guide's shoulder, and he wanders off once more.

I say I am sorry for the Nepali people, that I wish there could be peace. The guide says the people work hard. They have political parties, but no political party wants to work with the other. "The Nepali people could help each other, could do more," he says, "but the government fights against itself, against the people. Then the people don't work together."

It is time for me to go. He gives me his business card, invites me to meet him for tea any time. A six-month-old, black-and-white puppy bounces up to us, tail wagging, gets distracted, and turns away as a taxi just avoids hitting him. He continues bouncing along around the corner, following the trekking guide, looking for something, in and out of danger, safe only for the kindness of strangers.

I snap photos of graffiti as I wander, several areas scrawled with, *"How much they payin you to be their monkey?"* One rolling door is spray-painted with, *"Nature is dead."* I catch a shot of two boys playing on a skateboard, one seated, feet up, hugging his knees, being pushed from behind. Children need to be children even as their parents fear for their safety today. At one point I feel a dull clip at my right elbow as a motorcycle passes and shout to myself, "Are you kidding me?" Then I realize I'm walking almost in the middle of the street. The cyclist stops up ahead, raises his visor, holds out his left hand as he looks back at me.

"I'm sorry," I say as I approach him.

"I'm sorry, ma'am. I did not mean to hit you."

We need a little extra humanity today.

"No, no, I was in the middle of the street. I'm okay."

"No, no, I am sorry. You are okay?"

"Yes, I'm fine. I'm fine."

We say our goodbyes, and he travels on.

Tomorrow, when I relate this story to Devina and Suraj, they will be incredulous that the motorcyclist apologized for hitting me—incredulous that he stopped in the first place. I hadn't thought about that. Even though I've seen people get clipped several times, I've never seen the biker stop to check on the pedestrian.

A few minutes later, as I continue my walk, two very young boys race towards me and up into a shop to my right, laughing the entire time. A third comes after them. I stop and point into the shop. He skids to a stop just past me, looks back. I point again and he doesn't miss a beat. Up the stairs, into the shop after the other two.

The men who usually play badminton at the corner have relinquished the empty lot to a group of children. Four older boys play against eight much-younger ones, who seem to be trying their hardest. One of the older kids stops to tell me, "Seven to one." I look at the very tired younger boys, then back to this older boy. I point to his side, then to the other side, teasing, "One and seven?"

"No! No!" laugh the older boys. They point their racquets to themselves, "Seven!" Then to the other side, "One!" The four older boys pose, and I take a few photos.

One year from now, a building will stand on this lot. There isn't another place nearby for kids to play like this.

Behind me, the girl in the sundry shop calls out, and when I turn, she leans on the counter, smiling. She also wants her photo taken. One quick snap, and she is pleased. We wave goodbye, and I keep going.

&

Muna is not her normal, cheery self today. She makes tea for us, and we drink it in silence. I give her a squeeze around the shoulders when we're done, and she smiles, tells me she loves me.

Upstairs in my room, I mull over options as a small crowd gathers at the corner outside. I wonder how many of us are still holding our breath.

The streets are too quiet. At 4:00 p.m. it seems the strike has not struck. Up the street a truck drives by, music blaring, then a voice over the loudspeaker announces something, proclaims something—urging people to rise up, I imagine, or to stay still, perhaps.

I was out with my camera off and on all day, trying to capture the feeling in the streets, trying to photograph the sensation of going about one's day under a cloud of fear and concern. It is a compulsion. I kept grabbing my gear and walking around the neighborhood, heading in different directions each time, and each time I kept the fabric buff wrapped over my camera and my finger on the shutter, hidden from view, the camera casually hanging by my side yet strategically aimed. Armed police are everywhere today. Some have spied my camera and its strategic position and given me warning looks.

On another trip out today, I saw a pickup truck with tarps rising up from the sides of the bed. Twelve men dressed in drab olive uniforms and black berets stood in the bed of the pickup, looking out every direction, only their heads and shoulders showing above the tarps. I didn't dare point my camera at them, and when one man stared me down after spying my lens, my heart raced. *Keep walking, keep walking,* I told myself, even as I passed the officer in charge as he walked back to the truck, an official-looking man with ribbons on his chest and a maroon beret instead of black. *Don't do it!* I screamed in my head as the urge to capture a photo came over me.

This compulsion to document everything feels natural. I am in unbiased reporter mode, bringing the story of these elections to whomever back home wants to see. Somehow my safety isn't an important issue to me right now. I'm focused entirely on the story I see unfolding in these streets.

Now it has grown dark. Still in my room, reviewing photos, I hear the truck with the loudspeaker moving through our neighborhood. Muna and Akkal are preparing dinner. Without thinking, I am out the front door, unlocking the gate to the property from within, and closing it carefully behind me. As I swing the heavy metal gate shut, I see Akkal through the open front door, looking towards me, alarmed.

My actions are not merely careless, they are reckless. I stand in the middle of the road, several blocks from CGN's building, checking my camera settings in the light of a streetlamp, and I can hear the truck moving down one road. I pause to listen. Which direction is it headed? If I go down that street, can I meet up with the truck as it's coming towards me? These Maoists want their story to be heard, or so I think. I'll report that story for them, and for the world to see, while I also document the strife and fear they are forcing on their fellow Nepalis.

It isn't until I hear Akkal's voice behind me, pleading, that I realize just how inconsiderate and reckless my actions are.

"Didi! Didi! *Please* come back. *Please.* This is not safe!" he whispers, jogging towards me. His voice is quiet as he tries not to attract attention, and he looks panicked. *Oh, my God,* I think to myself, *I can't do this to him and Muna.* They lived through ten years of hell during that war, and they are reliving that hell tonight. I am making it worse for them.

Apologizing, I head towards him, apologize again as he tells me Muna is also worried. We jog through the empty streets. All the Nepalis are staying inside. Yes, it's just the idiot American out in the street tonight. Once back in the safety of CGN's grounds, Akkal flips the lock down on the gate after swinging it shut. Inside the building, he double-bolts the front door, top bolt and bottom, and pulls the latch across as well. Anything to seal us in. Anything to protect us, his family, from the violence he suspects might come tonight.

Muna is relieved to see me and squeezes my hand. I feel a twinge of disappointment that I'm not out there, photographing and documenting, but I can't do that to Muna and Akkal. They are my family, and you don't put your family through a hell like that.

☙

After dinner, as I brush my teeth and drift around the floor flicking off lights in rooms, I recall the angry man from Pakistan at the first elder care home. The man who yelled at me because I was American, and warned me that "there could be no India without Pakistan." I had no fight with him, but he had a fight with me. That night I came to realize that being American is not necessarily a good thing here. For some people here, my being American isn't even a neutral thing.

Still, I hadn't quite learned my lesson from my encounter with the man from Pakistan. Tonight, I was still naïve. Out there in those streets this evening, I was not just a simple tourist, nor was I some kind of photojournalist documenting the Maoists' story and the Nepalis' struggles. No, tonight I would have been fair game, pure and simple.

In the end, the Maoists will have their violence. They will set off bombs at various points around the outskirts of Kathmandu several times between the first round of elections this weekend, and the second round on December 7.

☙

Mao Tse-tung has been called "the greatest murderer in history." Some historical outlets estimate that forty-five million people were murdered during his reign, either through executions, beatings, starvation, or by being worked to death. Countless innocent people, including teachers and intellectuals, were identified as "enemies of the state." Many were rounded up, beaten, dragged to prison, beaten again, then executed. Others were simply executed in public after the accusations were leveled against them. Students from the cities were sent to "re-education" camps in the countryside, usually to be worked to death.

Since the death of Mao in 1976, subsequent political leaders in China have continued to embrace his philosophy, including the belief that "religion is poison." Here in Nepal, his followers call themselves Maoists.

⌀

During my first month here, I befriended Anna, the ex-pat from Cuba who'd invited me to dinner at Howard's place. We'd kept in touch, meeting at the farmers market or the coffee shop a few times a week. Anna had mentioned something once that made me think she'd been involved, somehow, with the Maoists here in Nepal. One day, I carefully asked her about that.

She was all at once wistful and far away. "Only in my heart," she said, holding her right hand over her heart, reminiscing about something.

It was a Saturday, and we were sitting at the farmers market in a rare spot of shade on the property. We leaned in close to each other, and she began her story.

The Maoists weren't violent in the beginning, she said, but they weren't being heard. She never joined them, Anna said. She only made the mistake of falling in love with what they represented, and with one of the men at the top of the organization.

They wanted the corruption to end, she said, and for the poor to be educated. They wanted a fair chance for all Nepalis, especially for the children, whom they honored as Nepal's future. The love of her life was dedicated to the movement, and dedicated to the cause, but she never personally signed up, she said.

What about the killing?

"We never kill nobody innocent," she said.

Did they kill?

"Yes, of course. But we never kill nobody innocent."

Much of the killing, she contended, was done by the government. Many of the citizens were killed by the Nepal Army. I pressed her on this, asking how the Maoists managed to kill only the guilty.

"Is it wrong to kill a man who harms a child?" she asked in response, assuming the answer.

Anna insisted they'd never wanted violence, that the origins of the group were peaceful, wanting change without bloodshed. Get any large group of passionate people together, though, and the perceived need for change forces divisions in even the most well-intentioned. When the group splintered over ideals, one fragment chose the path of violence. The members of this splinter group are proud of the torment they cause their fellow Nepalis, proud to take credit for the bombings.

Earlier this year, a merger took place between the mainstream Maoist Party and the Unified Marxist-Leninist party, forming the new Communist Party of Nepal. Now the Nepali public is even more confused as to what each party stands for. "Maybe they are not giving up," Anna said. "Maybe they just try to change things from inside."

The original Maoist Party had it right all along, she insisted. She wanted to be sure I understood that the group gave up everything when they signed the peace agreement in 2006. Everything. "The money," Anna said. "So much money. A million, maybe. Turned over to the government. And where did it go?" she asked, holding her hands up. Then she shrugged, disgusted.

"And the children," she added. The Maoists had been gathering children who'd been abandoned by their parents, or been separated or orphaned, or who had run away during the fighting, she said. They'd kept these children safe. Fed them. Educated them. Probably fifteen hundred children over several sites, she said. "The Maoists turn them over to the government. They trusted the government. No one said nothin', *nothin'* 'bout the children. What happen to them? *What did the government do with the children?*"

I heard what Anna was saying. I understood the agony of a small group of people trying to lift up an entire nation, but I'd also seen photos from the civil war, including photos of children tied tightly to posts because they were suspected of being traitors to the cause.

During my time in Pharping, I made the acquaintance of many of the locals. I once asked a man about the massive, abandoned cement building just outside the village, which was being destroyed bit by bit by bulldozers and a wrecking ball that all appeared inadequate for the job. I had wondered what the building had been and why it was being torn down. The man shook his head and looked off into the distance, disgusted. "Can you believe this?" he asked before he even began the story, lowering his voice as he spoke.

It had been a cement factory. The largest cement factory in the area, providing hundreds of jobs to the locals in Pharping and beyond. "Everyone was happy," he insisted, until the Maoists interfered.

Planting the seeds of unrest, the Maoists convinced the factory workers that the factory owner was taking advantage of them. Party representatives promised the workers their wages would be paid if they went on strike, and by the time they went back to work they'd have higher wages and health insurance.

It was a deal the workers couldn't refuse.

Weeks dragged into months, months into a couple of years.

The cement factory went bankrupt and the Maoists' money well ran dry, leaving the workers with no jobs and no income.

45.

Departure

I's 6:00 A.M., AND I am panicking as Akkal drives me to the airport. My insides are churning. I shouldn't be leaving, I tell him. I am leaving something important behind. He asks what. I tell him I don't know. Not a *thing*, but *something*. I tell him I feel as if I'm leaving unfinished business behind.

Akkal tells me I can stay. He asks if he should turn around. I tell him no, I can't. I shouldn't be leaving, but I can't stay.

He says again that it is okay, that everything is okay. He is reassuring me as I fight to contain the panic. My ears are buzzing, my head is fuzzy, and I sit on my hands to keep from leaping out of the moving car.

∾

Past two security checks and up to the ticket counter to check in at the airport, and the ticket agent tells me my bags are overweight. She tells me to move seven kilograms of items from my red duffel to my backpack.

I blink. How does that make sense? My bags would still be overweight if I do that. "Can't I just pay the fee?" I ask, but the young girl motions me off to the side, tells me to "take care of it."

I step out of the long line of passengers, and begin the exasperating task of taking clothes out of my red duffel, trying to fit them into my backpack, which already is loaded with souvenirs and my camera. I don't hide my annoyance and sigh as I pick at my belongings, making a big deal out of the task.

"Ma'am," the ticket agent says at one point to catch my attention, then gestures even farther away from the line. "Please go there," she tells me, instructing me to go to an empty ticket counter. I resist the urge to roll my eyes, but do as she says.

Moments later, a man in a reflective vest appears behind the counter and asks what I'm doing, and I tell him. I ask him why I can't just pay the overweight bag fee. The man motions for me to come to the counter and looks back down at his hands, still pretending to work.

He asks, in a low voice, how much I have on me.

"Excuse me?" I stammer, keeping my voice quiet. *What did he just ask me?*

He mumbles, "Two thousand rupees."

It takes a second to realize what's happening: He's asking for a bribe.

I only have one hundred rupees, I whisper. I have no rupees left.

He thinks for a moment. "Forty dollars," he says.

Forty US dollars equates to more than twice as much as he just demanded a moment ago! I panic. This man controls whether or not I get on the plane, and I don't even have forty US dollars on me.

Thinking fast, I remember I brought some Canadian dollars with me to Nepal. My brain fires in hundredths of seconds. I have thirty Canadian dollars. Do I tell him I only have twenty, to save myself some cash? But then if he sees the other ten dollars, I'm screwed. *Give it all to him,* my brain screams. *Just get on the damned plane.*

"I have thirty Canadian dollars," I whisper. He thinks for a moment, and I say, "It's more than forty US dollars," which is a lie, and I'm gambling he doesn't know this. "*Please,*" I add, just to help my case.

The man gives a quick nod and tells me to pack my bags, which I'm sure weren't overweight to begin with, and walks back to the first ticket agent's counter to wait for me. Before I leave my spot, I turn my back to the other passengers waiting in line, then reach into my money pouch. This man wasn't very obvious about demanding a bribe, so I'd rather not be too obvious about paying it. Moments later, I've slipped the money over the counter to him as the ticket agent prints my boarding pass.

One hour and three more security checks later, I'm seated on the plane, my mind reeling as I prepare to jump into another world, first at the airport in India, then back in Epsom on my way to the US.

The captain taxis out onto the runway, then we're all pressed back in our seats as he pushes the throttle forward.

VI. Aftershocks

"Making others happy, through kindness of speech
and sincerity of right advice, is a sign of true greatness.
To hurt another soul by sarcastic words,
looks, or suggestions, is despicable."

~ Paramahamsa Yogananda

"The consciousness in you and the consciousness in me,
apparently two, really one, seek unity and that is love."

~ Sri Nisargadatta Maharaj

46.

Re-Entry

RE-ENTRY IS BRUTAL. It's cold in Epsom. The temperature is down, and the Christmas decorations are up. As I step into the guest bedroom at Jon and Dee's, I can't figure out how Dee had time to change all the bedding and do all this decorating overnight. *I was just here*, I keep thinking. *I was just here on my way to Nepal*. It's jarring. All of it. Everything I see, hear, and touch. I can't determine what's real and what isn't. This world is so different from the one I just left. It's as if Nepal is a distant dream.

Dee loans me some warm clothes to wear so I can help scoop manure at the field where she and Jon board horses. We climb into her little work truck, and she pulls away from the curb. "I think I understand a bit of how our troops feel after coming home from a tour of duty," I tell her. It seems just yesterday I wore a t-shirt and shorts as I helped paint the shed at the field. Now I'm half-freezing. How is this possible? I blinked and lost three months.

After finishing with the horses, we stop at Sainsbury's to do some grocery shopping and have lunch, and I want to curl up in a corner and make myself small. The store is fresh, bright, clean, and white. I make a joke about keeping my arms close to my sides so I don't accidentally knock over an entire display of delicate Christmas decorations. Soft Christmas music is playing overhead. It's overwhelming, visually and aurally. I fight back tears. I feel ridiculous and lost and confused.

As I lie in bed that night, I realize I can't recall how I got to their house today. Was it today? I don't recall leaving, and I can't recall coming back. I just remember going to sleep and dreaming about Nepal, then waking up into winter.

࿇

The airport in Seattle feels both foreign and familiar. Kathmandu was just a dream. None of it was real.

For more than a week, I wake up several times every night and wonder when I will get home. I stand in the darkness at our kitchen window, and stare at the emptiness of the horse paddock. It feels as if parts of my body are going in different directions.

Nelson lets me sleep, keeps reminding me that I'm home. I have no patience for television, no focus for reading, very little memory of how to get around in a car. No one else can see that I'm different, and I don't know how to explain it. I'm the same person everybody sees from the outside, but inside I have someone else's memories. I'm adrift, lost on someone else's ocean.

࿇

Months later, although the confusion and brain fog have cleared, I begin to realize I'll never fully re-adapt to our overly busy and complicated way of life in the West, filled as it is with excesses. I will always feel out of place here. It's time for me to carve out a spot for myself in this world, time to reach my arms around the globe.

What began as a mere thought on the drive back from the elder care home in Pharping has grown into an overwhelming force to be reckoned with. That day, as Suraj cursed and muttered at the careless Nepali drivers around us, I had thought to myself, "I did this once. I could do it again."

Why not me?

I sit at my laptop for hours, searching and reading and picking away at how to start a global nonprofit. My older sister, a CPA with many years of experience working in this sector, walks me through some steps. For the most part, though, I'm on my own. She's not going to hold my hand. This is my journey through this maze.

We toss around ideas for the nonprofit's name, and I settle on The Global Humanity Initiative. Everything else falls into place. I choose a founding board based on their life experiences and philosophies, and their ability to tell me no when I need to hear it.

Our mission is simple: To improve the lives of impoverished elders around the world through food and housing support. It takes the IRS just thirty-one days to approve my nonprofit status. "Unheard of," my sister says. "It usually takes months to get approved, and sometimes even years of fighting."

It's a sign, she decides. A sign that I'm on the right path.

〜

Even with this progress on the nonprofit, I am stuck with a nagging feeling of unfinished business back in Nepal. It is a milder version of that all-consuming panic I experienced as Akkal drove me to the airport in November of 2017. *Nothing will be right with my life*, I keep thinking, *until I complete this unfinished business*. All I can think about is the dirt-poor little girl from that first elder care home who used to come to the services every night with her infant brother, hoping for food, but walking away into the dark streets empty-handed. Right up to my last night at the so-called elder care home, I'd been unsure of how I could possibly help her.

Now, though, I realize there is something I could do: I could pay for this girl's tuition at Suraj and Devina's school. At least if she were at their school, I'd know she'd be placed in the proper grade for her education, and that she wouldn't get picked on. The school has a strict no-bullying policy, and Devina enforces it with an iron fist. Children have been removed from the school for harassing other students, and staff have been fired for using a hostile or disparaging tone when speaking to the students. Suraj and Devina's primary goal is to create good humans. A high-quality education means nothing if a child is not raised to be a decent person. At least this girl could get a solid, Western education. I could give her a fighting chance.

I have no choice, really. My soul won't rest until I go back to Nepal and finish this.

47.

Back into Hell

In January 2019, I make a mad dash back to Kathmandu to check on the improvements in Pharping, and to try to find the little girl from the evening services at the first elder care home. I can't afford much time off work, so this will be an expensive, ten-day trip.

In advance of my travels, I reach out to Dil and Puja, my family. I send them a photo of the little girl, and they create some flyers. When they approach people at the evening services, however, everyone denies knowing the kids. Dil and Puja press multiple times: *Please look at this photo once again. It was taken here by an American last year.* The denials continue. No one has ever seen these children before.

Still, the regulars at the temple grounds allow flyers to be hung on a few walls. *If anyone sees these children*, the flyers read in the Devanagari script of Nepal, *please call this number so that we can speak to them.*

When Dil returns a few days later to follow up, the flyers have been removed.

Over dinner during my first night at the hotel, Puja and I talk about the temple grounds and Pradeep's elder care home. We are huddled together, eating a hot meal on the roof in the cold of a January night. Around us are one ex-pat who arrived in Kathmandu twenty-eight years ago and who refuses to leave, plus a couple of other hardcore and hardy travelers. Tarps hang around the frame up here to keep some of the chill out. I tell Puja that I will make one trip to the elder care home tomorrow evening, and that I'll take some food, which is always welcomed. This way, I can check on who is there and how I will be received. Puja nods in agreement.

Later we'll all gather back up here and hover around a steel drum filled with burning scraps of wood collected from the streets. We'll talk late into the night. After that, I'll head back downstairs to my cold room, and crawl under my winter bedding to sleep, fully dressed.

～

Sometimes we must break promises to ourselves and to others. I swore to myself that I would never set foot in this place again. Still, here I am, outside the temple grounds and this first elder care home from my Nepal visit over a year ago.

Taking a deep breath, I step through the gate into the courtyard. It never occurred to me that this place could feel more sinister than it did the day I walked out. This evening, it feels even darker.

It is almost 5:30 p.m. In the shrine room, someone is warming up on the tabla, and a woman is getting set up on the harmonium. There are only a few people in the audience tonight, and I recognize one or two of the regular attendees. Pradeep and Garima are nowhere to be found. The woman on the harmonium looks up at me. It's Sahdi, Pradeep's sidekick.

She jumps up from her seat and rushes over to see me, welcoming me like a sister. Opening the manila folder I brought, I show her an enlarged photo of the two children. This is the same photo that Dil and Puja used on their flyers.

Sahdi doesn't hesitate to tell me yes, they come here almost every service. We know who they are, she says. I tell her I want to talk to them the next time they come, and that I'll be back the next night just in case they are here. She nods in agreement.

When I look up, I see the man who scolded me a year ago for coming late to the service. He's looking at the photo. I remember how he blocked my view of the children as they headed out into the night and told me not to concern myself with them.

Now he points to the photo, then to me. "You will come here bholi, padch bajye?"

"Yes," I tell him. "Five o'clock tomorrow, I will come to see if they are here." He and Sahdi exchange a nod.

When I take the food I've brought up to the kitchen, the new couple who cook for the residents seem terrified with every move or sound around them. They keep their heads down, take the bag without making eye contact with me, and carry the aura of beaten dogs as they work. Hajuraama and Hajurbaa are no longer residents, nor are Mahti and Daya.

჻

Just before 5:00 p.m. the next evening, Puja and I head out to run errands. Spices and sundries for her, incense and bracelets for me. We browse, she visits with the shop owners, and I soak it all in. As it closes in on 5:30 p.m., though, Puja looks up at me. It's time. She links her arm through mine, and together we start the long walk to the elder care home. We talk strategy. This girl may not be a legal resident of Nepal, and so she wouldn't be allowed to enroll in school here. Although I'm optimistic about this visit, I need to be prepared for the possibility that she may not want my help, or that she may not be able to accept it.

As we approach the gate to the temple grounds, the hair on the back of my neck stands on end. No music. There should be music. The service should be well underway by now, but there is no sound.

Time seems to slow down as we turn and step in through the gate. The shrine room is closed and dark, the gate drawn across it. In the center of the courtyard is a steel drum filled with burning garbage and scraps of wood. Two women, bundled in heavy shawls, look up at me as Puja and I enter.

In a flash, I recognize the wide streaks of orange tika paint, starting from between their eyebrows and stretching up their foreheads and far into their hair. The same markings from the people who celebrated Chhath Puja while I was in Pharping. I've never found anyone who could tell me what tribe these markings represent. All I know is that these women are likely from India, not Nepal. Several young boys sit around the fire with these women, along with a young girl, who coos over a swaddled baby that she holds in her arms.

"Something is wrong," I murmur to Puja. She looks up at me, and we walk forward a few more steps. My stomach is churning. It feels as if the gates of Hell have opened from beneath the courtyard.

Sahdi is there, as is the man who scolded me last year. They stop pacing when they see us.

"This is not the girl," I mutter to Puja. "This is not her." I know it in an instant. I don't need to even think about it.

Sahdi and the man are happy to see us. The man gestures and says to Puja, in Nepali, that they have brought me the girl. He then asks her what I'm going to do with the children. Neither of us respond.

I begin walking around the circle of children and the two mothers huddled around the fire, wanting to get a better look at the girl, waiting to see her reaction to me. She doesn't even glance up. She just rocks the swaddled baby in her arms. My girl would always smile when she saw me. She brightened at my attention. When my camera was pointed at her, she would pose, living out her fantasy as a model.

Puja speaks to Sahdi, who gestures and tells her they have brought other children for me to see as well as the little girl and boy from my photo. I am silent, staring at the girl, trying to grasp all that is happening. It's not her. Why would they bring me a girl whom they know isn't the one I want? When Puja approaches me, I whisper again, "This is not the girl."

"You are sure?" she asks.

"Yes. I would know this girl as I would know my own daughter. This is not the girl." The words come out fierce.

At this point, Sahdi and the man are suspicious. The man is now agitated. He talks to Puja, and Puja shakes her head a little. Sahdi circles around to me. We are being divided, in the hopes of being conquered. Sahdi gets me to turn my back to the group by talking to me from behind. When she says, "We find the girl for you. This is the girl," she is forceful, demanding, pointing at the child holding the baby. The two women sitting around the fire are looking at me in anticipation of something. In anticipation of money. I'm sure of that. I can feel it somewhere in my bones.

It is all surreal, unreal, and—somehow—all too familiar.

I shake my head a little, tell Sahdi, "This is not the girl."

Now she becomes enraged. She steps towards me, jabs her finger within inches of my nose. "You are *incorrect!*" she screams, and I should not be surprised at her greed. "*Incorrect!* This is the girl!"

She snatches the manila folder I've brought with me and storms over to the girl, then holds up the photo next to the child's face. In an instant and without prompting, this girl strikes the same pose as the lost girl in the photo: right shoulder raised and slightly back with her elbow out to the side, chin down towards her shoulder, a coy smile on her face, and a mischievous glint in her eye.

"You have this shirt still, yes?" Sahdi asks the girl, getting a blank stare in response. Sahdi prompts her again. "This shirt! You have this shirt!" she yells at the girl, but I am already looking away, refusing to give Sahdi my attention.

This girl is younger than the one I'm searching for; her face is different, rounder; her eyes are smaller; her skin is darker; she does not behave with the same mannerisms—the list goes on in my head as to how I know she is not the girl, as if I need a list, because I don't, and not one ounce of this girl knows who I am.

Puja circles back to me. "What question would she know?" she whispers.

I think fast. "I gave her and her brother a stack of stickers last year. Lots of stickers."

"Can you take a picture of her?"

Nodding, I reach in my satchel for my phone.

Sahdi and the man are still berating us, pacing like caged animals, pausing to stab their fingers in our faces.

Puja approaches the girl, asks her a question in a low voice. I see the girl shake her head no, then Puja speaks to her again, and the girl responds with another no. As I hold my phone up to try to get a photo, Puja reaches with a gentle hand around the child's face, trying to get her to look up at me. One glance up at the camera pointed her way, and the girl pries her head out of Puja's hand. She doesn't like having her photo taken.

The man is working on me now, yelling at me in a mix of Nepali and broken English. I remain calm, collected. I will never cower before these people. "This is not the girl," I tell him in a cool, even voice.

Both Puja and I recognize the need to get away from the situation, and we walk towards each other.

"We will go," she says, as she takes my hand.

We pass through the gate, out to the road, as the yelling continues behind us.

＠

It is a silent walk back to the hotel. We wind through rush hour traffic, holding hands as much for comfort as to keep from getting separated from one another.

We turn into the alley that leads to Ganesh Temple and to Dil and Puja's hotel.

"You are sure?" Puja asks, questioning in a way that somehow doesn't question me, and I tell her yes, that I promise her it is not the girl, and that I will prove it to her. In my room, I turn on my little notebook laptop and plug in my external drive. Within moments, I am scrolling through at least fifty photos of this girl, and Puja is nodding, agreeing with my assessment.

"These people," she says, shaking her head in disappointment and disgust. "And on temple grounds," she adds. "They were greedy. They wanted money. It bothers me very, very much. This was very, very wrong." Puja puts a hand on her stomach, looks up at me. She says it makes her sick, then sighs, asks what I am going to do.

Outside, children are playing, and the bells at the temple ring as worshippers come and go. I look out the wall of windows in my room and take a deep breath. "I'm going to eat dinner," I tell her, and she smiles.

At dinner, Dil tells me the history of Pradeep's elder care home. We are alone on the roof tonight. I move my food around on my plate, pick at a few things. I'm not hungry. Dil says that he and Puja, along with others, had donated quite a bit of money to help build the elder care home. Soon after, the original founders died, and Pradeep, Garima, and Sahdi took over. Now all the original donors are disgusted at how the home has developed. This is why Dil kept encouraging me to stay at his hotel any time I needed to during the first month of my visit. He understood that I was in a bad situation.

ॐ

It's past midnight, and there's no good reason for me to be standing in my room, shivering in the cold, staring out at the homes and buildings around me. This would be a good time to stay under the covers, but I can't sleep.

Tonight, on grounds that should be holy, where people worship one of the higher forms of God in the Hindu religion, Sahdi and that man were willing to make a quick buck trying to sell children. I'm sure it didn't matter whether Sahdi felt she knew me and could trust me—I believe that, had I been a stranger, events would have unfolded precisely the same as they did tonight.

Now, standing in the semi-darkness of my room, I realize that any effort I make to find the lost girl would encourage others to hold her hostage, in some fashion, for money. Saying that I want to send her to school here would mean nothing to someone who wants to make a money off this child. At this point, I can't draw any more attention to her. If I reported Sahdi and that scolding man to the Ministry, what would happen? For starters, it would be Sahdi's word against mine. Plus, even if government officials were able to track down the children they tried to sell me tonight, let's not pretend that the kids would be protected. There is a vast underground here in the child sex-trafficking trade. Lastly, so much for ever reporting the elder care home to the Ministry of Women, Children, and Social Welfare. I did that and nothing changed, it seems. If anything, the place has grown worse.

When I sit down, the platform bed creaks, a heavy croak and groan beneath the weight of my confusion and guilt.

※

Suraj and Devina pull up to the curb outside the coffee shop. I slide into the back seat, and we begin the small talk of how our days have been as we head off to dinner. When I start to tell them about the incident at the elder care home, Devina becomes very quiet. It is their mission in life to create better human beings, and from this, a better Nepal. Protecting children, guiding them, giving them direction and freedom to discover who they are—this is what Suraj and Devina believe in. Offering children up for a fee on holy grounds is disturbing, and both are in equal parts saddened and angered by my story.

"I will tell you what happened," Suraj says, glancing at me in the rearview mirror. "These are people from India. These are not people from Nepal," he says of the women in the courtyard that night. I can still see them, looking at me with hope that I would rescue their children from this harsh land. Suraj proceeds to explain to me that Sahdi and the man must have approached these women and said they had a rich American who wanted to sponsor their children. For a finder's fee, Sahdi and this man would bring the women to meet me.

A naïve observer might hear the term "sponsor" and believe it means paying for the child's upbringing or education; to a more world-wise traveler, "sponsoring" simply means paying the parents a fee to adopt the child. That child is then taken back to the adopting person's country, supposedly for a chance at a better life, but usually never to be heard from again.

"Sponsoring" equates to selling children.

Suraj continues his rant against Sahdi and the man: "Now," he says, pointing at the road in front of us for emphasis, "they must pay back the fee to these women. This does not make them happy."

He clucks his tongue, swears under his breath in Nepali. Devina looks out her window in the passenger seat in front of me, lost in her own thoughts. I stare out my window, wondering how any country can survive if it's always every man for himself.

48.

Everything Changes

At the elder care home in Pharping, Slender Dhai is at Dakshinkali, and Dwarf Dhai is out for a stroll in town with his trusty walking stick. Dil brought me here late this morning, and now he and Reeta visit with Cheerful Aama near the pantry, while I sit with Pushpa on one of the old couches in the seating area. We cover our laps with a blanket and sit together like in the old days.

I glance around at the changes. In place of the ancient tube television, there is a small flat screen television hanging on the wall outside the pantry. Hanging from the support pole in the ceiling above us are small, colorful, origami animals. They appear to be made from some type of paper money.

Pushpa sees me staring at them, tilting my head every which way to make out the paper. She points and tells me, "Money." I ask what country and she smiles a bit, then says they were made by a volunteer from Japan.

I feel my eyebrows rise, and she smiles some more. Pushpa tells me that CGN has continued to send volunteers from other countries. The elder care home has hosted a young couple from Germany, who stayed for three weeks; a young man from Belgium, who stayed with them for two months; and another young woman from Japan, who stayed for a month.

Pushpa says, "Alena, you come here, the world opens. You are ..." Here she pauses to find the correct word, then says, "*bridge* to the world for us." I fight back tears, and she reaches over, pats my hand.

Peaceful Dhai, the newest resident whom I first saw during Chhath Puja, is still with the elder care home. Eternally grateful, he greets me as he always has before, placing both hands before him in prayer position, and nodding his head with a genuine smile.

The new wash facility has been completed, and the added grounds improvements are a shock. When the town heard I had donated money for a new wash facility, other people contributed to help expand the planned changes, and Padma, Suraj's mother and the visiting nurse here, collected even more money through her nurses' organization.

The result is that the grounds are now clean and safe. Previously, to get to the upper seating area where the elders would enjoy the sun and hang their wash, everyone had to make their way up uneven steps cut into the dirt. Now there is a smooth, cement ramp with a railing for the residents. The upper area used to be a rocky mess, and now it's a smooth sitting area, with decorative swirls of cement for the elders to walk on and where they can gather in chairs.

While the old wash facility has been left standing, the new facility is off to the side and is twice the size I expected. The plans called for one floor with three rooms: two rooms, each with a squat toilet, and a third room with hot and cold running water and the semi-automatic washing machine. Instead, they have a two-story building, with three toilet rooms and the washing machine room on the ground floor. The second floor is for storage of food donations and other goods, and the office was moved up there as well. All these changes free up two rooms in the dorm building. In short, Shaha can house six more residents. Now we can turn our focus to the next priority on the list: replacing the roof over the dorm building.

༄

The next day, I decide to pay Aabi, CGN's president and founder, a visit. He is surprised and pleased when I poke my head around his open door. He welcomes me in, and we laugh about his drapes finally being installed. At first our conversation is pleasant. We talk about Pharping and how well CGN's elder care program is going now. He thanks me again for all my efforts. As soon as I mention that I've formed my own NGO, though, his attitude towards me cools.

I want to talk with him about partnering on a project to film elders' stories all around Nepal. My idea is to pair college-aged, US volunteers with young adults from around Kathmandu. It would be a great way to introduce the elders' plight to the young, while giving them experience they can use in their careers.

Partway through my opening pitch, though, I feel as if I've stepped on a viper's nest. Aabi's tone is chill as he discusses the challenge of getting an uneducated person's agreement to be videotaped, especially if that person has dementia, and his conclusion is succinct: I should leave a project like that to the locals, and not include volunteers from the US. This is a project, he says, that should be done by CGN exclusively.

All at once, I am unwelcome. It's clear he feels I've overstepped my bounds as a former volunteer. As Aabi ends our conversation, he is also ending our relationship.

Somewhat defeated, I wander back down to the hostel on the second floor. I stop in the doorway of a room where two young women are chatting. They are from Norway, and here for six weeks working on a women's empowerment program. We talk in low voices as the young women complain about sleeping shoulder-to-shoulder with strangers in bunk beds that have been set side-by-side, and about having no place to store their gear or place their cell phones at night.

When I ask about the hot water system, they both groan. The system rarely works, they tell me. When it does, it only delivers room-temperature water. For the remainder of the time, the volunteers shower in cold water, and in a cold room now that winter is here.

Almost every item on my list of needed repairs has been ignored. In the bathroom, the window still doesn't shut all the way because the hinges have been painted over multiple times. As for the outlets, most of them have burned out, and the volunteers are left with few options for charging their electronics. Except for placing garbage cans in the bathrooms, none of the items on the list I gave Aabi were ever addressed.

Other volunteers, these young women tell me, have chosen to stay at a nearby youth hostel, or to go to a hotel, rather than stay at CGN's hostel. One young Japanese volunteer posted on Facebook about the situation and found a nearby family to whom she pays a daily rate for housing and food. She's having the immersion experience Aabi promises his volunteers, for which they have paid him generously. Because he won't provide suitable housing, these young people must find other places to stay, at their own expense. Apparently, Aabi doesn't care. After all, he got his money from them up front.

The young women sigh as they tell me these stories. "But this is what we signed up for, eh?" one of them says. I remember believing this same thing when I stayed at the first elder care home with all its toxic noise and aggravation. I remember believing that I, too, was meant to have a difficult journey here.

༄

The next morning, my backpack is heavy with bottles of water and food as I head off to the homeless encampment along the river. Back into No Man's Land, as I call it. Back into the neighborhood where I feel out of place, mistrusted, and unwelcome. This time I keep my head up, and keep my uncertainty in check until I pass something that looks like a play area behind a steel fence.

At first, I pass it, but then turn around out of sheer curiosity and walk through the gate. There are tables and stools cemented in place, and areas that look like they're going to be wading pools of some sort. It's all whitewashed, fenced-in, and empty except for a few young people who eye me with suspicion. I look through the fence and along the river, searching for the tent city. Did I miss it somehow? Did I walk right past it? Slightly confused, I leave the park and continue walking up the sidewalk.

As I pass the police station, though, I recall that two years ago I passed the tent city *before* I reached this station. I realize there's nothing ahead of me. No new tent city, no homeless elders, no police, and no safety. The homeless encampment is gone, replaced by an unused children's park. It looks like the

258

community has driven the homeless out, expecting them to migrate to the vast homeless camp on top of the garbage dump that I saw on my first trip to Dakshinkali. I have no other explanation as to why this unused park would be built here, in the middle of practically nowhere.

Backtracking again, I wander off down the river, and take the long way back to the hotel. As I walk, I find destitute men and women either begging or selling a few items from blankets on the ground. Each grateful elder gets water and food. Coming up around the corner towards Ganesh Temple and Dil and Puja's hotel, I spy the man in black sitting in his usual doorway up ahead.

Right away I can see that the man is different. He is nervous and edgy. I smile as I approach and greet him, but his eyes grow wide with concern. *Don't move too fast*, I tell myself, so I ease myself down as I sit in the doorway with him. It's not helping. He seems to grow even more fearful now that I'm sitting there and pulls his knees closer to his chest.

I offer him water, and he declines. I ask how he is, and he waves me off. He is focused on everything happening around him, checking for dangers with every move noted in his peripheral vision. I wonder what horrors he has endured since the last time I saw him.

My heart sinks. I stand up to leave, taking care not to move too fast, but he jumps a little anyway.

ॐ

It has been an abruptly short trip this time, filled with the usual emotional, rollercoaster ride that only Nepal causes in me. After my meeting with Aabi at CGN, I am acutely aware that I will have to use my own resources, my own Nepali family, to advance any programs in Nepal. That's not such a bad thing, really.

While I did not find the lost girl, the main purpose of this visit, my heart remains hopeful that we'll meet again one day. I will be where I'm supposed to be, when I'm supposed to be there, and we will recognize each other instantly.

Even though my bags are once again overpacked, there are no bribes to pay at the airport this time. Staring at the back of the seat in front of me, I take a deep breath in, then exhale out the last of Kathmandu, for now.

The captain taxis out onto the runway, then we're all pressed back in our seats as he pushes the throttle forward.

Epilogue

Six years have passed since I first set foot in Kathmandu. As I packed and repacked my bags all those years ago, I wondered if I'd recognize myself when I returned from that trip. I wondered how it would change me.

Looking back on those short three months now, it seems as if I was being drawn through a metamorphosis, as if the journey had already been written and I was being pulled along the path laid out for me. That trial-by-fire in Nepal finished forming me into the person I was supposed to be.

For at least a year after my return to the US, I felt like a stranger in my own body and in this world. I couldn't even process how I had changed. I just understood that I didn't quite know myself anymore.

During the long process of getting to know my new self, I kept returning to the moment I was grabbing my backpack to go across the street and meet the homeless man in black. I had trouble accepting that I was this person who would just walk across the street in a foreign country to offer a bottle of water to a complete stranger.

Now, recalling that disbelief, I wonder how I ever could have questioned myself. Trying to cross that road without getting hit by a car, focusing on that one man ahead, feeling my heart pounding out of my chest—that was a turning point for me. There really was no going back, only forward, to sit with him. When I heard the man describe himself as an orphan, and watched him place his hand on his chest as he said, "My religion is humanity," I finally understood the reason I was in Nepal. I was there to serve the elders in a broader sense than just doing elder care. I was meant to take all I had seen back with me, back home to the US, and work to help homeless and abandoned elders across the world. Six years after this trip, I still am coming to understand just what that mission means.

People have moved on from the 2015 Nepal earthquake. There is always another disaster competing for everyone's attention. After the world has turned its focus to the next tragedy, though, the elders remain behind, lost in a society that doesn't always cherish them. Today, my nonprofit continues to support the elder care home in Nepal, as well as one in Guatemala. Our supporters and donors are based around the world, with partners in Switzerland and the UK. We are fighting hard to keep up with the global demands of helping to provide care for our impoverished and abandoned elders, and struggling to grow quickly, but not *too* quickly, to ensure our success well into the future.

Our vision is grand, but attainable: For every elder, food and a home. We focus on geographic areas that have been hard-hit by natural and man-made disasters, and which have slipped through the cracks of society's minds. After identifying a potential need, we work with local nonprofits, or appropriate government agencies, to locate and rescue impoverished and homeless elders. We then assist in constructing an elder care home in a manner which respects the local culture and environment, and help to set up a sustainable food program so the home can become more self-reliant. We never require repayment from the elder care homes, and they continue to receive our support for as long as they meet our standards of care.

In 2023, we launched a sustainable food program in Nepal's impoverished, remote Tamang villages, to help the families there continue to support themselves and their elders. We also worked with our partner elder care home Guatemala to set up their own sustainable food program. In addition, we began doing outreach in both countries, to help get abandoned elders to safety.

❧

In Nepal, many things have changed from six years ago, while many things remain the same.

Coffee shops are popular now, complete with milkshakes, smoothies, and Western menus. Garbage is no longer piled up in the streets, but now picked up at designated locations. Three-wheeled motorcycles and scooters offer greater mobility for those who can't use the traditional two-wheelers, while a few stop lights have been installed around the city and are obeyed by drivers. Traffic seems calmer, more civilized.

Pedestrians, however, still don't have the right of way, not even at a marked crossing. As before, a young mother, clutching her infant, still can't get a break when navigating a crosswalk.

Beggars, young or old, once used to hold out their hand to tourists, but are now regularly cleared from the streets. Now security guards have permission to keep a beggar from sitting on a stoop to rest, anywhere, anytime, or to keep a beggar from finding a spot in the shade on a hot day. Businesses in Thamel don't want the tourists bothered, don't want tourists to know there are poor, homeless elders in the streets.

Thamel's message to beggars remains the same: Keep moving. Life must appear happy and carefree in Shangri-La.

༄

At the elder care home in Pharping, life continues with only a few changes. Six years ago, we would see just one family each month come to the elder care home with food or blankets to celebrate a child's birthday. Now, we see several a week. It's not just on a child's birthday, either: Sometimes we see widows bringing their family to remember the deceased father's birthday.

Through the years, age has taken its toll on the bodies and minds of the elders at the home. and Death has called to collect on its claim: We've lost nearly every elder I encountered during this first visit. Folded Aama left us while being kept comfortable, clean and dry, with a personal caregiver paid for by our nonprofit.

Of those living at the elder care home now, many have been abandoned by their children. I think about those adult children from time to time. Did

Black Aama's son wonder if she survived the 2015 earthquake? In Guatemala, the trend is to leave your parent in the hospital and never go back. Do those children ever wonder what's happened to the person who did their best to raise them? Do they ever feel guilty for just walking away?

Each day, it seems, the news brings another story about "granny-dumping" somewhere around the world. My heart weeps every time I read about someone leaving their loved one by the side of a remote road. The caregiving family member feels overwhelmed with their responsibility, doesn't know where to turn, and the elder suffers as a result. The road ahead for my nonprofit is unending, and we do the best we can. Setbacks arrive as frequently as improvements, but there is no turning back. There is no stopping. There is only forward.

I cannot bear the thought of elders being abandoned by their children, and being left to fend for themselves. I dream of a world where every elder has food and a home, and I believe that our global society can reach that goal. While plenty of organizations do laudable work empowering women to become independent, and helping to give children a better future, no one seems to remember the elders, who are dependent on others, and whose future is behind them.

There is a great truth in the words of the Nepali trekking guide whom I met during the general strike in 2017: We could all do more for each other, but don't. We need to start trying. We are one human race. *Just one.* We can't be focused on getting ahead at the expense of someone else, keeping others down as we claw our way up to what we think is the top. In the bigger scheme of things, that ends up merely holding all of us back.

If we want to move our global society *and ourselves* forward, we need to live as one human race. Kindness and generosity are the qualities that anchor us in our humanity, and they will move us, as one, into our future.

This...*this* we can do. Together.

About The Global Humanity Initiative

The Global Humanity Initiative is a registered 501(c)(3) nonprofit organization based in the US. Our focus is simple: To rescue homeless and abandoned elders around the world, give them a new family, a safe place to live, and unconditional love.

We are committed to preserving the heritage and culture of any environment in which we work, provided the culture does not condone harm to others, and we are actively engaged in the fight for human rights within any country in which we work.

Our donors are spread across the globe—from Japan, to Switzerland, to the UK, and the US. We currently support elder care homes in Nepal and Guatemala; many of the elders in the homes we support have been abandoned by their families. In addition, we run sustainable food programs to help impoverished elders improve their food security.

During our travels, we collect stories and photos of homeless and impoverished elders, both in the US and abroad, and share them on social media and on our website. We hope to educate others with these stories, and to remind everyone that we are all one human race. No one sets out in life with the plan to be homeless in their twilight years.

Please visit our website at GlobalHumanityInitiative.org. Any help you wish to give is deeply appreciated. Fifteen percent of all sales of this book go to support our efforts.

Thank you for reading. Thank you for caring. Let us resolve together to create a safer and happier world for the forgotten elderly.

Acknowledgements

Three women helped me breathe life into this book, and have supported my efforts from the start. For that, I am grateful.

Ronni J. Sanlo, PhD, one of the bravest women I know. Before I left on this journey, you suggested we publish my journal when I returned. I laughed. You didn't. You believed in me and in whatever message needed to be told as a result of these three months. Thank you for that, and for your ongoing friendship.

Connie Young, the best cousin-sister a girl could ever ask for. Your enthusiasm about both my physical journey to Nepal and my journey as a writer kept me going during the toughest times. I am grateful for your insight, for your prayers, and for your friendship.

Jessi Rita Hoffman, the perfect book editor for this story. You called out my lazy writing, demanded more from me, and served as a critical sounding board on all things Vedic. Throughout this journey, you have become a true friend. I thank you deeply.

Deep gratitude goes out to so many others—too many to name, but I shall try. To both of my sisters for all those times you asked how the book was going and heard me weep in response. To Angela and to Tim, for believing in me and in my work. To Maia, Lana, Suzie, and Cathy for your support and love. To Cindy, Sherry, and Diane, for listening to me groan unceasingly. To Theresa Cassiday, for rescuing me more times than I can count. To Barbara Gottlieb, who took my ideas and made them shine.

A special shout-out goes to both Ron Falzone and to Mary Mitchell, for your invaluable friendship, advice, and insight. I adore you.

The most important person to acknowledge, however, is my husband. Without you, none of this would have ever been possible—not this first trip, nor the nonprofit, or this book. You have been my biggest fan. Thank you for keeping me grounded, for your unconditional love, and for helping me to be a better person.